Lewis Richards

Build up
to IELTS

Ayad

Author acknowledgements

The first draft of this book was co-written with Joel Burchett and Rebecca Scott, and I would like to express my gratitude for all their ideas, input and work in the initial stages of the book.

Thank you to everyone at DELTA and Klett, in particular Nick Boisseau and Bettina Höfels. I would also like give special thanks to the editor of this book, Catriona Watson-Brown. Her incisive comments on the drafts, along with her support and sense of humour, contributed greatly to the final manuscript.

All the material in the book has been developed in my IELTS classes at Language Specialists International Portsmouth, where I've worked for the last 16 years. I'd like to thank all the students, staff and teachers at LSI for being so supportive and encouraging of this project.

Finally, I would like to dedicate this book to Marine Joly.

Picture credits:
11 Getty Images (svetikd), München; **12** Getty Images (10';000 Hours), München; **16** Getty Images (Lumi Images/Dario Secen), München; **17.1** Getty Images (Caiaimage/Paul Bradbury), München; **17.2** Getty Images (Caiaimage/Paul Bradbury), München; **17.3** Getty Images (PhotoAlto/Gabriel Sanchez), München; **17.4** Getty Images (Hoxton/Sam Edwards), München; **19.1** Getty Images (221A), München; **19.2** Getty Images (georgeclerk), München; **29** Getty Images (Tom Merton), München; **31.1** Getty Images (Jacobs Stock Photography Ltd), München; **31.2** Getty Images (Hinterhaus Productions), München; **31.3** Getty Images (Jacobs Stock Photography Ltd), München; **32.1** Getty Images (Image Source), München; **32.2** Getty Images (Morsa Images), München; **36** Getty Images (IPGGutenbergUKLtd), München; **44** Getty Images (sorbetto), München; **46.1** Getty Images (Alistair Berg), München; **46.2** Getty Images (Thomas Northcut), München; **49** Getty Images (courtneyk), München; **59** Getty Images (Hill Street Studios), München; **64** Getty Images (Jacobs Stock Photography Ltd), München; **66** Getty Images (SolStock), München; **70** Getty Images (skynesher), München; **71** Getty Images (AnthiaCumming), München; **78** Getty Images (5xinc), München; **83** Getty Images (prognone), München; **88** Getty Images (Halfpoint), München; **94** Getty Images (tonefotografia), München; **113** Getty Images (borchee), München; **117** Getty Images (extravagantni), München; **121** Shutterstock (nayef hammouri), New York; **124** Getty Images (martin-dm), München; **129** Getty Images (Alfredo Maiquez), München; **131** Getty Images (Muslim Girl), München; **136** Getty Images (KevinDyer), München; **143** Shutterstock (jutamas), New York

| Download the free DELTA Augmented app onto your device | Start picture recognition and scan the **the first page of each unit** | Download the audio tracks and use them now or save them for later |

Apple and the Apple logo are trademarks of Apple Inc., registered in the US and other countries. App Store is a service mark of Apple Inc. | Google Play and the Google Play logo are trademarks of Google Inc.

1st edition 1 ⁵ ⁴ ³ ² ¹ | 2023 22 21 20 19

The last figure shown denotes the year of impression.

Delta Publishing, 2019
www.deltapublishing.co.uk
© Ernst Klett Sprachen GmbH, Rotebühlstraße 77, 70178 Stuttgart, 2019

Editor: Catriona Watson-Brown, CWB Editorial Services,UK
Cover: Andreas Drabarek, Stuttgart, Germany
Layout: Andreas Drabarek, Eva Mokhlis, Stuttgart, Germany
Illustrations: Sven Palmowski, Barcelona, Spain
Typesetting: Swabianmedia, Stuttgart, Germany
Cover picture: stock.adobe.com (Daria), Dublin
Printing and binding: Elanders GmbH, Waiblingen, Germany

ISBN 978-3-12-501571-5

Contents

Reading	Listening	Speaking
Reading: Matching information • Skills focus	**Listening Part 2: Multiple-choice questions** • Skills focus • Skills application	**Speaking Part 1** • Talking about what you do • Grammar: tenses
Reading: True / False / Not Given questions • Skills focus • Skills application	**Listening Part 1: Distractors** • Skills focus • Skills application	**Speaking Part 3** • Giving opinions
Reading: Identifying information • Skills focus • Skills application	**Listening Part 1: Predicting answers** • Skills focus	**Speaking Parts 1 and 2** • Common questions related to health and fitness **Speaking Part 3** • Giving examples from your experience
Reading: Matching headings • Skills focus • Skills application	**Listening Part 2: Predicting answers** • Skills focus • Skills application	**Speaking Parts 2 and 3** • The news • Communication
Reading: Note completion • Skills focus • Skills application	**Listening Part 3: Multiple choice and sentence completion** • Skills focus • Skills application	**Speaking Parts 2 and 3** • The environment
Reading: Matching • Skills focus • Skills application	**Listening Part 4: Sentence completion** • Skills focus 1 • Skills focus 2	**Speaking Part 3** • Tourism
Reading: Summary completion with a wordlist • Skills focus	**Listening Part 3: Sentence completion** • Skills focus	**Speaking Parts 1, 2 and 3** • Talking about jobs • Grammar: Cleft sentences • Grammar: Using comparatives
Reading: Table completion • Skills focus • Skills application	**Listening Part 4: Predicting answers** • Skills focus • Skills application	**Speaking Part 2** • A city you enjoyed visiting **Speaking Part 3** • Talking about improvements
Reading: Matching headings and multiple-choice questions • Skills application	**Listening Part 3: Matching information** • Skills application	**Speaking Part 3** • Future predictions **Speaking Part 1** • Your future plans
Reading: Completing a flowchart • Skills focus • Skills application	**Listening Part 2: Sentence completion** • Skills focus • Skills application	**Speaking Part 2** • Grammar: Linking phrases • Grammar: Modal verbs to talk about the past

Introduction

Aim and approach

This book is designed for students who want to achieve a score of 5.5–6.0 in the Academic IELTS exam. It covers all four parts of the IELTS exam (Reading, Listening, Speaking and Writing) in detail and aims to improve your IELTS score in each section. However, special focus has been given to the Writing section, as this is the area that many IELTS candidates experience the most difficulty with. All the exercises in this book have been developed in the classroom, and the material has helped many IELTS students to achieve the scores they need.

Organisation

The book is split into ten units, each covering a different topic. These topics (e.g. education, the environment, media and technology) are some of the most common areas of language that you will need for the exam. All the tasks that directly practise the exam format are indicated by ⌖.

Writing
The Writing sections take up approximately half of each unit and are split into two types:

- **Units 1–5** look at different types of Task 2 essays (advantage/disadvantage essays, opinion essays, problem/solution essays, two-part questions and discussion essays).
- **Units 6–10** cover the different type of Task 1 questions you may be asked to write about in the exam (trends, comparatives, maps, mixed questions, future graphs and processes).

Each Writing section begins with a **model essay**, designed to show you how to organise and write a good answer at this level. The following pages guide you through a step-by-step process for writing a good Task 1 or 2 answer. These exercises practise different parts of the essay (e.g. introduction, main body, conclusion), as well as highlighting key grammar and vocabulary for each type of writing question.

At the end of each unit, there is a practice question (or sometimes two) for you to apply what you have learned to a different essay question. Sample answers for all of these are provided in the key, so that you can compare your writing with another model.

Reading and listening
Each unit also contains sections for developing your reading and listening skills for IELTS. The exercises cover the main question types and skills for both Reading (e.g. matching headings, True/False/Not Given, table completion) and Listening (e.g. dealing with distractors, multiple-choice questions, matching information). There are *Skills focus* exercises, which show you the techniques required to tackle different types of reading or listening question, and *Skills application* exercises, which give you the opportunity to practise the techniques you have learned.

Speaking
The book covers all three parts of IELTS Speaking, providing you with strategies (e.g. using linking words to organise your answer in Part 2), as well as grammar and vocabulary which you can use in the Speaking exam. You will hear model answers recorded by native speakers, to show you what is required to gain a good speaking score.

Each unit ends with a section entitled *Pulling it all together*, which reviews key language and skills from the unit, and concludes with the final Writing task. The book concludes with a summary of advice for the exam.

The book comes with 33 audio tracks that can be download from the DELTA Augmented App (available for iOS and Android) for free. Simply scan the first page of each unit to download or stream the tracks of the particular unit on your device.

There are full transcripts of the audio tracks at the back of the book.

I hope that you enjoy using this book, and I wish you every success in the IELTS exam!
Lewis Richards

Living home and away

Writing Task 2: Advantage/disadvantage essays

Model essay

 In this unit, you're going to look at how to write a Task 2 advantage/disadvantage essay. In the exam, you will have **40 minutes** for Task 2, and you have to write a minimum of **250 words**.

1 **Discuss these questions in pairs.**

1 Have you ever lived in a foreign country?
2 Would you like to live in a foreign country in the future? Why?/Why not?
3 Do you know anyone who has lived in a foreign country? Did they like it?
4 Why do you think many people these days spend time living abroad?

2 **Write down two advantages and two disadvantages of living in a foreign country. Compare your answers in pairs.**

Advantages	Disadvantages
1	1
2	2

3 **Read the exam question and model essay, and see if the ideas are the same as yours.**

These days, more and more people spend time living abroad, either to learn a language, to study or to work. What are the advantages and disadvantages of living in a foreign country?

In recent years, it has become much more common for people to live in another country. Many people believe that there are significant benefits of doing this, while others argue that there are also drawbacks connected to living abroad. This essay will look at both points of view, and then I will give my opinion.

One advantage of living abroad is that you improve your language skills. This means that when you return to your own country, it will make it easier to get a better job. For example, many young people study in an English-speaking country for a few months or years, and when they come back, they have more job opportunities. Another benefit of living abroad is that you can learn about new cultures. For instance, you will learn about customs, habits and food. The consequence is that people tend to become more open-minded.

On the other hand, there are also some disadvantages. One drawback of living abroad is that people may feel homesick. They often miss their family and friends, and find it difficult to make new friends. Another important drawback of living abroad is that it can be difficult at first to adapt to the new country. This is because the way of life may be very different, and people often become frustrated, because they do not understand the new culture and the language very well.

To sum up, having looked at this topic in detail, it is clear that there are both advantages and disadvantages of living abroad for a while. In my opinion, the benefits outweigh the drawbacks. Although it is true that it can be difficult at first, on balance I think that if you live abroad, you will have new experiences which will stay with you for the rest of your life.

(300 words)

4 **Answer these questions about the model essay.**

1 Were the ideas in the essay the same as yours?
2 How many paragraphs are in the essay?
3 How many advantages and disadvantages are mentioned?
4 Where is the writer's opinion included?
5 Do you agree with the writer's opinion?

Topic sentences for advantage / disadvantage essays

 A topic sentence is usually the first sentence of each paragraph of the main body of the essay. It is used to introduce the main idea of the paragraph. For example, the topic sentence in the second paragraph of the essay on page 7 is: *One advantage of living abroad is that you improve your language skills.*

1 Look at the model essay on page 7 and <u>underline</u> the other three topic sentences.

2 Complete these topic sentences without looking at the model essay.

1 One a____ of l____ abroad is that you improve your language skills.
2 A____ b____ of living abroad is that y____ can learn about new cultures.
3 One d____ of living abroad i____ t____ people m____ feel homesick.
4 Another i____ drawback of living abroad is that i____ c____ be difficult at first to adapt to the new country.

3 Correct the mistakes in these topic sentences.

1 One advantage of study English is that you can get a better job.
2 Another benefit for studying English is that you can communicate with people all round the world.
3 One advantage of living in the countryside is that peaceful.
4 Another benefit of living in the countryside it is friendly.
5 One disadvantage live in the countryside is that it can take a long time to get to work.
6 Another downside of living in the countryside that there is not much to do in the evening.

4 Complete these topic sentences with a suitable ending.

1 One advantage of living with your parents …
2 Another advantage of living with your parents …
3 One drawback of living with your parents …
4 Another downside of living with your parents …

5 Look at this plan for an advantage / disadvantage essay about going abroad on holiday. Write four topic sentences using the notes.

Advantages	Disadvantages
come into contact with a new culture	*language barrier*
the weather – better than at home?	*long time to get there*

Supporting the topic sentence

 After you write your topic sentence, you need to support it by writing one or two more sentences to give more detail, describe a result or explain why something happens. Writing good support sentences will enable you to build interesting paragraphs and increase your chances of getting a high mark for Writing Task 2.

1 Match these support sentences with their function (a–c).

1 **If** you live abroad, it is likely that **you will** learn the language of the country to a high level.

2 **This means that** when you return to your own country, it will make it easier to get a better job.

3 **In other words**, you will come into contact with people from different cultures and come across different ways of life and of doing things.

4 **The consequence is that** people tend to become more open-minded and learn more about the world.

5 It can be difficult to be separated from your loved ones for a long time while living overseas, **and the result is that** many people feel lonely and depressed.

6 Another important drawback of living abroad is that it can be difficult at first to adapt to the new country. **This is because** the way of life may be very different, and people often become frustrated.

a Gives more detail about the topic sentence
b Describes a result
c Gives a reason for something

Giving more detail

Look at four possible ways of giving more detail about this topic sentence:

One advantage of living abroad is that you can broaden your horizons.

- **If you live abroad, you will** *come into contact with people from different countries, with different opinions and ideas.*

- **In other words,** *you come into contact with people from different countries, with different opinions and ideas.*

- **Living abroad means that you** *come into contact with people from different countries, with different opinions and ideas.*

- **By living abroad, you** *come into contact with people from different countries, with different opinions and ideas.*

---

2 Write a sentence giving more detail about each of these four topic sentences.

1 One advantage of having a mobile phone is that it is easy to contact people. Having a mobile phone …

2 Another benefit of owning a mobile phone is that it is useful if you need information quickly. By having …

3 One drawback of having a mobile phone is that it is expensive. If …

4 A further disadvantage of having a mobile phone is that it can be addictive. In other words …

Describing results and reasons

The following phrases can be used to describe results and reasons:

1 The result / consequence is that …
2 As a result / consequence, …
3 This means that …

4 This is because …
5 The reason is that …

---

3 Decide whether each of the phrases in the box above introduce a result or a reason.

4 **Complete these essay extracts with suitable phrases from the box above.**

1 One of the main advantages of working from home is that you can save a lot of time.
   ＿＿＿ you do not have to spend time driving to the office every day.
2 Another main drawback of studying abroad is that students often get homesick.
   ＿＿＿ they are not able to enjoy their experience and may not benefit from it.
3 One drawback of working from home is that it is easy to get distracted from your work.
   ＿＿＿ you do not have a boss checking that you are doing your work properly.
4 Another disadvantage of living in the country is that it can take a long time to commute
   to work every day. ＿＿＿ you can get home late and be tired at the end of the day.

5 **Complete these support sentences with your own ideas.**

1 One advantage of learning English is that it improves people's chances of finding a good job.
   This is because …
2 Another advantage of learning English is that it is spoken all over the world. As a result,
   if you learn English …
3 One disadvantage of having a part-time job while you are studying at university is that it
   takes up a lot of study time. The consequence is that …
4 Another disadvantage of running your own business is that it can be stressful.
   The reason is that …

6 **Write suitable support sentences for these sentences.**

1 One advantage of living with your parents as an adult is that you can save money.
2 Another advantage of living with your parents as an adult is that you can help them around
   the house.
3 One drawback of living with your parents as an adult is that you have less privacy.
4 Another downside of living with your parents as an adult is that you have to follow their rules.

Giving examples

Writing Task 2 questions always ask you to give relevant examples, so you need to be prepared to
write one or sentences doing this.

1 **Read this paragraph from a Task 2 essay about studying English abroad. Then decide which of the
   example sentences below (a–c) are suitable and which are not. Give your reasons.**

One advantage of studying English abroad is that you can improve your English quickly. Living in an
English-speaking country means that you have to listen to English all the time, and speak to native
speakers every day. As a result, your level will improve dramatically in a short period of time.

a Take my cousin Juan, for example. When he went to the USA last year, his English was poor, but he
  worked really hard and now his English is great.
b For instance, according to statistics, if you study English abroad, you will learn 30% faster than in your
  country.
c For instance, many young people go to study in the UK or the USA for a few months after they finish
  university so that they can improve their speaking quickly and pass an exam in English.

2 Complete these phrases for giving examples.

1 For e_____ , …
2 For i_____ , …
3 T_____ the UK, for example. In the UK, …
4 A g_____ example is …
5 A c_____ in point is …

3 Add an appropriate example to each of these paragraphs.

1 One advantage of living in the countryside is that it takes a long time to travel to work. The reason is that you have to drive to the nearest city twice a day, and often there is a lot of traffic. …

2 Another benefit of living with your parents as an adult is that you can help them around the house. By living with your parents, you are always available to give them assistance with shopping, cooking and cleaning. As a result, their life will be easier and they will be more relaxed. …

3 One drawback of having a mobile phone is that it is easy to become addicted. You can find that you are checking your mobile phone many times a day, even during class or at the dinner table.

4 One disadvantage of living in a big city is that it can be very expensive. Living in a capital city means that house prices, transport and going out are much more expensive than in small towns or villages.

Introductions for advantage/disadvantage essays

It is important to write a paragraph to introduce your essay. It does not have to be too long, but you need to rephrase the essay question using different words and explain what your essay will do.

1 Discuss these questions in pairs.

1 What information should you include in an introduction to an advantage/disadvantage essay?
2 How many sentences should you write?
3 Should you repeat the essay question word for word?

2 Read the introduction to the model essay again. Are your answers to the questions in Exercise 1 still the same?

[1]In recent years, it has become much more common for people to live in another country. [2]Many people believe that there are significant benefits of doing this, while others argue that there are also drawbacks connected to living abroad. [3]This essay will look at both points of view, and then I will give my opinion.

3 Match the sentences in the introduction (1–3) with their function (a–c).

a This sentence says what the essay will do.
b This sentence describes the two different opinions about the topic.
c This sentence rephrases the question and introduces the topic.

4 Complete these introductory sentences with an appropriate tense of the verbs in brackets.

1 In recent years, it _____ (*become*) more common for people to live abroad.
2 Today, many people _____ (*want*) to study English in another country.
3 In recent decades, the number of people who study English abroad _____ (*increase*) significantly.
4 These days, many people _____ (*choose*) to live abroad for work or study.
5 The number of people who decide to live abroad _____ (*increase*) all the time.
6 The number of people who choose to work from home _____ (*rise*) over the past few years.

5 Complete the table with the tenses in the box.

> present continuous ▪ present perfect ▪ present simple

Rules	Tense
1 Facts about now	
2 Recent changes	
3 Things changing now	

6 Complete this introduction.

In recent years, it has become much more common for people to live in another country for an extended period of time. ¹M_____ people ²b_____ that there are significant ³b_____ of doing this, ⁴w_____ others ⁵a_____ that there are also drawbacks ⁶c_____ t_____ living abroad. This ⁷e_____ will ⁸l_____ at both ⁹p_____ of ¹⁰v_____ , and then I will ¹¹g_____ my opinion.

7 Complete the introduction below about working from home with the words and phrases in the box.

> believe ▪ disadvantages ▪ doing ▪
> points of view ▪ rising ▪
> significant ▪ this ▪ while ▪
> who ▪ will ▪ will

The number of people ¹_____ choose to work from home is ²_____ year on year. Many people ³_____ that there are ⁴_____ benefits of ⁵_____ this, ⁶_____ others argue that there are also ⁷_____ connected to working from home. ⁸_____ essay ⁹_____ look at both ¹⁰_____ and then I ¹¹w_____ give my opinion.

8 Write an introduction for this topic: 'What are the advantages and disadvantages of having a mobile phone?'

Conclusions for advantage / disadvantage essays

The most important thing in the conclusion of an advantage/disadvantage essay is to give your opinion. Do you believe there are more advantages or more disadvantages of the topic? You have to make it clear to the examiner what you think.

1 Discuss these topics in pairs. Do you think there are more advantages or more disadvantages for each one?

1 Living with your parents as an adult
2 Working from home
3 Living in the countryside
4 Having a mobile phone

2 Discuss these questions in pairs.

1 What should you write in a conclusion to an advantage/disadvantage essay?
2 How many sentences should you write?

3 Match the sentences in the conclusion of the model essay (1–3) with their function (a–c).

¹To sum up, having looked at this topic in detail, it is clear that there are both advantages and disadvantages of living abroad for a while. ²In my opinion, the benefits outweigh the drawbacks. ³Although it is true that it can be difficult at first, on balance I think that if you live abroad, you will have new experiences which will stay with you for the rest of your life.

a Stating your opinion
b Saying that the other side of the argument has some good points, and then giving more detail about your opinion
c Saying that you have examined both sides of the argument

4 Choose the correct words so that the sentences mean the same.

1 In my opinion, the benefits outweigh the drawbacks.
   = I believe there are more *advantages* / *disadvantages*.
2 In my opinion, the drawbacks outweigh the benefits.
   = I believe there are more *advantages* / *disadvantages*.

5 Complete the conclusion with the words in the box.

> advantages ▪ although ▪ balance ▪ clear ▪ detail ▪ disadvantages ▪
> experiences ▪ having ▪ opinion ▪ outweigh ▪ sum

To ¹____ up, ²____ looked at this topic in ³____ , it is ⁴____ that there are both ⁵____ and ⁶____ of living abroad for a while. In my ⁷____ , the benefits ⁸____ the drawbacks. ⁹____ it is true that it can be difficult at first, on ¹⁰____ I think that if you live abroad, you will have new ¹¹____ and learn valuable new things, which will stay with you for the rest of your life.

6 Write conclusions for these two topics.

1 What are the advantages and disadvantages of working from home?
2 What are the advantages and disadvantages of living in the country?

Listening Part 2: Multiple-choice questions

Skills focus

> One of the most common types of listening question in the IELTS test is multiple-choice questions. These questions can be difficult because at least two of the options are usually mentioned. You need good listening technique in order to identify which option is correct and which options are incorrect, and why. You will find multiple-choice questions in all parts of the IELTS Listening test; the questions in this unit are similar to those you might have to answer in Part 2.

1 **You are going to listen to a presentation about studying and working abroad. Before you listen, read questions 1 and 2.**

a Underline the key words in the questions and the options.
b Think of possible synonyms for the key words that you have identified.

1 Overseas Opportunities moved into a new building in
   A 1992.
   B 1978.
   C 2001.

2 Overseas Opportunities send people abroad for
   A less than a month.
   B a maximum of a year.
   C more than a year.

2 🎧1 ✒ **Listen to the first part of the presentation and choose the correct letter, A, B or C, for questions 1 and 2.**

3 **Read the audioscript on page 147 and** underline **the sections that gave you the correct answers. With a partner, discuss why the other two options in each question are incorrect. Then check your answers to Exercise 2 in the key on page 156.**

4 Underline **the key words for questions 3–9 and think of possible synonyms.**

3 Volunteers on a charity placement do not have to pay for
   A their shopping.
   B the house they stay in.
   C taking the bus or train to other parts of the country.
4 People who want to do a voluntary placement should
   A have done a similar placement before.
   B be happy to live in a simple way.
   C speak some of the local language.
5 Overseas Opportunities now sends the highest number of volunteers to
   A South-East Asia.
   B India.
   C Sub-Saharan Africa.

6 Most of the internships arranged by Overseas Opportunities
   A do not pay a salary.
   B pay a good salary.
   C pay a limited salary.
7 If you are offered a work placement, you should
   A pay Overseas Opportunities once for arranging it.
   B not pay anything at all.
   C pay the company you are going to work for.
8 The speaker says that the number-one thing people can get from doing a work placement is
   A saving money.
   B having a better work record when you look for a job.
   C doing new things.

Skills application

1 🎧2 ✒ **Listen to the second part of the presentation and choose the correct letter, A, B or C, for questions 3–8. When you finish, check your answers in the audioscript on page 147.**

2 **Discuss this question.**

Would you be interested in doing voluntary work overseas? Why?/Why not?

Speaking Part 1

Talking about what you do

In the first part of the speaking exam, the examiner will ask you a few personal questions, including questions about what you do. These questions are really important because they give you the chance to show the examiner how good your English is. To do this well, you will need to have a good range of grammar.

1 **Discuss these questions in pairs.**

1 Do you work or are you a student?
2 How long have you been working or studying?
3 What do you enjoy most about what you do?
4 What did you do before?
5 What are your future plans?

2 ○3 **You are going to hear a man answering the questions in Exercise 1. Listen and make notes about what he says.**

3 ○4 **Listen to a woman answering the same questions. Make notes about what she says, then compare in pairs what you heard from both people.**

4 ○3,4 **Complete what the speakers said with the correct form of the verbs in brackets. Then listen again and check.**

Speaker 1

1 So, at the moment, I _____ (study) English in a language school.
2 I have great teachers, and I _____ (live) with a great host family.
3 I _____ (study) English for about three months and I've got one month left before I finish my course.
4 What I really like about studying English is that I _____ (meet) lots of interesting people.
5 Before I _____ (come) here, I _____ (work) as a shop assistant in a supermarket, but I _____ (decide) that I _____ (want) to get a better job, so I _____ (quit) and I _____ (come) here.
6 I _____ (plan) to study at university in the UK.
7 If I get good results in IELTS, I _____ (start) an MBA in London in September.

Speaker 2

1 I _____ (work) as a nurse in a local hospital. I _____ (specialise) in caring for young children who are in intensive care.
2 I _____ (work) as a nurse for nine years. I _____ (work) for six years in a hospital in another city, and I _____ (work) in this job for three years.
3 What I really _____ (like) about my job is that you can make a difference to people's lives.
4 When I _____ (finish) school, I _____ (take) a gap year and I _____ (travel) around Asia and Australia for about nine months.
5 Next year, I _____ (apply) for a promotion to senior nurse.
6 If I get it, I _____ (have) more responsibility, and of course more money, which will be great.

5 **What verb tenses did the speakers use? Discuss in pairs why each tense was used and whether there is more than one tense that could be used.**

Grammar: Tenses

1 **What is the difference between these two sentences? Discuss in pairs.**

1 At the moment, **I'm studying** English in the UK.
2 **I work** as a nurse.

2 **Look at this extract from Speaker 1. If you want to talk about things you did in the past which are finished, which tense do you need?**

*Before I **came** here, I **worked** as a shop assistant in a supermarket, but I **decided** that I **wanted** to get a better job, so I **quit** and I **came** here.*

3 **Read these sentences. Which ones talk about finished actions (F), and which ones talk about unfinished actions (U)? Which tense is used in each sentence?**

1 I worked as a shop assistant for a year.
2 I've been working as a nurse for nine years.
3 I worked for a few months on a farm in Australia.
4 I've been studying English in the UK for three months.

4 **What is the difference between these sentences which talk about the future?**

1 Next year, **I'm going to** apply for a promotion.
2 If I get it, **I'll have** more responsibility.
3 **I'm planning to** study at university in the UK next year.
4 If I get a good result in IELTS, **I'll start** an MBA in London in September.

5 **Complete these sentences with the correct tense of the verbs in brackets.**

1 When I _____ (*finish*) school in 2014, I _____ (*take*) a break from studying for a year, and I _____ (*work*) as a volunteer in a care home.
2 At the moment, I _____ (*do*) a part-time job in a café, but in September I'm going to start university.
3 If all goes well, I _____ (*start*) my own business in the next year.
4 When I finish university next year, I _____ (*plan*) to take six months off and go travelling.
5 I started working as a doctor when I finished university, and I _____ (*work*) for six years. I love it, it's a great job!
6 Right now, I _____ (*live*) in a host family, and they are very nice, but next month I _____ (*look*) for my own place to live.
7 I _____ (*work*) as a dentist. I qualified ten years ago, and I _____ (*work*) as a dentist ever since.
8 Before I _____ (*come*) here, I _____ (*spend*) five years working in an office job, but I _____ (*not like*) it very much, so I _____ (*give*) it up, and now I'm studying English.
9 I _____ (*apply*) for a place at university last month, and they accepted me. I _____ (*start*) in October.
10 I _____ (*graduate*) in French last June and I _____ (*get*) my first job a month later, so I _____ (*work*) for nine months now.

6 **Make notes about the questions in Exercise 1 on page 15. Use a variety of tenses.**

7 **Ask and answer the questions in pairs.**

Reading: Matching information

Skills focus

One of the key skills you need for IELTS Reading is to skim paragraphs quickly and match information. You can do this by:
- highlighting the key words in each statement
- skimming each paragraph quickly and trying to match the words in the statement with similar information in the text
- underlining where you have matched the information in the text.

1 Read the title and introduction to the article on page 19. What do you think the four people will say about living in the country?

2 Read the whole article quickly and check your ideas.

3 Look at the underlined text in the first question in the exam task in Exercise 4, then look at the underlined text in Arthur's section of the article. How are the two bits of text related?

4 ⊙ The article relates the experiences of four different people. Answer these questions, choosing from Rose, Arthur, James or Maria. Before you start, underline the key words in each question, then underline the answer in the text when you find it.

Which person

1 spent their childhood in the countryside, but doesn't live there any more?
2 says that it is easier to have good job prospects in a big city?
3 feels happier now that they are living in the countryside?
4 found living in a city stressful and bad for their health?
5 works in a city, but lives in the countryside?
6 says there is no entertainment in the countryside?
7 enjoys the fact that you can meet foreign people in a big city?
8 says that they get bored easily if they spend time in the countryside?
9 enjoys the air quality in the countryside?
10 says living in the countryside is great for family life?
11 didn't enjoy the long journey to work every day?
12 says that it's more expensive to live in a big city, but it's worth it?

Rose

Arthur

James

Maria

5 Find words or phrases in the article with a similar meaning.

Rose
1 There were too many people on the Tube. *The trains were overcrowded.*
2 a long daily journey to work and back
3 a house
4 The air is clean.
5 making the most of the fact that there is not much noise

Arthur
6 things to do in the evening for fun
7 when people talk about other people's lives
8 It's more expensive.
9 with people from all over the world

James
10 work possibilities
11 I've got lots of jobs and my CV is great.
12 places to look at paintings and art
13 the fact that life is quick

Maria
14 forget about city life
15 raise kids
16 connected to the people in the village
17 not always having friendly people around

6 Complete the questions with words and phrases from Exercise 5. Then discuss the questions in pairs.

1 Do you enjoy the fast p____ of l____ in big cities?
2 Would you be prepared to do a long c____ to work every day?
  Or would you prefer to live near to your work?
3 Do you enjoy going to m____ and g____ ? When did you last visit one and look at art?
4 Do you think it's true that people in big cities can feel alone and i____ ?
5 Do you think it's true that people in small villages like to exchange g____ about other people's lives?
6 What's the n____ like where you live? What do people normally do in the evenings?
7 How important is it to you to live in a place with f____ air? Is the air quality good where you live?
8 Would you rather b____ u____ children in a city or in the countryside?
  Where were you brought up?
9 Would you move to a big city because of the better job o____ ?
10 Is the c____ of l____ in the capital city much higher than in the rest of your country?
  Is it difficult to have a good quality of life in the capital?

Living in the countryside: heaven or hell?

Fed up with living in a big city, with all the stresses and strains of urban life? Four people give their take on what it's like to live in rural Britain.

'I moved out to the countryside about a year ago, and I haven't looked back. I'd been living in London for about ten years, and although it was great to be in the centre of things, I found it increasingly difficult to live there. It was always so busy, noisy and full of people, and it made me really stressed to have to deal with the constant noise and speed of the city. Every morning, I used to get the Tube into work, and the carriage was always completely packed with people, with nowhere to sit down. The trains were overcrowded, hot and uncomfortable, and I found myself hating the journey to work. It also took me at least an hour and a half to get to work every day, and the commute was really tiring. I also found the air pollution hard to deal with; I kept getting colds and feeling sick, and in the end it really got me down. So I decided that I would look into relocating to the countryside, and after thinking it over for several months, I changed my job so that I could work at home, and I bought a property about an hour from London, in a small village. I love it! There's fresh air, it's quiet and there's hardly any traffic. I just love summer evenings, sitting outside the local pub, having a drink and enjoying the peace and quiet.'

Rose

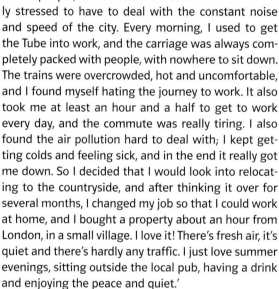

'I was born in New York City, and I can't imagine living anywhere else. For one thing, I love the fact that there are so many job opportunities in New York. I'm a journalist, and if you want to be a writer in the US, New York is the place to be. There is a lot of competition for work, but if you're good, there are so many different organisations you can write for. I've been able to build a really good career so far, and I'd never be able to do that in a small town. I also love the museums and galleries – sometimes if I have time I visit one of the galleries on the way home and just spend an hour looking at great art. When I leave the gallery, I feel inspired and I forget about any stress or trouble I have in everyday life. Another thing I really like is the fast pace of life – everything is quick, but I love it, it makes life interesting. Sometimes I go for a long weekend to the New Hampshire countryside, and it's beautiful, especially in the fall, but after about three days I run out of things to do, and I need to come back to New York.'

James

<u>'I was brought up in a small village,</u> and I know it's really beautiful, but it was also really boring. In the village where I lived, there's one shop, one pub and nothing else. If you want good nightlife, or even to watch a film at the cinema or go somewhere new, it's not the place to be. On top of that, it's so small that everyone knows each others' business, the whole village is full of gossip, and you can't really be yourself. <u>As soon as I turned 18 and passed my exams at school, I moved to London. I've been there for six years now,</u> and I've just started working as a trainee lawyer in a big law firm. It's true that the cost of living is much higher in London, and I have to be careful with money, but I feel alive in London, and I wouldn't change it for the world. The other thing I really like in London is that it's really cosmopolitan. You come across people from all over the world here, and that's really interesting. Even being able to try food from other countries or go to watch foreign films makes me feel like I'm more open-minded, and I'm able to enjoy the cultural life. I'd never go back.'

Arthur

'I think I have the best of both worlds. I live in a small village outside Paris, and it only takes 40 minutes by train to get into the centre of the city. I work in an advertising agency near to the city centre, and I need to be in Paris for work, but I've always lived in the village, and I've never been tempted to move into Paris. I love the fact that at the end of the day, when I get home, I can just switch off from the stress of the city and relax. We have a big garden at the back of the house, and it's a great place to bring up children. My husband and I have three kids, and it's great for them to grow up in the fresh air, with space to play and to explore the countryside. At weekends, we sometimes go out for a walk in the woods near our house, and it's beautiful. The main thing I find is that people in the village are so friendly, probably because they have time. They'll always stop for a chat, and it feels great to be part of a community. I think in Paris people are a bit isolated – even though they are surrounded by people, it's easy to feel alone and that nobody cares, whereas here you can drop into the local bar for a drink and everyone knows your name and says hello.'

Maria

Pulling it all together

Review

1 Write three topic sentences about living abroad.

One advantage of living abroad is that you improve your language skills.

2 Write a support sentence for each of the sentences you wrote in Exercise 1.

If you live abroad, it is likely that you will learn the language of the country to a high level.

3 Write four more phrases for giving examples in Writing Task 2.

For instance, ...

4 Answer these questions about introductions for advantage/disadvantage essays.

1 How many sentences should you write in the introduction?
2 What should each sentence do?

5 Complete these introduction sentences with the correct form of the verb in brackets.

1 In the last few years, it ____ (*become*) more common for people to work from home.
2 These days, many people ____ (*choose*) to take a gap year between school and university.
3 The number of people who decide to work from home ____ (*rise*) at the moment.

6 Answer these questions about conclusions for advantage/disadvantage essays.

1 How many sentences should you write in the conclusion?
2 What should each sentence do?

7 Complete these conclusion phrases.

1 To s____ up, ...
2 H____ looked at this topic in d____ , ...
3 It is c____ that there are b____ advantages and disadvantages of living abroad.
4 A____ it is true that it can be difficult at first, __
5 On b____ , I think the benefits o____ the d____ .

Final practice essay

> *Some people find living in the country enjoyable and relaxing, whereas others would not like to live in the country, and prefer living in a big city instead.*
> *What are the advantages and disadvantages of living in the countryside?*

1 🎯 Write an essay for the exam task above. You should:

- include your four main points
- provide supporting ideas for your main points (details/reasons/examples)
- use a range of vocabulary
- write at least 250 words.

2 Compare your answer with the sample answer on pages 157–158.

Writing Task 2: Opinion essays

Model essay

 In this unit, you're going to look at how to write a Task 2 opinion essay. In the exam, you will have 40 minutes for Task 2 and you have to write a minimum of 250 words.

1   Discuss these questions in pairs.

1   Do students in your country have to pay for education, or is it free?
2   Why do you think some people believe that students should pay for university?
3   Why do you think other people believe that university should be free?
4   Do you think students should pay for university, or should the government pay?

2   Read the exam task and model essay, and see if the ideas are the same as yours.

Systems of funding university education are different from country to country. While some countries charge students for studying at university, others offer university education for free.
Do you think students should pay for higher education?

These days, more and more young people go to university, and as a result, the cost of funding higher education is greater than in the past. It is argued by some people that students should pay for university themselves. However, my view is that higher education should be free for students and should be paid for by the government. This essay will explain my opinion in more detail.

One reason that I believe university education should be free for students is that it allows everyone to go to university. If students have to pay for university, many people from low-income backgrounds will not be able to afford it. As a result, poorer young people will be excluded from learning and future job opportunities, which is not fair.

Another reason to support free university education is that it benefits society in general. For example, if the government invests in training more doctors, there will

be better health care in the future, once those doctors are working in hospitals. In addition, those doctors will pay higher tax on their income, and that tax can be used to pay for university education for future generations.

Having said that, there are those who argue that students should pay for their own university education. They believe that university education is an investment and that it is not fair to ask society in general to pay for it. They think that poorer students should borrow money to pay for the tuition fees, because later on they will get a better job and earn more money.

In conclusion, having looked at this topic in detail, although it is true that graduates generally earn more money than people who do not go to university, on balance I am of the opinion that governments should pay for higher education. The main reason is that education should be available to everyone, not just to people who have enough money to pay for it.

(323 words)

3   Answer these questions about the model essay.

1   Does the writer give an opinion in the introduction?
2   How many paragraphs in the main body support the writer's opinion in the introduction?
3   What does paragraph 4 do?
4   How is the main body of this opinion essay different from the advantage/disadvantage essay in Unit 1?

Introductions for opinion essays

 For opinion essays, your introduction should be slightly different to the introduction for advantage/disadvantage essays. This section will show you how to tailor your essay introduction to suit the task type.

1 Read the introduction to the model essay again. What is the main difference between this and the introduction to the advantage/disadvantage essay on page 7?

[1]These days, more and more young people go to university, and as a result, the cost of funding higher education is higher than in the past. [2]It is argued by some people that students should pay for university themselves. [3]However, my view is that higher education should be free for students, and should be paid for by the government. [4]This essay will explain my opinion in more detail.

2 Match the sentences in the introduction in Exercise 1 (1–4) with their function (a–d).

a Gives the writer's opinion.
b Rephrases the question in different words.
c Says what the rest of the essay is going to do.
d Shows that some people have a different opinion to the writer.

3 In the introduction, you can explain the different sides of the argument. Look at the phrases in bold.

It is argued by some people that *students should pay for university themselves.* ***However, my view is that*** *higher education should be free for students, and should be paid for by the government.*

Put these words in the correct order to form other phrases for doing this.

1 argue | people | that | some … , is | opinion | my | but …
2 believe | people | many | that … . think | I | that | However, …
3 argument | put | some | people | forward | the | that … . disagree | I | believe | and | this | with | that | I …
4 thought | by | some | people | is | it | that … . view | I | that | hold | the | However, …

4 Practise using the phrases from Exercise 3 with these pairs of contrasting opinions.

1 People should pay for healthcare./The government should make healthcare free.
    Some people argue that people should pay for healthcare, but my opinion is that the government should make healthcare free.
2 All criminals should be sent to prison./It depends on the crime and the age of the criminal.
3 Children should go to single-sex schools./Children are more successful in mixed-sex schools.
4 All adult men should have to join the army for a period of time./It should be people's choice if they want to sign up for the military.

5 Complete the introduction about healthcare below with the words in the box.

> argued ▪ by ▪ detail ▪ essay ▪ explain ▪ however ▪ longer ▪ result ▪ should ▪ view

These days, people are living longer and [1]_____ , and as a [2]_____ , the cost of funding healthcare is higher than in the past. It is [3]_____ by some people that individuals [4]_____ pay for health care themselves. [5]_____ , my [6]_____ is that healthcare should be free for everyone, and should be paid for [7]_____ the government. This [8]_____ will [9]_____ my opinion in more [10]_____ .

6 Complete these opinion essay introductions.

1 Topic: Mixed or single-sex schools?
    It is common these days for the majority of students to go to schools where boys and girls study together. Some people argue that it is better to send children to single-sex schools, but …

2 Topic: Send all criminals to prison?
    In the modern world, crime rates are rising, and people feel increasingly under threat from crime. It is argued by some people that the answer is to send all criminals to prison. However, …

7 **Write introductions for these opinion essay questions.**

1 Should all adult males have to join the army for a period of time?
2 Should shops be closed on Sundays to give workers a break?

Topic sentences for opinion essays

> When you write an opinion essay, your topic sentences are slightly different from an advantage/disadvantage essay. In paragraphs 2 and 3 of an opinion essay, you should give reasons to support the opinion you wrote in the introduction.

1 **Look at the topic sentences in paragraphs 2 and 3 of the model essay on page 21.**
   How are they different from the ones in the model essay in Unit 1?

2 **Complete these topic sentences that can be used for paragraphs 2 and 3.**

1 One r_____ that I b_____ university education should be free is …
2 One a_____ in f_____ of making university free is …
3 The m_____ reason that I t_____ university education should be free is …
4 A_____ reason to s_____ free education is that …
5 Another argument in f_____ o_____ making university free is …
6 A s_____ argument to support free university education is that …

> You can use the structure *Not only … but also …* to give emphasis when writing Task 2 essays. One way that you can do this in opinion essays is to repeat the argument from paragraph 2, starting with *Not only … ,* and then introduce the new topic sentence using *but also*:
>
> **Not only** *does free university education allow everyone to go to university,* **but** *it* **also** *benefits society as a whole.*
>
> Note that:
> • you need to change the word order of the sentence after *Not only* so that it follows the word order of a question, adding the auxiliary *do/does* if necessary;
> • the word order after *but also* does not change, but the subject of the sentence needs to be placed between *but* and *also.*

3 **Rewrite these sentences, changing the word order after *Not only*.**

1 Not only the government should invest in public transport, but it should also build more cycle lanes.
2 Not only mobile phones are addictive for children, but they also stop children from communicating face to face.
3 Not only you save money on travel costs if you work from home, but you also do not have to spend time commuting.
4 Not only banning cars from city centres on Sundays would reduce pollution, but it would also make it safer to cycle.

4 **Rewrite these sentences using *Not only … but also …***

1 Healthcare should be free, and it should be available to everyone.
2 The government should increase tax on junk food, and ban junk-food advertising.
3 Military service is expensive, and it does not benefit young people.
4 Sending criminals to prison protects society, and deters potential criminals from breaking the law.

5   **Write two topic sentences using these notes and the sentence beginnings below.**

Opinion in the introduction: All adult men should do military service.
Argument in paragraph 2: Military service teaches young people respect.
Argument in paragraph 3: There will be more trained people to defend the country if there is a conflict.

One argument …
Not only …

Giving opinions

 You will need a range of phrases to give your opinion, both for Writing Task 2 opinion essays and also in Speaking Part 3.

1   **Complete the phrases below for giving opinions with the words in the box.**

> am ▪ concerned ▪ opinion ▪ point ▪ see ▪ view ▪ would

1   As far as I am _____ , …   3   My _____ is …   5   My _____ of view is …
2   In my _____ , …   4   I _____ argue that …   6   I _____ of the opinion that …

When you are giving your opinion in speaking or writing, you can use a range of grammar structures and patterns:

- *should* + verb:
  *I believe that joining the army **should be** optional.*

- *ought to / need to* + verb:
  *The government **ought to pay** for university.*
  *The council **needs to take** responsibility for the state of the roads.*

- *I would recommend / support* + -ing:
  ***I would recommend/support paying** workers more on Sundays.*

- *I would advise* + -ing / someone to + verb:
  ***I would advise taking** the matter more seriously.*
  ***I would advise the government to invest** more in public transport.*

2   **Complete the sentences below giving opinions with the words in the box.**

> advise ▪ need ▪ ought ▪ should ▪ starting ▪ support

1   I would recommend _____ school at six, so that children get an extra year to play and develop before going to school.
2   In my opinion, the government _____ reduce the number of tests the children have to do.
3   My view is that schools _____ to provide more opportunities for students to study subjects like art and music.
4   I would _____ schools allocating more time to arts subjects, especially in primary school.
5   I would _____ schools to start teaching foreign languages from about six or seven years old.
6   I think governments _____ to raise teachers' pay, so that more talented people go into teaching.

3   **Choose one or two of these questions related to education and discuss them in pairs. Use the language from Exercises 1 and 2.**

1   At what age do you think children should start school?
2   What do you think is the best age to start learning a foreign language?
3   How important do you think it is to study subjects like music and art at school?
4   Do you think teachers in your country are paid enough money?
5   Do you think exams are a good way to test students?
6   Do you think children should go to mixed or single-sex schools?

Conclusions for opinion essays

In the conclusion of an opinion essay, you need to give your opinion again, and say which of your two arguments is the most convincing. It is also important to show that you have understood the other side of the argument.

1   **Read the conclusion below.**

Identify …
1   the writer's opinion;
2   the most convincing argument to support the writer's opinion;
3   the part of the conclusion which shows the writer has understood the other side of the argument.

In conclusion, having looked at this topic in detail, although it is true that graduates generally earn more money than people who do not go to university, on balance, I am of the opinion that governments should pay for higher education. The main reason is that education should be available to everyone, not just to people who have enough money to pay for it.

You can use the structure *Although it is true that … , on balance …* to say 'I understand the other side of the argument, but this is what I think':

Although it is true that single-sex schools can be good for girls' confidence, **on balance** I believe that children should go to mixed schools.

2   **Write sentences using these prompts and the structure *Although it is true that … , on balance …***

1   Other side: Working from home can save you money.
    My opinion: It is better to work in an office.
2   Other side: Living in the countryside is relaxing.
    My opinion: It is better to live in a big city.
3   Other side: University education is expensive for the government.
    My opinion: It should be free.
4   Other side: Mobile phones can be addictive.
    My opinion: They are really useful for communication and getting information.

3   **Complete this conclusion.**

In ¹c____ , ²h____ looked at this topic in ³d____ , ⁴a____ it is true that graduates generally earn more money than people who do not go to university, I ⁵a____ of the ⁶o____ that governments ⁷s____ pay for higher education, and not students. The ⁸m____ ⁹r____ is that education should be available to everyone, ¹⁰r____ of their parents' income, and this can only be done by making it free.

Identifying opinion and advantage / disadvantage questions

> *i*   You can identify the difference between an opinion essay question and an advantage/disadvantage essay question by reading the second part of the essay question carefully and deciding if you are being asked to give a direct opinion or to consider both sides of the argument first.

1   Decide in pairs if these are opinion essays or advantage / disadvantage essays.

1   *The trend in education is to give more tests to children, and from an earlier age. It is believed that the earlier children start to get used to doing exams, the more successful they will be when they are older.*
    Discuss the pros and cons of testing children in primary school.

2   *Children should not start school until the age of six or seven, because they need to have more time to play and develop before they go to school.*
    To what extent do you agree or disagree with this statement?

3   *Some people think that subjects like maths, science and languages are the most important school subjects, and less time should be spent on subjects like music and art. Others believe that schools should spend more time on subjects like music and art, because children need to have a broad range of knowledge and skills.*
    Discuss both views and give your opinion.

4   *It is common for young people to go abroad to study at university, instead of studying in their home country.*
    Do the advantages of studying at university in another country outweigh the disadvantages?

2   Discuss the first essay question in Exercise 1 in pairs.

1   Why do you think some people argue that children should be tested in primary school?
2   What are the arguments against testing children in primary school?
3   What is your opinion?

3   Make a plan for the essay. Write down the main ideas and some supporting points.

Example:

Type of essay: *advantage / disadvantage*

My view: *I disagree with testing children in primary school.*

Main point	Support
Disadvantage 1 Children should enjoy primary school without the stress of tests.	It's important for children's development to play and learn in a fun and relaxed environment without being tested and put under pressure.
Disadvantage 2 Children should be tested when they are older and they are able to benefit from tests.	Around 11 or 12 is a good age for children to start being tested.
Advantage 1 People believe that children need to start being tested early to get better results later on.	There is more and more competition in the world for jobs, and children need to start learning as early as possible.
Advantage 2 If children are tested, they will study harder.	Tests make children revise and study more, and therefore get better results.

4   Discuss the other three essay questions in Exercise 1 in pairs. Make notes about the main ideas.

5   Make essay plans for the other three essay questions in Exercise 1.

Reading: True / False / Not Given questions
Skills focus

- One of the most common question types in the IELTS Reading exam is *True / False / Not Given* (T/F/NG) questions. You can answer these questions more effectively if you use the right strategy and technique.
- Remember that T/F/NG questions are generally in order in the text, so answer one question at a time.
- You may also come across *Yes / No / Not Given* questions in the exam. These are similar and can be tackled in the same way, but Y/N/NG questions usually identify views and opinions, whereas T/F/NG questions generally ask questions about information or facts.

1 **Discuss these questions in pairs.**

1 Do you find T/F/NG questions difficult? If so, why do you think that is?
2 Do you have a technique for T/F/NG questions? If so, what is it?

2 **Read this extract and the six questions. Then study the technique below for answering T / F / NG questions.**

Teaching in Spain

In 1998, I got a job teaching English in Spain. I spent 18 months teaching in a city called Córdoba in the south of Spain. It was my first teaching job and it was an amazing experience. The city was beautiful and the students were really friendly. In summer, though, it was too hot – it can get up to 48 degrees Celsius in August. It was impossible to go out in the afternoon, because it was just too hot. In May, there is a fantastic festival in Córdoba, where the people dance and eat and drink for a week, and dress up in traditional flamenco costumes. Not many people speak English in Córdoba, so it is really important to learn Spanish when you live there.

1 The writer taught English in Córdoba for a year and a half.
2 The writer had never worked as a teacher before they got this job.
3 In summer, the temperature is sometimes over 50 degrees.
4 The Córdoba Festival lasts for seven days.
5 The writer wore traditional flamenco clothes when they went to the festival.
6 The writer learned good Spanish when they were in Córdoba.

1 Read Question 1 and underline the words that contain the most important information (key words):
   The writer <u>taught English</u> in <u>Córdoba</u> for <u>a year and a half</u>.

2 Divide the key words into the following two categories:
   a **Topic key words**: These help you locate quickly the sentence or part of the text where you will find the answer. In this case, the topic key words are *taught English* and *Córdoba*.
   b **Detail key words**: These help you decide if your answer is True, False or Not Given. In this case, the detail key words are *a year and a half*.

3 If there is more than one topic key word, think about which one would be easier to find quickly in a text. Then write 'T1' above this topic key word, 'T2' above the other one, and 'D' above the details key word:
   ```
            T2              T1              D
   ```
   The writer <u>taught English</u> in <u>Córdoba</u> for <u>a year and a half</u>.

4 Think of synonyms of the key words if possible.
   taught English = was a language teacher
   a year and a half = 18 months

5 Search the text for the topic key words or their synonyms. When you find them, <u>underline</u> them.

6 Now look carefully for the detail key words. If the answer is True, you might find the word itself or a synonym. If the answer is False, you may find words related to the detail key words (e.g. *a year and a half*). So if the answer is False, you might find another period of time in the text.

7 If you think the answer is True or False, underline the word(s) in the text which tell you the answer. If you can't find anything, then the answer is probably Not Given.

This is how your question paper should look after you have answered Question 1:

Teaching in Spain

T2   D (Q1)
In 1998, I got a job <u>teaching English</u> in Spain. I spent <u>18 months</u> teaching in a city

    T1
called <u>Córdoba</u> in the south of Spain.

   T2   T1   D
1 I <u>taught English</u> in <u>Córdoba</u> for <u>a year and a half</u>.   **Answer = True**

3 Follow the technique in Exercise 2 for Questions 2–6 in Exercise 2. Then check your answers in pairs.

4 Read the text below and use the same technique to say whether these statements are True, False or Not Given.

       D   T1   T2
1 <u>Over twice as many schools</u> teach <u>well-being</u> as <u>a decade</u> ago.
   Possible synonyms: double, happiness, ten years   *Answer = True*
2 More than 100 schools are thinking about bringing in well-being classes next year.
3 Two-thirds of students who went to university in 2008 from Wilson's school did not complete the course.
4 Not as much time is spent on well-being classes as on maths and English in Wilson's school.
5 There was a slight drop in exam results after well-being classes were introduced.
6 Teachers in the school are pleased that well-being classes have been introduced.

Can you teach children to be happy?

This may seem a ridiculous idea, but schools in the UK are increasingly starting to include lessons on 'well-being', or happiness, in the curriculum. Worried by the alarming rate of teenage depression and self-harm, schools across the country have started to include classes which aim to teach children things like fitness, relaxation, positive thinking and self-esteem. In the last ten years, the number of schools who have well-being lessons as a regular part of the curriculum has more than doubled, and at least 100 more schools are considering introducing well-being lessons next year.

'The main reason that we introduced well-being lessons into the school,' says Andrew Wilson, head of a large secondary school in London, 'is that I was really concerned that children were leaving us at 16 or 18 unable to cope with modern life. Even those children who got great grades at A Level and went on to university were often unprepared for real life, and suffered from depression and stress-related illnesses.

Of the young people who left our school in 2008 and went to university, around 30 percent dropped out before the end of the first year. I wanted to try and do something about this.'

What followed was truly remarkable. Well-being classes now constitute around ten percent of class time at Andrew Wilson's school, and although this is still less time than is spent on traditional subjects like maths and English, the benefits are substantial. The school noted that truancy rates fell by 80% in the first year, and the number of days lost to pupil sickness halved. Teachers also reported that most students were more positive in lessons, more motivated and the average grades were up ten percent on the year before.

'It just shows that education is not simply about knowledge and facts and passing exams, it's about the whole person, about feeling good and feeling happy in yourself,' says Andrew Wilson. 'It's the best thing I've ever done.'

5 What do you think about the ideas in this text? Do you think well-being lessons are a good idea?

Skills application

1 🎯 Read the text below and say whether these statements are True, False or Not Given.

1 It has been decided to bring in tests for five-year-olds in the UK.
2 Exam results in the UK are better than ever before.
3 Exam results for seven-year-olds are now transparent to parents and school administrators.
4 Those who believe children should not be tested before 11 argue that the qualities required to work successfully are different from in the past.
5 In countries where there are no tests until 11, exam results at 18 are better.
6 The majority of parents would like to keep the same number of tests in schools.

Testing, testing …

It is estimated that by the time a person finishes school at the age of 18, they will have had to sit between 100 and 120 exams and tests in their school career, and this number is rising all the time. Once, children were spared tests until the end of primary school, aged 11; now the first SATs in the UK take place at age seven, and there are rumours that exams for five-year-olds are on the way, with a decision expected next year. But is this a good thing? Does it work?

Those who are in favour of lots of tests claim that the reason that school-leaving exam results are higher than at any time in the past is because children start taking exams early on and work harder as a result. They point to the fact that 20 or 30 years ago, where there were no tests until age 11, most children were able to go through primary school without worrying about how well they were doing and, more significantly, teachers were not held accountable by results for children's progress. As a result, it is argued, those teachers who were good at their job taught children well without exams, but those who were perhaps less motivated could put less work into their lessons, knowing that there was no way of measuring how the children were doing. By contrast, now that parents and school managers can see the results of the age-seven tests in black and white, teachers are held accountable and know that if their children all do badly, they will have to answer to parents and bosses as to why.

However, there are also those who believe that testing children at seven is not effective, and does not help children learn, at least not in the right way. They argue that children need to use the period between the ages of five, when they start school, and 11, when they move on to secondary school, to learn more important things than simply how to get through exams. They need to be encouraged to be creative, to play, to experiment, to express themselves. In the modern world, the skills that people will need when they grow up and enter the workplace are soft ones – interpersonal skills, team-working, empathy – as well as creativity. Knowing your times tables or memorising dates and facts are not enough to equip young people for the future world of work. People who want to get rid of tests at seven say that by doing so, therefore, we are actually improving the quality of education and our children's future job prospects.

So, what of the future? Is the way forward more tests, more hard work for children and possibly better exam results in the end? Or is the danger that you can develop a system with great results in maths and science, and yet high rates of teenage burnout, depression and even suicide? According to a recent survey of parents, around three-quarters would like there to be fewer tests in schools. Will this happen? One thing is for sure – everyone has to go to school, so this is a topic that will continue to be discussed and argued about passionately for years to come.

2 Discuss these questions in pairs.

1 At what age did you start having tests at school?
2 What do you think is the best age to start testing children?
3 Have you ever got 100% in a test?
4 Were you good at exams at school?

Listening Part 1: Distractors

Skills focus

> i In the first part of the listening test, you will normally hear a telephone conversation in which someone is phoning to ask for information. There are ten questions and you need to write down the answers as you listen. Don't forget, you will only hear the conversation **once**.

1 🎧5 The conversation that you hear will include some 'distractors'. These are words which could be the answer, but they are not correct. You have to listen carefully and ignore them. Listen to the first part of a conversation between a receptionist at a gym and a man phoning to ask about gym classes and sport facilities and complete the notes.

- Types of membership available:

  – ¹_____ : unlimited access to class and two sessions with a personal trainer at no extra cost

  – ²_____ : two gym classes a week included, but no personal training

  – ³_____ : access to the gym only; no classes

- The man chooses a ⁴_____ membership.

- Membership costs ⁵_____ a year (= less than ⁶_____ a week)

2 Look at this extract from the audioscript. Circle the words that gave you the answer for gap 4 in Exercise 1 and underline the two distractors. Why are they not correct?

Man: *OK, well, as I said, I think I'll probably only go to one or two classes a month, so I won't need the full membership. I think the standard membership is the one I'll go for. If I sign up for the basic, I'll end up paying for the classes anyway, so I might as well have them included in the price.*

3 🎧6 Listen to the second part of the conversation. Complete this form and make a note of any distractors that you hear.

University Gym

Gym classes

The most popular class is ¹_____ .

Before you can attend a class, you need to reserve an ²_____ with a personal trainer.

Personal details

Name: Geoff ³_____

Date of birth: ⁴_____ /_____/_____

Credit card number: ⁵_____

Security code: ⁶_____

First session with the trainer

Geoff is going to attend a session with a trainer on ⁷_____ at ⁸_____ pm.

---

4   Highlight the distractor in each of these sentences and discuss in pairs why they are not correct.

1   The standard membership is £215 per year. It was £200 last year.
2   We've had to raise the price by £15. But that still works out at less than £5 a week.
3   We're currently not running yoga classes, but we're planning to add a class to
    the programme in the new year.
4   Our most popular class is boxfit … Previously, our number-one class was always Pilates,
    but it's been overtaken this year.
5   **Receptionist**: Great, and I just need the security code on the back.
    Man: OK, it's 585. No, hang on, it's 588.
6   **Receptionist**: We have a slot at two o'clock on Wednesday. Would that suit you?
    Man: Wednesday … no sorry, I can't do that I'm working.
7   **Man**: How about Thursday? Would four o'clock work?
    Receptionist: Let me have a look. Could you make it quarter past four on Wednesday?
    Man: Yes, that's fine.

5   Match the distractors in Exercise 4 (1–7) with these reasons (a–e). You can use each reason more than once.

a   The speaker hesitates and corrects what they first said.
b   The question is about now and the speaker talks about the future.
c   The question is about now and the speaker talks about the past.
d   The first possible option is rejected by one of the speakers.
e   The speaker mentions two similar numbers, relating to different things.

6   Discuss these questions in pairs.

1   Are you a member of a gym?
2   Have you ever been a member of a gym?
3   Have you ever been to a gym class? What kind of class was it?
4   Have you ever had a personal trainer?
5   Would you like to have a personal trainer in the future?
6   Do you enjoy going to the gym?
7   Do you prefer doing exercise alone or with other people?
8   What time of day do you normally exercise?

Skills application

1   🎧7   ⊙ You will hear a conversation between a woman enquiring about English classes and the receptionist at the South Coast School of English. Listen and complete the form.

> **i**   In the real exam, you have to answer ten questions, but there are 16 questions here to give you extra practice.

South Coast School of English

Type of course
The woman is going to study a ¹____ course.

Types of GE course available
•   Intensive
•   ²____
•   ³____
The woman decides to study the ⁴____ course.

Times
Her course will start at ⁵____ and finish at ⁶____ .

Prices
The course costs ⁷____ per week.
You pay ⁸____ less if you book for eight weeks.
There is also a ⁹____ of £50.

Doing the test
The woman is going to visit the school on Friday at ¹⁰____ to do a placement test.

IELTS Preparation Courses
Students have to pay an additional ¹¹____ per week.

Personal details
Name: Jana ¹²____
Nationality: ¹³____
Date of birth: ¹⁴____ /____/____
ID card number: ¹⁵____
Phone number: ¹⁶____

2 When you finish, go through the audioscript on pages 148–149 and highlight all the distractors. Think about what type of distractors they are, and why they are wrong.

Speaking Part 3
Giving opinions

In Part 3 of the Speaking test, the examiner will ask you to give your opinion about a few questions on the same topic. Part 3 lasts for between four and five minutes.
Some of the things that the examiners will be looking for in Part 3 are:
- using a range of phrases to give your opinion (see page 24);
- extending your answer and explaining your point clearly;
- giving examples, including personal examples;
- showing that you can deal with complex questions.

1 **Discuss these Speaking Part 3 questions in pairs.**

1 Do you think that it is a good idea to test children?
2 Do you think children in your country are tested too much?
3 How could the education system of your country be improved?

2 🎧8 **Listen to someone answering the three questions in Exercise 1. Make notes about what you hear.**

3 🎧8 **Now read the extracts from the listening. Can you remember what goes in the gaps? Listen again and check.**

- Do you think that it is a good idea to test children?
  Yes, I do, but only up to a ¹p_____ . As I ²s_____ it, testing is a really good way to measure progress, and you can see how you're doing, and your ³s_____ and ⁴w_____ by doing a test. ⁵N_____ o_____ that, my ⁶v_____ is that it motivates students to work harder if they know there is a test coming up. But it's important to ⁷s_____ a b_____ between having tests, and allowing children to enjoy learning without being tested all the time.

- Do you think children in your country are tested too much?
  Yes, I think so. In my ⁸c_____ , for ⁹e_____ , we had tests all the time, especially from the age of about 13 upwards, and I remember feeling ¹⁰s_____ and under ¹¹p_____ most of the time between about 13 and 18. As far as I'm ¹²a_____ , it's even worse now, there are more and more tests, and I think sometimes they were just about learning by ¹³h_____ and ¹⁴m_____ information, and not about really learning and thinking for yourself.

- How could the education system of your country be improved?
  Well, I think ¹⁵f_____ o_____ thing, it ¹⁶w_____ be ¹⁷g_____ if the government reduced the number of tests, as I ¹⁸s_____ b_____ , and maybe replaced some of those tests with ¹⁹c_____ or a presentation or a project. And ²⁰f_____ a_____ , I'd like to ²¹s_____ the government ²²s_____ or at least cut ²³t_____ fees for university, because it's really expensive, and it means that poorer kids sometimes can't afford to go.

4 **Go through Exercise 3 and highlight the phrases you think are useful to learn.**

5 **Find a word or phrase from Exercise 3 with a similar meaning to these. The answers are in the same order as you hear them.**

1 Things you are good at and things you are not good at *strengths and weaknesses*
2 Find a middle way
3 As far as I know
4 Remembering information such as dates by repeating it again and again in your head (two phrases)
5 Work which is assessed during the year, not in an exam at the end of the year
6 The money students pay for university

6 🎯**Think about the questions in Exercise 1 again. Make some notes and try to answer them with some of the language from Exercises 3–5.**

Pulling it all together

Review

1 How many sentences should you write in the introduction of an opinion essay, and what should you write in each sentence?

2 Write some more phrases for explaining the two sides of the argument.

Example: *Some people argue … , but my opinion is …*

3 Write down at least four more ways of introducing a topic sentence.

Example: *One reason that I believe university education should be free is …*

4 Rewrite these topic sentences using *Not only … but also …*

1 Exams help students see their strong and weak points, and also exams motivate students to work harder.
2 Exams are really stressful for children, and also children can have a bad day and therefore the result is not fair.

5 Complete these phrases for opinion essay conclusions.

1 In c____ , …
2 H____ l____ at this topic, …
3 In d____ , …

4 A____ it is t____ that …
5 On b____ , I am of the o____ that …
6 The m____ r____ is that …

6 Complete these phrases for giving opinions.

1 I think the government s____ spend more money on education.
2 I would r____ investing more in universities.
3 I would a____ schools t____ start teaching foreign languages from the age of six.
4 My view is that schools o____ t____ spend more time teaching creative subjects like art and music.
5 I would s____ reducing the amount of time students have to spend doing tests.

7 What are 'distractors' in IELTS Listening? What different type of distractors are there?

8 What technique should you use to tackle *True/False/Not Given* questions in the Reading test?

Final practice essay

Every school system in the world includes regular tests and exams, and many people think that it is important for students to take lots of exams.
What is your opinion?

1 🎯 Write an essay of at least 250 words for the exam task above. You should:

- include a clear opinion in the introduction
- include two paragraphs to support your opinion
- include one paragraph which looks at the other side of the argument
- include more detail about your opinion in the conclusion
- include phrases and vocabulary from this unit.

2 Compare your essay with the sample answer on pages 159–160.

Health and fitness

Writing Task 2: Problem / solution essays

Model essay

Another common essay type in Task 2 is a problem/solution essay, where you will be asked to explain the causes of a common problem and then make suggestions about how to solve the problem. As with all Task 2 essays, you have to write a minimum of 250 words in 40 minutes.

1 Discuss these questions in pairs.

1 What do you do to keep fit?
2 Do you think you have a healthy diet?
3 Have you ever smoked?
4 In general, do you think you lead a healthy lifestyle?

2 Read the exam question and model essay, then answer the questions below.

In many countries, people's average weight is rising, and their general levels of health and fitness are decreasing.

What are the main causes of these problems, and what can be done to tackle them?

In recent years, governments and health experts around the world have become increasingly concerned about the general health of the population. They are particularly worried about problems such as obesity, the lack of exercise and high rates of smoking and drinking. This essay will look at these problems in more detail and propose some solutions.

One major problem connected to health is obesity. These days, many people eat a lot of processed meals, junk food and take-aways, and as a result, obesity rates are increasing all the time. This is a significant problem in the UK, for example, where sales of this type of food are higher and higher every year. To try to solve this problem, governments should increase tax on unhealthy food.

Another issue is that many people do not do enough exercise. The main reasons for this are the high cost of gym membership and a lack of sports facilities. The answer could be for governments to subsidise going to the gym and to build more sports facilities. If they did this, it would make it easier for people to keep fit.

A final problem is the high rate of smoking and drinking alcohol. The number of people who suffer from serious illnesses connected to cigarettes and alcohol is on the rise in many countries. One way to address this issue is for governments to spend more money on publicity campaigns to educate the public about the dangers of smoking and drinking too much.

To sum up, there is no doubt that the problems of poor health connected to people's lifestyle are becoming increasingly serious. Unless action is taken urgently, these problems will only get worse. My opinion is that responsibility for improving people's health lies mainly with the government but also with individuals.

(297 words)

1 Which problem is mentioned in paragraph 2, and what reason is given for it? What is the writer's solution?
2 Which problem is mentioned in paragraph 3, and what reasons are given for it? How many solutions are proposed?
3 Which problem is mentioned in paragraph 4? What is the result of this problem? What does the writer suggest should be done?
4 Where in the essay can you find a specific example to highlight the writer's point?
5 What is the writer's opinion in the conclusion about who should tackle these problems?

3 Discuss these questions in pairs.

1 Does your country have a problem with obesity?
2 Apart from taxing unhealthy food, do you there is anything else that can be done to tackle obesity?
3 Is there a problem with high rates of smoking and drinking in your country? Apart from educating the public, is there anything else that could be done to encourage people to quit or cut down?
4 Do you think people in your country generally do less exercise than in the past?
5 Are there any other ways to increase the fitness of the population?
6 Do you agree with the writer's opinion in the conclusion of the essay?

Topic sentences for problem/solution essays

> When you write a problem/solution essay, you should write about two or three key causes of the problem in the question. To introduce each idea, you need to write a topic sentence, which will help organise the main body of your essay.

1 Complete these topic sentences from the model essay.

1 One _____ problem _____ to health is obesity.
2 Another _____ is _____ many people do not do enough exercise.
3 A _____ problem _____ the high rates of smoking and drinking alcohol.

2 Complete the topic sentences below with the words in the box.

> additional · cause · contributing · explain · explanation · factor · for · related

1 One _____ of stress in modern life is job insecurity.
2 One reason _____ teacher shortages in secondary schools is the low rates of pay.
3 An _____ cause of teacher shortages is that some pupils are very badly behaved.
4 One _____ for water shortages is that some people waste a lot of water when washing or cleaning their teeth.
5 A further way to _____ shortages is that a lot of the water pipes are old and leak water.
6 Another _____ behind air pollution in cities is the high level of traffic in city centres.
7 One _____ factor to high crime rates is the lack of police officers on the streets.
8 One issue _____ to homelessness is the lack of hostels for people who have nowhere to live.

> When you write a topic sentence, you can either use a noun phrase or a sentence with *that* + a clause:
> *One reason for stress in modern life is **job insecurity**.*
> *One reason for stress in modern life is **that many people have jobs which are insecure.***

3 Rewrite these topic sentences with either a noun phrase or *that* + a clause.

1 One reason for the shortage of nurses is the low salary.
2 One cause of air pollution in cities is the lack of green areas and parks.
3 Another way to explain obesity is poor diet.
4 One contributing factor to traffic congestion is that public transport is very expensive.
5 One issue related to high rates of alcohol consumption is that alcohol is very cheap in supermarkets.
6 A final cause of homelessness is that there are very few jobs for unskilled workers.

4 Write full topic sentences using the prompts.

1 Teacher shortages | have to do a lot of marking in their free time.
2 Obesity | lack of ability to cook healthy food.
3 People's lack of fitness | drive to work instead of walking or cycling.
4 Crime | lack of CCTV cameras on the streets.

5 Write two or three topic sentences about this exam task.

Many people feel that modern life is faster, busier and more stressful than in the past. More and more people are suffering from stress in their daily life, and the rates of stress-related illness are increasing.

What are the main causes of stress in modern life?
How can these problems be tackled?

Example: *One reason for stress in modern life is job insecurity.*

Language for writing about solutions

In each paragraph of the main body of a problem/solution essay, you will need a sentence which introduces your solution or suggestion. You can learn and practise specific chunks of language for doing this:
The solution might be to *raise the tax on cigarettes.*

1 Complete these sentences for introducing solutions from the model essay.

1 To try to _____ this problem, governments _____ increase tax on unhealthy food.
2 The _____ could be _____ governments _____ subsidise going to the gym.
3 One _____ to address this _____ is for governments to spend more money on publicity campaigns to educate the public about the dangers of smoking and drinking too much.

2 Complete the solution phrases below with the words in the box.

> be · could · deal · for · forward · order · solution · tackle

1 To _____ with this problem, councils _____ invest more in bus services.
2 The way _____ might _____ for governments to cut the price of gym membership.
3 The _____ is _____ people to cycle or walk to work, instead of driving.
4 In _____ to _____ this issue, governments should ban smoking in vehicles.

3 Add a solution phrase from Exercises 1 and 2 to these sentences. Use the words in brackets to complete the sentences.

1 One cause of teacher shortages is low pay. (*raise salaries*)
   The way forward might be to raise teachers' salaries.
2 One reason for air pollution in cities is a lack of controls on factory pollution.
   (*governments* | *stricter pollution limits*)
3 One explanation of rising crime is a shortage of police officers. (*governments* | *employ more*)
4 One reason that many people do not cycle to work is that the roads are too dangerous.
   (*local councils* | *create more cycle lanes*)

4 Write a solution sentence for each of these problems, using language from this section.

1 There is a shortage of qualified nurses.
   One way to address this issue is to give student nurses a salary while they are studying.
2 Trains and buses are over-crowded at rush hour.
3 People do not recycle newspapers, bottles and plastic enough.
4 Children often check their mobile phones during school lessons.

Vocabulary for writing about solutions

> ℹ You can improve the language in your problem/solution essays by building up a bank of vocabulary about solutions to common problems.

1 Write down a possible solution to each of these problems. Then compare what you wrote in pairs.

A It is dangerous to cycle on many roads in city centres.
   The government could build more cycle lanes to make cycling safer.
B There are too many cars in cities.
C Class sizes in primary schools are too high.
D Many accidents are caused by people using their mobile while driving.
E Public transport is too expensive for many people.
F Families do not eat together as much as they used to.
G Not everyone recycles their household rubbish.
H House prices are so high that many people can't afford to buy a house.
I There are long delays for hospital treatment.
J Supermarkets use too much plastic packaging.
K Homelessness is an increasingly serious problem.

2 Match the sentence halves.

1 Governments could bring in a law …   a who do not recycle.
2 The government should fine people …   b to make them cheaper.
3 The government could allocate more money …   c to healthcare.
4 The government should introduce a congestion charge …   d for people who drive into the city centre.
5 They should set aside an hour a day …   e primary-school teachers.
6 The government could offer cheap loans …   f to first-time buyers.
7 The government could subsidise trains and buses …   g on producers of plastic packaging.
8 The government could open more shelters …   h to have dinner as a family.
9 Schools could employ more …   i for people sleeping rough.
10 Governments should impose higher taxes …   j to ban people from using mobiles in cars.

3   Match the solutions in Exercise 2 with the problems in Exercise 1 (B–K).

4   Find words or phrases in Exercises 1–3 that mean the following.

1   The number of pupils in a class
2   Give more of the government's money to something
3   Introduce a new law
4   You have to wait a long time to see a doctor at the hospital.
5   Make people pay money as a punishment
6   Sleeping on the streets
7   Places where homeless people can stay
8   Raise tax
9   Make something illegal
10   People who want to buy their first home

5   Discuss these questions in pairs.

1   Do you think governments should fine people who do not recycle?
2   Do you agree with imposing higher taxes on plastic packaging?
3   What was the average class size when you were at school?
4   Are there long delays for hospital treatment in your country?
5   What can be done to help people who are sleeping rough?
6   Do you think it is a good idea to give cheap loans to first-time buyers?
7   Do you think introducing a congestion charge in big cities is a good idea?
8   Do most people in your country set aside time every day to eat together?

6   Discuss the problems in Exercise 1 again. Use language from this section to improve your solution sentences.

Conclusions for problem / solution essays

When you write a conclusion to a problem/solution essay, you can do two or three of these things, depending on the topic:
- say how serious the problem is
- say who you think should solve the problem
- summarise the ideas in the main body
- make suggestions about what to do in the future
- say what will happen if nothing is done to solve the problem.

1   Read this conclusion and match the sentences (1–3) with the meanings below (a–c).

[1]In conclusion, it is clear that people are facing a range of health problems connected to their lifestyle, such as poor diet, lack of exercise, and smoking and alcohol consumption. [2]These problems need to be addressed quickly, otherwise they will only get worse. [3]I believe that both governments and individuals have a role to play in improving everyone's health.

a   Who should solve the problem
b   A summary of the ideas in the main body
c   What will happen if nothing is done to solve the problem

2   **Complete the phrases below for problem / solution conclusions by adding the words in the box in the correct place.**

> act · addressed · duty · increasingly · lies · range · simple · ~~taken~~

taken

1   Action needs to be ⌄ urgently.
2   This is an serious problem.
3   The main responsibility with the government.
4   To sum up, there is no doubt that these problems need to be quickly.
5   I think that everyone has a to recycle and care about our environment.
6   There are a of problems facing people who live in the countryside.
7   There is no solution to the problem of teacher shortages.
8   Governments need to now before the problem gets even worse.

> You can use *unless* and *otherwise* to show what will happen if no action is taken to solve the problem: *We need to take action urgently,* **otherwise** *more people will suffer from lifestyle-related illnesses.* **Unless** *the government invests more money in health education soon, these problems will become even greater in the future.*

3   **Read the example sentences in the box above and answer these questions.**

1   Where in the sentence should you write *otherwise*, and which tense comes after it?
2   Which tense follows *unless*? Which tense comes in the second half of a sentence which starts with *unless?*
3   In the first half of the sentence with *otherwise*, which tense is used?
4   In the example sentence, *unless* comes at the beginning. Is it possible to change the order of the sentence and start with *These problems …*?

4   **Write sentences using *unless / otherwise* as shown and the correct form of the verbs in brackets.**

1   If we don't raise teachers' pay | fewer and fewer people (*choose*) to go into teaching. UNLESS
2   Governments should ban the use of mobiles while driving | If they do not do this, there (*continue*) to be a large number of accidents. OTHERWISE
3   If governments do not make recycling compulsory | many people (*continue*) to throw recyclable material away. UNLESS
4   If supermarkets continue to use so much packaging | the seas (*continue*) to be full of plastic. OTHERWISE

5   **For each of these suggestions, discuss in pairs *What will happen if we don't …?* Use *unless / otherwise* in your answers.**

1   Charge people to drive into city centres
2   Increase the price of plastic bags in supermarkets
3   Cut waiting times for hospital operations
4   Make public transport cheaper

Writing about the result of the solution

> You can finish a paragraph in the main body of a problem / solution essay by writing a sentence to describe the result of the solution. You do not need to do this in every paragraph, but try to include at least one result in each essay:
> *The answer could be for governments to subsidise going to the gym and to build more sports facilities.* **If they did this, it would make it easier for people to keep fit.**

1 Rewrite these phrases for writing about the result of the solution in the correct order.

1 *this | doing | by*, more people would take up sport.
By doing this, more people would take up sport.
2 *that | this | mean | would* people would eat more healthy food.
3 *done | this | was | if*, people would be more aware of the dangers of a lack of exercise.
4 *that | this | be | of | would | the | result* more people would give up smoking.
5 *the | did | government | if | this | the*, people would probably cook more often from scratch.

2 Add a result to each of these sentences, using the words in brackets.

1 Governments should allocate more money to homeless shelters. (*they | did*)
2 To tackle this issue, teachers' working hours could be reduced. (*was | done*)
3 The answer is for the government to give everyone an extra week of paid holiday every year.
(*would | mean*)

3 Add a result to each paragraph. Use any result phrase you like.

1 One problem is that advertisers of unhealthy snacks and drinks target children's television programmes.
To solve this problem, governments could ban junk food advertising at certain times of the day.
2 Another issue is that many people work long hours and are too tired to do exercise after work. One way
to address this issue is for companies to encourage their staff to go the gym in their lunch hour.

Introductions for problem / solution essays

In the introduction to a problem/solution essay, you do not need to give an opinion about the
problems or solutions. You just need to rephrase the question, then say what the rest of the essay will
do.
You can write an introduction in three stages:
1 Rewrite the question, focusing on why the problem is being discussed. Is it a problem that has
become more serious or widespread recently? You can often use a sentence with the present
perfect to talk about this.
2 Give a little bit more detail about the issue, perhaps outlining the main causes or problems briefly.
3 Say what your essay is going to do.

1 Complete these introduction sentences with the present perfect of the verbs in brackets.

1 In recent years, the number of people admitted to hospital with obesity-related illnesses ____
dramatically. (*rise*)
2 The issue of teacher shortages ____ increasingly serious and urgent in the last decade or two. (*become*)
3 There ____ a sharp increase recently in the percentage of the population who are officially
overweight or obese. (*be*)

2 Complete the introduction below with the words in the box.

addressed · detail · examine · face · major · over · propose · reached · related · tackle

[1]____ the last few years, agreement has been [2]____ among governments and medical professionals that
societies [3]____ serious problems [4]____ to lifestyle. Obesity, lack of exercise and problems connected to
smoking and drinking are now [5]____ health issues and need to be [6]____ urgently. This essay will [7]____
these problems in more [8]____ , and [9]____ some ways to [10]____ them.

3 Write an introduction for the exam task on stress on page 37.

Reading: Identifying information

Skills focus

> A common question type in IELTS Reading gives you a list of topics and asks you to decide **which paragraph contains the information** in each topic.
> To answer this type of question effectively, you should follow these steps:
> 1 Read all the questions before you start, because they are not in order.
> 2 Underline the key words in each question and think of possible synonyms.
> 3 Read the first paragraph of the text. Try to match one or more of the topics with information in the first paragraph.
> 4 If you think you have found an answer, highlight your answer in the text. Make sure there are synonyms which prove your answer is correct.
> 5 Read the rest of the text paragraph by paragraph and find the rest of the answers. Remember that you may find more than one answer in the same paragraph.

1 **Highlight the key words in these topics and think of possible synonyms.**

1 A country with a long tradition of a vegan and vegetarian diet
2 An explanation of why veganism has recently grown in popularity
3 A positive change in attitude towards veganism
4 An environmental reason for becoming vegan
5 Possible dangers of a vegan diet

2 **Read the text and match the topics in Exercise 1 to the correct paragraphs. Highlight the sentences that gave you the answers.**

Example: 1 Paragraph C

The vegan revolution

A According to recent figures, around 20% of the UK population are now either vegetarian or vegan. This is a dramatic change compared to even a generation ago. Twenty years ago, the typical image of a vegan was an odd bearded hippy, wearing sandals and eating lentils. It was certainly not popular, and children whose parents brought them up as vegans in the 1970s or 1980s were seen as weird or strange at school, and often tried to hide their veganism from classmates. Now, though, veganism is seen as a positive lifestyle choice. Veganism among people under 25 is approaching 40%, and it now has a trendy and cool image.

B What lies behind this trend? Surveys suggest that the primary motivation for this mass conversion to veganism is health-related. A vegan diet is seen as better for you, with less saturated fat, no red meat, of course, and no high-fat dairy products, and with an emphasis on vegetables, nuts and grains. A minority of those asked in a recent survey also said that they became vegan in order to protect the planet, the reason being that so much land, water and resources are taken up with feeding livestock for meat and dairy production. If everyone in the world went vegan, they argue, it would save massive amounts of resources and help feed the population far more cheaply and efficiently.

C Despite the fact that veganism has become popular relatively recently, it is not new. Vegans have existed as long as human beings have existed, and a vegan or vegetarian diet has been a fundamental part of some cultures and religions for thousands of years. India, for instance, has had the highest rate of non-meat eaters in the world since records have been kept.

D So what should be taken into account if you are thinking of going vegan? There is no doubt that vegan food is now widely available, both in supermarkets and restaurants, so there is little difficulty in finding non-meat based products. Do be aware, though, that in order to get sufficient protein in your diet, it is necessary to do a little bit of research. Without animal protein, if you do not eat vegan foods in the right combinations, for example rice and beans together, there is a risk of your diet lacking essential nutrients and proteins. There are also other options if you are not ready to give up animal products entirely: also popular is the concept of a 'flexitarian' diet, meaning a diet that is mostly vegetarian or vegan, but contains the occasional piece of meat and fish.

3 Discuss these questions in pairs.

1 Is veganism growing in popularity in your country?
2 Do you eat meat, fish and dairy products? If so, would you consider becoming a vegan in the future?
3 What do you think about the idea of a flexitarian diet?

Skills application

1 🎯 Read the text on page 44 and do this exam task using the techniques on page 42.

> ***Which paragraph (A–F) contains the following information?***
> ***NB: You may use any letter more than once.***

1   The effects of over-work on family life
2   A law which is not enforced properly
3   A comparison between employment conditions in the past and now
4   A lack of separation between life at work and life outside work
5   Problems caused by long journey times
6   The impact of the internet on how people work
7   Pressure to do what your co-workers do
8   A consequence of short-term work contracts

2 Find words or phrases in the text with a similar meaning.

1 Improvements in technology (paragraph A) *technological advances*
2 Not enough time (paragraph B)
3 Spending a lot of time at work (paragraph B)
4 A major reason for stress (paragraph B)
5 I feel that I should do what everybody else is doing (paragraph C)
6 I work too much and I have very little free time. (paragraph C)
7 Being unable to forget about work (paragraph D)
8 Travelling long distances to work and back every day (paragraph E)
9 Work contracts with no time limit (paragraph F)
10 Work contracts for a fixed time (paragraph F)
11 Work contracts where no work is guaranteed (paragraph F)

3 Complete these questions with the correct form of the words and phrases from Exercise 2.
Check your answers, then discuss the questions in pairs.

1 How important is it to have a good w_____–l_____ balance?
2 Is it common in your country for people to have a z_____-h_____ contract? What do you think about this time of contract?
3 Do you find it easy to s_____ o_____ from work or study?
4 Do you think people in your country generally have long w_____ h_____ ?
5 How would you feel about c_____ more than two hours to work every day? Would you be willing to do it?

4 Write down three key causes of stress in modern life and ideas to tackle them.

Example: *Cause of stress: Many people have zero-hours contracts.*

Solution: The government should bring in a law to ban zero-hours contracts.

Stress in modern life 'on the increase'

More people are seeing doctors with stress-related conditions than ever before, according to a new survey by the Sleep Foundation.

A Modern life is causing 'major stress' and sleepless nights for an ever-increasing number of people, says a report which surveyed over 5,000 people in the UK over a 12-month period. The report says that although many labour-intensive and stressful jobs that in the past had to be done by hand are now done by computers or electronic devices, modern life is actually more stressful than in the 1950s.

B The major cause of stress, according to the report, is a feeling of a lack of time. 86% of the people surveyed felt that they were under time pressure in their lives, in a variety of ways. Many cited long working hours as a key source of stress. By law, workers are not allowed to work more than 48 hours a week in the UK, but 42% of people reported that they worked more than 48 hours a week on a regular basis, with a resulting cost to their physical and mental health.

C Sally Jones, a marketing executive from North London, is a case in point. 'My contracted hours are 8.30 a.m. to 5.30 p.m., but I don't think I've ever left the office on the dot of 5.30 p.m. Extra work comes in late in the day, I have to go to meetings which go on sometimes until 6 or 7 p.m., and there's also a culture of staying late in the office, which I feel pressure to fit into. Everyone else stays late, so if I went home at 5.30 p.m., I feel like my boss would think I was lazy.' As a result, she says, she normally doesn't get home until 8 or 8.30 p.m. 'I have a very poor work–life balance – I hardly ever see my husband, and when I do get home, I'm normally exhausted and I'm in bed by 9.30. It's really bad for our relationship.'

D Another issue which affects many people is the inability to switch off from work. This is caused by internet technology. In the past when people left work, it was impossible for their boss to contact them; now many people are checking work emails in evenings and weekends, and never really get a chance to stop working. As a consequence, many workers have no chance to really relax and to forget about work and do other things.

E For people in big cities, travelling to and from work is a big issue. In London, for instance, it can take two hours to get from one side of the city to the other, and people often get stuck in traffic jams if they are driving or have to travel in over-crowded and busy buses or trains if they are using public transport. Half of those surveyed said that spending several hours a day commuting to work and back was their number-one source of stress.

F A final factor in the report is the fact that many jobs these days do not offer permanent contracts. In previous generations, many people got their first job and then had a job for life, with no need to worry about losing it. However, in today's job market, many workers are employed on temporary and short-term contracts. In the IT industry, for instance, it is common for workers to be employed for six months, then they are either given another six months or they are not offered another job. In many jobs, people are also employed on zero-hours contracts, whereby they do not have any guaranteed hours and have to wait and see week by week how much work, if any, they will get. The result of all of this is to place workers under great amounts of stress and pressure, and often leads to people working too much, in order to try to make sure they get work at the end of the contract or even in the next week.

Listening Part 1: Predicting answers

Skills focus

> In Listening Part 1, as well as thinking about distractors (see Unit 2), it is also very important to think about what kind of answer is most likely, and also to look at the key words in the question.

1 Look at the exam task below and discuss these questions in pairs.

1 What do you think are possible answers for questions 1 and 2?
2 What is the key word in question 2, and can you think of a synonym of this word? What do you predict the answer will be?
3 Which is the most likely answer for question 4: 2, 20 or 200? Why?
4 What is a synonym of the word *available* in question 5? If the tickets are not available, how might the speaker say this?
5 If you hear £50, £35 and £70 for question 6, which would be the correct answer?
6 For question 7, which of these family names would be correct and why: *Smith* or *smith*?
7 How many digits do you think you will have to write in question 9?
8 For question 10, what is a synonym of *arriving*? What type of answer do you expect to hear?
9 What do you think the answer to question 11 could be?

You will hear a man telephoning a ticket agency to buy some tickets for a sports event in London. Write NO MORE THAN TWO WORDS AND/OR A NUMBER for each answer.

Tickets for sports events in London

Tickets available:	football, athletics, [1]____ , [2]____
Maximum number of tickets per person:	[3]____
Number of tickets required:	[4]____
Next date available:	[5]____
Cheapest ticket:	[6]____
Name of buyer:	Mr John [7]____
Address:	34 [8]____ Road, Manchester
Credit card number:	4156 3245 [9]____
Tickets arriving:	[10]____
If customer cancels tickets, there are no [11]____ .	

---

2 🎧 09 🎯 Listen and do the exam task above.

3 Use the audioscript on page 149 to check your answers.

4 Look through the audioscript again and highlight any distractors that you find.

5 Discuss these questions in pairs.

1 Do you like watching sport on TV? If so, what are your favourite sports to watch?

2 Have you ever been to a live sports event? What did you see?

3 Are you planning to go to any sports events in the future?

4 How much money would you be willing to pay to watch a big sports event?

5 Have you ever paid a lot of money for a ticket for a different type of live event, such as a concert?

Speaking Parts 1 and 2

Common questions related to health and fitness

1 Complete the Part 1 questions below with the words and phrases in the box.

> been ▪ cook ▪ cut down ▪ encouraged ▪ enough ▪ food ▪
> in shape ▪ individual ▪ member ▪ moderation ▪ taken part ▪ team ▪ trainer

Sport and fitness

1 What exercise do you do to keep _____ ?
2 Are you a _____ of a gym?
3 Have you ever had a personal _____ ?
4 Do you prefer _____ sports or _____ sports? Why?
5 Have you ever _____ in a competition or sports event?
6 Were you _____ to do sport by your parents when you were a child?

Health and diet

7 Have you ever _____ on a diet?
8 Is there anything that you eat too much of, and you need to _____ on?
9 Do you think it's OK to eat things like chocolate and cake in _____ ?
10 Do you think schools should teach children to _____ ? Did you have lessons when you were at school?
11 Do you think you generally get _____ sleep?
12 Is there one _____ item that you just could not live without?

2 Discuss the questions in Exercise 1 in pairs.

3 Use language from this unit to prepare an answer for these Speaking Part 2 questions. Take one minute to make notes and think about what you're going to say.

> *Talk about an enjoyable sporting event you have watched or taken part in.*
> > *You should say:*
> > > *what the event was*
> > > *when and where it took place*
> > > *who you were with*
> > *and why you enjoyed it.*

> *Talk about someone you know who you think has a healthy lifestyle.*
> > *You should say:*
> > > *who the person is*
> > > *how long you have known this person*
> > > *why you think they have a healthy lifestyle*
> > *and if there is anything you could learn about being healthy from this person.*

4 🎯 Speak about each Part 2 question in Exercise 3 for two minutes.

Speaking Part 3

Giving examples from your experience

In Speaking Part 3, you will be asked to give your opinion about different topics. To make your answers longer, better and more interesting, you can add in examples from your own experience, talking about your country, people you know or yourself.

1　Read these Speaking Part 3 answers (A–C) and underline all the sentences which talk about:

- the speaker's personal experience
- the experience of people the speaker knows
- examples from the speaker's country.

A　**Do you think children should have to do at least half an hour of sport a day at school?**
In my opinion, I think it's important for children to do regular exercise, so I agree that children should have to do sport every day at school. Children in my country only have sport once or twice a week, and it's not enough. I also think that parents should encourage their children to do sport in their free time. In my case, for example, my parents took me to football training every Saturday morning.

B　**Why do you think many people give up eating meat?**
I think there are different reasons. Some people stop eating meat for health reasons, because they think a vegetarian or vegan diet is better for you. Other people think that it's wrong to kill animals for food as a principle. My brother, for instance, gave up meat when he was 14 for this reason. For me personally, I gave up meat two years ago and it was definitely for health reasons.

C　**Why do you think many people don't do enough exercise?**
Well, I think one reason is that people are often just too busy. If I think about my father, for example, he has a really stressful job and he works really long hours, and he never really has time to do any exercise after work. Another thing is that it can be quite expensive. Where I'm from, you have to pay quite a lot of money to join a gym, which means that a lot of people I know can't really afford it.

2　Complete the phrases below for talking about personal experience with the words in the box.

> average · case · country · experience · instance · know ·
> personally · take · think · where

1　In my ＿＿＿ , …
2　For me ＿＿＿ , …
3　If I ＿＿＿ about my best friend, he …
4　＿＿＿ I'm from, …
5　A lot of people I ＿＿＿ …

6　People in my ＿＿＿ generally …
7　My sister, for ＿＿＿ , …
8　From my ＿＿＿ , I would say …
9　The ＿＿＿ person in my country …
10　＿＿＿ my brother, for example. He …

3　🎯 Ask and answer these questions in pairs, giving examples from your own experience.

1　Why do you think many people eat unhealthy food, or don't cook as often as they could?
2　Do you think schools should teach children about healthy eating and nutrition?
3　Do you agree that life was less stressful in the past than it is now?

Pulling it all together

Review

1   Rewrite these topic sentences by changing the grammar of the underlined part of the sentence.

1   One cause of stress in the modern world is <u>the fast pace of life.</u>
2   Another reason for stress is that <u>people spend a long time at work every day.</u>
3   One contributing factor to teacher shortages is that <u>the number of students in a class is rising all the time.</u>
4   One issue related to obesity is <u>a lack of exercise.</u>

2   Complete these ideas for writing about solutions.

1   I____ a congestion charge in cities.
2   B____ in a law to ban mobiles in cars.
3   E____ more teachers and nurses.
4   I____ higher taxes on older cars which pollute the environment.
5   F____ people who do not recycle.
6   Set a____ an hour a day to eat together as a family.
7   Open more shelters for people sleeping r____ .
8   Offer cheap loans to f____-t____ buyers.
9   A____ more money to healthcare.
10 S____ buses and trains to make them cheaper.

3   Rewrite these conclusion sentences using the word in brackets.

1   Action needs to be taken immediately, otherwise the healthcare system will face a crisis. (*unless*)
2   Unless the government invests substantial resources in healthcare, people will continue to face a long wait for hospital treatment. (*otherwise*)

4   Write a list of phrases that you can use for writing about the result of the solution.

Example: Governments should allocate more money to healthcare.
<u>By doing this</u>, waiting times for operations <u>would</u> fall.

5   What steps should you follow when you are answering a Reading question that asks you to identify specific information?

Final practice essay

1   🎯 Write an answer for this problem/solution essay about stress that you looked at earlier in the unit.

> *Many people feel that modern life is faster, busier and more stressful than in the past. More and more people are suffering from stress in their daily life, and the rates of stress-related illness are increasing.*
> *What are the main causes of stress in modern life?*
> *How can these problems be tackled?*

2   Compare your essay with the sample answer on page 162.

Media and technology

Writing Task 2: Two-part essay questions

Model essay 1

> Sometimes Task 2 questions can be two-part questions. Instead of having just one question to answer, you need to deal with both. This means that the organisation of your essay will be slightly different from when you only have to answer one question.

1 Discuss these questions in pairs.

1 How do you think the internet has changed how people get information? How was it different in the pre-internet age?
2 Are there any drawbacks of information and websites being freely available to people?
3 When you were a child, did your parents control what you could look at on your computer? If so, how?
4 Do you think there should be controls on what adults can look at on the internet? If so, how could we do this?

2 Read the two-part essay task below and think about these questions.

1 How would you organise your answer?
2 What would you write in the introduction?
3 How many paragraphs would you write, and what would you write in each paragraph?
4 What would you write in the conclusion?

In the modern internet age, information is freely available to anyone who has a computer and an internet connection. In the pre-internet age, information was more tightly controlled and regulated by governments. However, these days there is virtually no control by governments of what people can read and look at on the internet.

Is this unlimited access to information on the internet a good thing?
Should there be any controls on what information adults and children can have access to on the internet?

3 ⊙ Try writing an answer for the task in Exercise 2.

4 Read the model essay, then compare it to the one you wrote in Exercise 3.

As a result of the development of the internet, people can now search for anything they want and find it at the touch of a button. In my view, having access to information online is generally a positive thing, but I also believe that it is important to place some limits on what children can look at on the internet. This essay will explain my opinion in more detail.

One benefit of having access to information online is that it is much easier for people to gain knowledge than in the past. To take one example, people who cannot attend a face-to-face university course now have access to online courses and can study at home, whenever they want. It is also easier to get information as a consumer. People can read online reviews and compare different products and services online, and therefore make better choices about what to buy.

However, there are also disadvantages of having unlimited information online, particularly for children. The biggest downside of the internet is that children can sometimes access websites with adult content. It is much easier than in the past for children to come across violent or sexual images, and this can have a negative effect on their well-being. Therefore, I believe that there should be controls and limits on what children can watch online. One way to do this is for parents to use a filter on their children's computers which blocks adult content.

In conclusion, my view is that although it is generally a good thing that people have access to information online, there should also be some controls on what children can watch. However, I believe that adults should be trusted to decide what to look at online, and it is important that governments do not prevent adults from getting information about whatever they like.

(304 words)

5 Analyse the model essay by answering these questions.

1 How many sentences are there in the introduction, and what does each sentence do?
2 Has the writer given an opinion about one or both of the questions in the introduction?
3 What is the main idea of paragraph 2?
4 How many examples are used to explain the main idea in paragraph 2?
5 What are the main ideas in paragraph 3?
6 Does the conclusion answer one or both of the questions?
7 What is the writer's conclusion? Do you agree with it?
8 How is the organisation of this essay different from the essays in Units 1, 2 and 3?

6 Read the model essay again and find words or phrases with a similar meaning.
The answers are in order.

1 Because of the development of the internet, …
   As a result of the development of the internet, …
2 find something very quickly online
3 For example, …
4 where you study with a teacher in a classroom
5 the main disadvantage
6 see violent or sexual images by accident
7 This is bad for their happiness.
8 a computer application which stops adult content being seen by children
9 stop adults from finding out information

ℹ When you are planning to write an essay for a two-part Task 2 question, you should:
   • make sure you mention both questions in the introduction;
   • divide the main body of the essay into two paragraphs. Answer the first question in the first paragraph, and the second question in the second paragraph of the main body;
   • make sure that your conclusion talks about both questions.

Grammar: Noun phrases

One way to make your Task 2 answers more interesting and more academic is to use noun phrases. A standard sentence is based around a verb and is called a **verb phrase**:
*One change in recent years is that **the internet has developed.***

To make a noun phrase, change the verb *developed* into a noun, then use the structure *the* + noun + *of* + noun:
*One change in recent years is **the development of the internet.***

1 Change these verb phrases into noun phrases.

1 One change in recent years is that internet access has expanded.
One change in recent years is _____ .
2 One development in the last few years is that universities have introduced free online courses.
One development in the last few years is _____ by universities.
3 A key transformation in recent decades is that business has become more global.
A key transformation in recent decades is _____ .
4 One improvement to the way we watch television in the last few years is that catch-up television has been invented.
One improvement to the way we watch television in the last few years is _____ .

2 Match the halves of these noun phrases. Most follow the pattern of *the* + noun + *of* + noun, but some are slightly different.

1 the expansion of	a the mobile phone
2 the invention of	b well-paid jobs
3 increasing competition for	c internet access
4 the shift towards	d flights in Europe
5 the shift away from	e working from home
6 the need to	f speak English for work
7 the accessibility of	g having one job for life
8 the low cost of	h information on the internet

Another common noun phrase structure is:

In the last few years, there has been …   a rise / a fall / an increase / a decrease in the number of
The last few years have seen …   people who …

In the last few years, there has been a rise in the number of people who work from home.
The last few years have seen a fall in the number of people who study subjects like history or literature at university.

3 Write complete sentences using these prompts.

1 In the last few years | increase | people who go abroad to study English.
2 The last few years | rise | people who change jobs several times in their career.
3 In the last few years | fall | women who stay at home to look after children.
4 The last few years | decrease | people who can afford to buy a house in London.
5 In the last few years | rise | people | study free online courses.
6 The last few years | increase | people | want to move out of big cities and live in the countryside.

Noun phrases can be used to give reasons or explanations. Common linking phrases to do this are:
Due to …
Because of …
As a result of …
As a consequence of …

Communication between people has become much faster, **due to the invention of the mobile phone.**
Because of the introduction of low-cost airlines, *it is now much easier for people to visit other countries for a short break.*

4 **Complete these sentences with noun phrases formed from the words in brackets.**

1 As a result of ____ (*the internet has been invented*), almost unlimited information is available to most people at the touch of a button.
2 More are more people are choosing to study abroad, due to ____ (*speaking English is necessary to get a good job*).
3 As a consequence of ____ (*the cost of a house is rising*), more and more young people are forced to go back and live with their parents after they finish university.
4 There are more and more water shortages these days, because of ____ (*global temperatures have increased*).

5 **Discuss these questions in pairs.**

1 Do you remember what it was like before the invention of the mobile phone? How was life different?
2 How would your life be different without the internet?
3 Do you think the introduction of catch-up television is a good thing? Has it changed how you watch TV programmes?

Model essay 2

1 **Discuss these questions about mobile-phone use in pairs.**

1 How often in a normal day do you think you check your mobile phone?
2 Have you ever worried about overusing it?
3 Do you think addiction to mobile phones is a problem amongst children?
4 Have you ever tried to go without your mobile phone for a few days? If so, how was it? If not, would you try it?

2 **Read the exam task and model essay, then answer the questions on page 53.**

These days, even primary-school children often have their own mobile phone, and many parents are increasingly worried about their children becoming addicted to their phones. To deal with this problem, some primary schools have decided to ban children from using their phones during the school day. Children have to hand over their phones to their teacher when they arrive at school and cannot use the phone until they leave school.

Do you think this is a good idea?
In what other ways can parents stop children from using mobile phones too much?

In some primary schools, the last few years have seen the introduction of a rule to ban mobile phones during school hours. Some people argue that this is too strict, but my view is that this is good for children. I also believe parents should set clear rules and limits on how long children can use mobile phones outside of school. This essay will explain my opinions in more detail.

One advantage of banning mobiles during school time is that it encourages children to talk, play and interact. If children have their mobile phones during school, it is likely that they will check their phone frequently and send messages, instead of chatting with their classmates. As a result, they tend not to develop such good interpersonal skills. In addition, I believe that it is harder for children to concentrate on their lessons if they have their phone in their pocket.

In terms of what parents can do, I am of the opinion that parents should strictly monitor and control how long children use mobile phones. For instance, parents could allow their children to use their phones for an hour a day, at a set time, and then insist that they turn the phone off. By doing this, parents can strike a balance between allowing the child to communicate with friends and use social media, and doing other things, such as talking to their parents or doing sport.

To sum up, having looked at this topic, my opinion is that stopping primary-school children from using phones is a good idea, mainly because they will learn and interact better without a phone. However, I think it is important to allow children to use phones at home, as long as parents set clear boundaries and time limits on how long children use them for.

(301 words)

1 How is the second part of this essay question (*In what other ways can parents stop children from using mobile phones too much?*) different from the second part of the question on page 49?
2 How many sentences are there in the introduction, and what does each sentence do?
3 What is the writer's opinion about banning mobiles in schools?
4 What does the writer suggest that parents could do?
5 What is the topic of paragraph 2?
6 What is the topic of paragraph 3?
7 How many opinions does the writer give in the conclusion?

3 Read the model essay again and find words or phrases with a similar meaning.

1 tell children exactly how long they are allowed to use their phones
2 look at their phone often
3 skills such as working together, getting on with other children and so on
4 focus on the lesson
5 a linking phrase to show that you're going to start talking about the second question
6 If they did this, …
7 have a good balance between two things
8 sites like Facebook and Instagram
9 a phrase which means 'the most important reason I believe this is'
10 Parents tell children what is allowed and what is not.

You can see from the model essays on page 49 and this page that you should:
• answer both questions in the introduction;
• divide the main body into two parts – one per question;
• talk about both questions in your conclusion.

It is also important to identify what type of questions you are being asked. For example, in the essay on page 49, you had to answer **two opinion questions.**
However, in the essay on this page, the first question is an **opinion question** and the second question asks for **suggestions or solutions.**

These two possibilities are very common in two-part questions. You can practise with the essay questions on page 62.

Language for avoiding generalisations

> One way to improve the quality and style of your Task 2 writing is to try to avoid generalising, by using phrases like *tend to* in your writing.

1 What is the difference between these two sentences? Why is sentence b better?

a People who study abroad get homesick.
b People who study abroad tend to get homesick.

2 Work in pairs. Write down any other words or phrases you can use to qualify what you write.

3 Improve these sentences by adding the phrase in brackets in the correct place. There is sometimes more than one possible answer.

1 People who cycle to work are fitter than those who drive. (*generally*)
2 People who live in the capital city spend a long time getting to work each day. (*often*)
3 Children who use mobile phones too much become less sociable. (*can*)
4 People who live abroad for a year or two become more open-minded and tolerant. (*generally speaking*)
5 People who do a lot of exercise and eat healthily do not become overweight or obese. (*tend not to*)
6 People who get good degrees from a top university get good jobs. (*more often than not*)
7 If children have their mobile phones during school, they will check the phone frequently and send messages to people. (*it is likely that*)
8 Children whose parents read a lot at home will enjoy reading too. (*in most cases*)

4 Add phrases from Exercise 3 to these sentences.

1 People who work from home get easily distracted.
2 People who run their own businesses make more money.
3 Those who work in jobs like teaching enjoy their jobs more than people who work in business.
4 People who do not do sport suffer from illnesses later in life.
5 People who live in the countryside have more peace and quiet than those who live in cities.
6 Access to unlimited information on the internet is a good thing.
7 Students who take a gap year after they finish high school are more mature and more successful when they go to university.
8 If smoking is banned in public places, more people will give up smoking.

5 Write sentences about these topics. Use different phrases to avoid generalisations. You can also write another sentence to explain the first.

1 Working in a big company
   Generally speaking, people who work in big companies tend to have more opportunities for promotion than people who work in smaller organisations. This is because the company may have a large number of branches, and so there are more high-level positions available.
2 Moving to another city to study at university
3 Living at home with your parents when you go to university
4 Studying a subject like medicine or law, compared to philosophy or art
5 Working in a small family-run company
6 Living near the sea

6 Find examples of avoiding generalisations in the model essay on page 53.

7 Read through your last two or three Task 2 essays. Did you use any language to avoid writing statements which are too general? If not, think about where you could add some phrases from this page into your essays.

Reading: Matching headings

Skills focus

One of the most common types of Reading question in IELTS is matching headings to paragraphs. Two useful techniques for answering this type of question are:
1   analysing paragraphs and identifying the topic sentence of the paragraph;
2   matching synonyms in the heading and the paragraph.

Technique 1: Analysing paragraphs and identifying the topic sentence of the paragraph
One of the key techniques which will help you answer matching headings questions is to practise finding the topic sentence of the paragraph. The topic sentence is a sentence which sums up the rest of the paragraph. However, some paragraphs do not have a topic sentence. In this case, you should read carefully and decide what you think the main idea of the paragraph is, and then match this idea with the correct heading.

1   Identify and underline the topic sentence in each of these paragraphs (if there is one).

1   Opinion is divided about the benefits for children of watching television. However, many experts believe that television has a positive effect on children. They argue that watching television stimulates the brain and senses, particularly for young children. Not only that, but it is argued that teenagers can learn a lot from television, especially if parents choose to let them watch documentaries or educational programmes. Television also, educational academics believe, has the advantage of providing a common topic for children to discuss together. Children all watch the same programme at home in the evening at home and then talk about it in the playground the next day.

2   If you have exams coming up next summer, make sure you start studying early and work steadily over the year, rather than trying to cram in information at the last minute. If you have a part-time job, make sure you don't work too many hours in the weeks before the exam. Make a study plan and stick to it. Take breaks and try to balance time for studying with time to have fun with your friends. Seek advice from parents, teachers or friends if you find yourself getting stressed. Planning ahead is the route to success.

3   Environmental organisations such as Greenpeace use a range of strategies to get their message across. One way is to take out advertisements about their campaigns in newspapers, to bring people's attention to the issue of the day. They also work with students at universities, setting up environmental groups to get young people interested in green issues. Another tactic used by such organisations is to undertake high-profile campaigning stunts, like abseiling up the side of an oil rig with a large banner protesting about fossil fuels, in order to get media coverage. They also employ 'chuggers', people who are paid to approach shoppers in the street and to try to persuade them to pledge money to the organisation.

4   To begin with, for many people, having a pet such as a cat or dog helps combat loneliness. Dogs in particular are very loyal, and for many older people living alone, having a dog is a form of companion-ship. Pets can also help protect people from potential burglars. A barking canine is often all that is needed to ward off possible intruders and keep properties safe. Not only that, but there is research to suggest that having a pet reduces stress. Stroking Fluffy or Rover is scientifically proven to lower blood pressure and to be relaxing. Finally, having a pet can be a wonderful way of teaching young children about responsibilities to others.

2   Compare your answers in pairs, then discuss these questions.

1   Why did you choose the topic sentences that you did in Exercise 1?
2   Are there any paragraphs which don't have a topic sentence? If so, what is the main idea of the paragraph?
3   Check the correct answer in the key on page 163. Read the paragraphs again and discuss why those are the correct answers.

3 Choose the best heading for each paragraph in Exercise 1.

Paragraph 1
a The benefits of watching television
b The benefits of watching television for children
c The pros and cons of watching television for children

Paragraph 2
a Don't study just at the last minute.
b Don't work in the last few weeks before your exam.
c Organise yourself well in advance

Paragraph 3
a Strategies used by environmental groups like Greenpeace
b How environmental groups like Greenpeace get funds from the public
c How environmental groups like Greenpeace use the media to get their message across

Paragraph 4
a Using pets for protection of your property
b Pets can be good for your physical health
c The benefits of having a pet

4 Compare your answers to Exercise 3 in pairs, then discuss why you rejected the other two possible headings in each case.

> **Identifying topic sentences: tips**
> 1 Some paragraphs (like paragraph 3 above) have a topic sentence with a general idea (*a range of strategies*) in the first sentence, and then details about those strategies in the rest of the paragraph.
> 2 Some paragraphs have a topic sentence at the end (e.g. paragraph 2), which sums up the specific points made in the rest of the paragraph.
> 3 If you think a paragraph does not have a topic sentence (e.g. paragraph 4), read it a second time and think about what think the paragraph is about.

Technique 2: Matching synonyms in the heading and the paragraph

Before you read the text, underline the key words in the heading and think of possible synonyms:
<u>Benefits</u> of television for <u>young people,</u> according to <u>researchers</u>

Key word(s)	Possible synonyms
benefits	*advantages, pros, positives*
young people	*children, teenagers*
researchers	*academics, scientists, experts*

Then read the text quickly and try to match the key words and synonyms with the words in each paragraph. If you find some matches, it is much more likely that you have the correct heading.

5 Look again at paragraph 1 from Exercise 1 and match the key words from the heading in the box above with synonyms in the paragraph.

→ = researchers

Opinion is divided about the benefits for children of watching television. However, many experts believe that television has a positive effect on children. They argue that watching television stimulates the brain and senses, particularly for young children. Not only that, but it is argued that teenagers can learn a lot from television, especially if parents choose to let them watch documentaries or educational programmes. Television also, educational academics believe, has the advantage of providing a common topic for children to discuss together. Children all watch the same programme at home in the evening at home and then talk about it in the playground the next day.

6 <u>Underline</u> the three key words in this heading and think of synonyms for them.

The drawbacks of running a business in your 20s.

7   Read this paragraph and highlight the matches between the key words/synonyms
    you chose in Exercise 6 and the paragraph. Then check your answers.

Many young people think that when they graduate from university, it is the best time to set up a company, because you are young and energetic. However, evidence suggests this is not true. One potential problem of becoming your own boss before your 30th birthday is that you have no real work experience. This means you have never really seen how a company works and so you haven't learned what to do in a whole range of situations. Another downside is that it can be hard to get money from a bank to found your company. Banks like to see a track record of success and that you know what you're doing, and they are reluctant to lend to young people fresh out of college. Finally, it can be tough to have the authority to manage staff much older than you. In conclusion, it's far better to go and work for someone else for a few years, save up some money and then open a business later on.

Skills application

1   🎯 The text below has ten paragraphs, A–J. Choose the correct headings for paragraphs A–J from this list of headings.

List of Headings

i An unexpected popular success	vi An unplanned consequence
ii An explanation of why television audiences were so high	vii An opinion about the nation becoming less united
iii An event which united a nation *Paragraph A*	viii A dramatic change in audience figures
iv Today's television is an improvement on TV in the past	ix A revolutionary change
v A trend that looks set to continue	x Narrowing social differences

Is 'water-cooler television' dead in the UK, and if so, does it matter?

A From the moment that television began to have mass popularity in the UK, which many social historians believe was the coronation of Queen Elizabeth II in 1953, television started to play a role in bringing the nation together. It is believed that over a million British households went out and bought a TV in order to watch the investiture ceremony of the current monarch. Although the picture quality may not have been very high, millions of families sat glued to the TV at a moment of national change.

B An unintended consequence of this was what became known later as 'water-cooler television'. As the British began working in offices, there became space for people to talk and compare notes about what they had seen on the television the night before whilst standing around the water-cooler machine in the office. It may not have been anyone's intention to provide the nation with something to talk about, but that is what happened.

C The shared experience of people watching the same programmes at the same time and then discussing them was facilitated by the fact that, in the 1950s, there were only two television channels in the UK; a third channel, BBC2, was launched in 1964. What this meant was that there was very little choice for viewers, and so people watched the same programmes at the same time. If a programme was popular, half the nation could be watching it.

D It is hard to believe now, but a single programme in the 1960s and 1970s could attract between 25 and 30 million viewers. To put that into context, these days a TV show is considered a success by both broadcasters and advertisers if five million people watch it. And this does not mean five million people watching a programme at the same time. This includes everyone who watches that programme, whether at the time of broadcast or later.

E Media historians believe that, despite the downsides of the lack of choice, television in this period played a key role in a number of significant social changes. First of all, as has been mentioned, it brought workers from different social classes together, as they discussed what they had seen the night before at work. Not only that, but many believe that the differences between the different regions of the UK shrank, as people from the south coast to Scotland, from Belfast to Wales, all watched the same programmes and felt part of something.

F However, since the 1980s, this picture of a cohesive nation watching television together and then talking about it around the water cooler has altered dramatically. Viewers now have a staggering array of choice about what to watch. Hundreds of digital TV channels, online subscription services such as Netflix, on-demand TV that can be watched at any time – all these have completely transformed our viewing habits.

G It is now a very rare series which attracts mass attention and has people talking the next day at work about it. One show which has achieved mass popularity, and therefore passed the 'water-cooler test', is *The Great British Bake-Off*. Who would have thought that a gentle show where 12 contestants bake cakes in a tent could have the nation talking to itself again?

H However, *The Great British Bake Off* is unusual. We do not now have a national conversation very often about 'must-watch' television shows. Does it matter? Henry Stevens, a media historian, believes that it does. 'I think the decline of mass audiences has led to a fragmented nation. What keeps us together any more? Without television to bind the country together, aren't we in danger of having nothing to talk about?' he says.

I Others disagree. 'I think it's great that we now have so much choice,' says Jackie Brown, a journalist based in London. 'People talk about the good old days, when 30 million of us sat around a TV watching the same programmes, but what you have to remember is that most of the programmes were pretty rubbish, and you had no choice at all. It's much better now.'

J So, there you have it. Is the water-cooler moment dead? Most commentators predict that TV audiences will continue to fragment, and that we will have even more choice of what to watch, and how and when to watch it in the future, but that there will always be room for a really popular programme to cut through and get the nation talking.

Listening Part 2: Predicting answers

Skills focus

Listening Part 2 is generally one person talking about a subject for between two and three minutes. It is often a talk on the radio or a short speech to a group of people.
You will hear distractors, as in Listening part 1, but you will also need to predict the type of answer that you need to listen for.

1 You are going to hear an extract from a radio talk about the London Museum of Film and Television. Before you listen, look at the exam task and discuss the questions below in pairs.

The London Museum of Film and Television

1   The museum has been closed for ____ as long as planned.

2   The new exhibition room is significantly ____ and larger than the old one.

3   You can look out over the ____ from the north side of the museum.

4   A new feature of the museum is the ____ room for kids.

5   A highlight of the kids' room is the ____ TV studio, where children can pretend to be TV presenters.

6   Some of the children of the museum ____ have tried out the new kids' room and they really like it.

---

1   What kind of word could be followed by *as long as*? What do you think the answer is?
2   What kind of word goes in the gap? Will it be a similar word, in terms of grammar, to *larger*? What's your guess for this answer?
3   What can you *look out over*? What do you think it might be?
4   What kind of word (noun, verb, adjective, etc.) goes in the gap? What kind of room would you imagine children would like in a museum?
5   What type of TV studio do you think it is? If children 'pretend to be presenters' there, what do you think the answer might be?
6   Whose children do you think have tried out the kids' room?

2   🎧 10 Listen and complete the exam task in Exercise 1.

3   Read this extract from the audioscript and check your answers.
    Discuss if your predictions were correct in pairs.

Man: Hi, everyone, and welcome to the programme. Today's guest is Sally Jones, manager of the London Museum of Film and Television. As many people know, the museum was badly damaged in a fire three years ago, but after a lot of hard work, it is about to re-open next month. Welcome, Sally. Tell us about what's been happening with the museum.

Sally: Thanks for inviting me, it's a pleasure to be here. Well, the first thing to say is that we're really happy to be finally opening. We had originally planned to be closed for just 18 months, but it's taken us twice as long, so that's three years. However, we're really happy with the new museum, and we think people will like what's inside.
So, our main collection of exhibits is now a room which is considerably larger and brighter than the old space, which means we can include a lot more things for people to enjoy. There

are beautiful views now of the river from the north side of the museum, so I think people will really enjoy that, too.

Something which is completely new is our interactive room for children. Once we got the go-ahead from the government to rebuild the museum after the fire, we had a six-month period of consultation with the public, where we asked people what they thought of the old museum, and how we could make it better. Something which came up a lot was making the museum more fun for kids, so we've built a whole new section of the museum for children. It's got all sorts of exhibits that they can touch, sit on and get involved with.

The highlight is a mock TV studio where children can pretend to be TV presenters. They can read a script from an autocue, and then have their news bulletin filmed and watch it back. We've tried it with some of the children of the staff, and the kids absolutely love it.

Skills application

1 🎧11 **Look at the next part of the Listening task and predict possible answers. Then listen and check if you were correct.**

The London Museum of Film and Television

The new buffet restaurant is more informal and [1]____ than the old restaurant.

You can buy finger food, [2]____ , cheaper meals and sandwiches there. There is also a large choice of [3]____ .

The museum bar has the same [4]____ as in the past, but the colour of the décor is different.

The public felt that the old bar was a bit [5]____ , so the new bar will be cheaper.

The opening date is [6]____ .

The original number of guests was [7]____ or ____ , but now there will be 150 people coming to the opening night.

The museum will be open every day of the year except [8]____ and Christmas Day.

Entrance fees:

- Children: £2
- Students: £3 (as long as you show a [9]____ student card)
- Adults: £5
- Free entrance for the under-fives and over-[10]____

2 **Read the audioscript on page 150 and check your answers.**

3 **Discuss these questions connected to museums and galleries in pairs.**

1 What kind of museums and galleries do you enjoy going to?
2 Do you think museums should be free to the public, or should they charge a fee?
3 Is there a museum or gallery somewhere in the world that you've always wanted to visit?

Speaking Parts 2 and 3

The news

 In the IELTS Speaking exam, Parts 2 and 3 are connected. After you finish Part 2, you will be asked questions related to the topic of Part 2. This means that you will discuss one topic area for two-thirds of your Speaking exam.

One way to improve your Speaking score, therefore, is to build up your vocabulary on common topic areas in Parts 2 and 3 of the Speaking exam.

1   Look at this Speaking Part 2 task and make notes. Think about what you want to say and use a dictionary to look up any vocabulary you think will be useful.

> **Talk about an interesting news story that you have read or watched recently.**
>
> **You should say:**
> > **what the story was about**
> > **when you read or watched it**
> > **how you read or watched it (e.g. in a newspaper, on TV, online)**
> > **why you found the story interesting**
> > **and if you talked about this story with anyone else.**

2   Talk about the task in Exercise 1 for two minutes.

3   Complete the phrases below for talking about the news with the words and phrases in the box.

> bias • browse • catch • community • fake news • headlines •
> informed • lose touch • trust • up-to-date

1   I think it's really important to keep ____ with the news, so that you know what's happening in the world.
2   I think it's essential to be ____ about the political news, so that you know what's happening in your country.
3   When I have time, I like to ____ the website of my favourite newspaper and read some interesting stories.
4   I try to ____ the evening news when I come home from work, just so that I'm aware of the main news stories of the day.
5   I think it's a shame if people ____ with the news, because everyone should know what's happening.
6   I often pick up a newspaper on the train to work and look quickly at the ____ of the main stories.
7   I read more news about my local ____ , because it's connected to my life, but I also try to follow the main world events, too.
8   I think people are afraid of '____' and they don't believe what they read on some websites.
9   I know if I follow the news on an organisation like the BBC that I can ____ what they say more than some other news organisations.
10 It's important to be aware that most newspapers have a political ____ and they write stories from the point of view of their political opinions.

4   Discuss these Speaking Part 3 questions in pairs. Try to use some of the expressions from Exercise 3.

1   How important do you think it is to follow the news?
2   How do you generally follow the news? Do you get most of your news online?
3   Do you read or watch more local or international news? Why?
4   Why do you think some people find it difficult to believe what the news tells them?

Communication

1   Look at this Speaking Part 2 task and make notes. Think about what you want to say and use a dictionary to look up any vocabulary you think will be useful.

> **Talk about an important conversation that you have had.**
>
> > **You should say:**
> > > **who the conversation was with**
> > > **when the conversation was**
> > > **what the conversation was about**
> > > **why the conversation was so important**
> > **and what happened after the conversation.**

2   🎯 Talk about the task in Exercise 1 for two minutes.

3   Complete the phrases below for talking about communication with the words and phrases in the box.

> apologised ▪ argument ▪ debates ▪ get on with ▪
> interrupt ▪ misunderstand ▪ presenting ▪ relationships ▪ therapist

1   Although my sister and I disagree about politics, we always have interesting ____ when we talk about it.
2   Last year, my friend and I had a big ____ and we didn't speak for a few weeks …
3   … then we met up for a chat and ____ to each other, and now we're friends again.
4   In the future, communication skills such as ____ ideas to an audience and building good working ____ with colleagues will be more and more important.
5   If you have a problem, it can be useful to talk to a professional ____ , so you can discuss the problem with someone who isn't close to you.
6   It's a key skill to be a good listener and not ____ people when they are telling you something important.
7   When you are speaking to people from other countries, it is easy to ____ what they are saying, because people communicate differently in different cultures.
8   In the future, it will be even more crucial to be able to ____ people from all different cultures and backgrounds.

4   Discuss these Speaking Part 3 questions in pairs. Try to use some of the expressions from Exercise 3.

1   What do you think are the most important communication skills?
2   How important is it to have good communication skills in the workplace?
3   Have you ever had an argument with someone close to you? What happened?
4   Do you agree that it is easy to misunderstand people from other cultures?

Pulling it all together

Review

1 Review some of the vocabulary from this unit by completing the sentences belowwith the words and phrases in the box.

> balance · button · concentrate · filter · limits

1 These days, any information you want can be found online at the touch of a ____ .
2 One way to stop children coming across unsuitable content online is for parents to put a ____ on their child's computer.
3 To make sure children do not stay on their computers for too long, parents can set clear ____ on the amount of time per day that children are allowed to be online.
4 Parents need to be realistic about their children's use of the internet, and strike a ____ between being online and doing other things.
5 If children are constantly checking their phone in class, it will be difficult for them to ____ on the lesson.

2 Use language from page 54 to make these statements less general.

1 People living in big cities spend longer getting to work than people living in the countryside.
2 People who work for themselves find it harder to switch off from work at the end of the day.
3 People who work for private companies now have less job security than in the past.
4 Children who spend too long in front of the television become badly behaved and overweight.

3 What two techniques for tackling Matching headings reading questions were covered in this unit?

4 Complete these sentences containing noun phrases and linking expressions.

1 The l____ few years have s____ an increase in the number of people studying abroad.
2 One interesting d____ in recent years is the t____ of the way people shop online.
3 It is much easier to communicate with friends and family these days, d____ t____ the invention of the mobile phone.
4 As a c____ of cheaper air fares, there has been a sharp r____ in the number of people going abroad for short trips and holidays.

Final practice essays

> 1 *In most countries, the major museums are owned by the government, and some governments have decided not to charge people to enter those museums.*
> *What are the pros and cons of making museums free to enter for everyone?*
> *Do you think all governments should make major museums free for everyone?*

> 2 *It is increasingly common for young people to take a gap year between school and university, or after graduating from university and before starting work.*
> *Why do you think people like to take a gap year?*
> *What do you think is the best way to spend a gap year?*

1 Write essays for the two exam tasks above. You should:

- mention both questions in the introduction
- write two paragraphs in the main body, one for each question
- talk about both questions in the conclusion
- write at least 250 words.

2 Compare your essays with the sample answers on pages 163–164.

Writing Task 2: Discussion essays

Model essay

> Another task type in Writing Task 2 is a discussion essay. This is where you are presented with two different sides to an argument; you have to explain both of them in more detail, then give your opinion. In your conclusion, you can agree more with one side of the argument or you can say that you agree with parts of both opinions.

1 Discuss these questions in pairs.

1 What do you think are the biggest environmental issues facing society?
2 What do you think governments can do to tackle these issues?
3 Do you think you lead quite a green lifestyle?
4 Is there anything you could do to be more environmentally friendly?
5 Have you ever joined an environmental organisation?

2 Read the essay task and model essay, then answer the questions on page 64.

Some people say that governments are responsible for dealing with environmental issues.
Other people believe that it is the individual's responsibility to take action to protect the environment.

Discuss both these views and give your opinion.

There is no doubt that the world is facing many serious environmental problems, such as climate change, polluted air and marine pollution. It is often argued that environmental issues should be tackled by governments. However, there are also those who argue that these problems can only be solved by individuals. This essay will examine both points of view.

One reason that people believe governments should tackle environmental issues is that governments have the power and money to do so. Governments can make laws to reduce the use of fossil fuels and increase renewable energy, for example, and they also have the resources to invest in green technology. Another argument that can be put forward is that major environmental change needs international co-operation. Governments from different countries need to work together and make agreements on reducing carbon emissions, for instance.

On the other hand, there are many people who believe that individuals can make the biggest difference in terms of the environment. They say that each of us should take responsibility for the environment, by recycling, reducing the use of the car or by buying local produce instead of food flown in from the other side of the world. In addition, it is argued that individuals can work together in local communities to make a real difference. For example, they can get together on a Sunday and pick up litter from the local beach or park, or lobby local councils to spend more money on recycling.

In conclusion, having looked at both opinions, my view is that both the government and individuals have a responsibility to protect the environment. Each person should try to act in a green way in their everyday life, but we also need the power of government action to make major environmental changes.

(296 words)

1 Does the writer give an opinion in the introduction?
2 How many sentences are there in the introduction, and what is the function of each of them?
3 How many arguments are there in paragraph 2, and what are they?
4 How many arguments are there in paragraph 3, and what are they?
5 What is the writer's opinion, and do you agree with it?

3 Find word or phrases in the model essay with a similar meaning.

1 The process by which the world's temperature is rising
2 Pollution of the sea
3 Oil, gas and electricity
4 Energy sources from the sun, wind or the sea
5 Money, funds
6 Countries working together
7 Decreasing greenhouse gases
8 Food that comes from near where you live
9 Rubbish that is dropped outside
10 Try to persuade someone in power to do something

4 Discuss these questions in pairs.

1 Have you ever taken part in a beach clean? Would you like to?
2 Do you try to avoid using a car if you can?
3 Do you try to buy local produce?
4 Is there a good system of recycling in the town or city where you live?

Language for introducing ideas

> You can see from the model essay that in the main body of a discussion essay, you need to write about four points. You should write two points about each opinion in the question.
> To do this effectively, you need to learn and practise language for introducing ideas. You can do this with some set phrases and also by using the impersonal passive grammar structure:
> ***It is argued that*** *individuals can work together in local communities to make a real difference.*

1 Rewrite these sentences, changing the underlined words into the impersonal passive.

1 <u>Some people say that</u> individuals should try to use their cars less often.
  It is said that individuals should try to use their cars less often.
2 <u>Many people believe</u> that recycling should be made compulsory.
3 <u>People often claim</u> that renewable energy is cheaper than energy from fossil fuels.
4 <u>People often put forward the argument</u> that only governments can make major environmental changes.
5 <u>People generally think</u> that supermarkets use too much plastic in their packaging.
6 <u>People often say</u> that people should think globally but act locally when it comes to the environment.
7 <u>A common argument is</u> that environmental problems cannot be solved by one government acting alone.

2   Write these set phrases for introducing arguments in the correct order.

1   *argument | is | that | an | there* individuals cannot make much difference to the environment without government action alongside it.
2   *believe | reason | people | one | that | that* governments should tackle environmental issues is because they have the power and resources to do so.
3   *people | many | who | think | there | are | that* governments should invest more in electric car technology.
4   *those | that | there | say | who | are* governments from different countries need to work together to tackle climate change.
5   *line | of | one | argument | is | that* governments should impose heavy fines on people who drop litter.
6   *view | point | that | a | there | is | of* nuclear power is a cleaner form of energy than energy from fossil fuels.

3   Use set phrases from Exercise 2 to expand these sentences.

1   Governments should double their investment in solar and wind power.
2   Governments should close down nuclear power plants because they are too dangerous.
3   Governments should help people save energy by providing money to insulate homes from the cold.
4   Water companies should charge people for the amount of water they use.
5   Local councils should set up park-and-ride schemes in order to reduce car use in city centres.
6   People should take showers instead of baths in order to reduce their water consumption.

Grammar: Relative clauses

You can use a relative clause at the end of a sentence to give more information about the main idea of the sentence and/or your opinion about it.
You can also learn and practise some common verbs and phrases which are used in this type of relative clause:
In some countries, such as Denmark or Holland, councils have built a large network of cycle lanes, **which is a positive development, because it means that it is safe and easy to cycle to work**.
In many countries, the government gives scholarships to children from low-income families, **which makes it possible for them to go to university.**

1   Match the sentence halves.

1 Nowadays, it is free to enter the major museums in London,	a which would encourage companies to transport goods by rail instead of road.
2 Modern technology means that workers can continue to check emails after they leave the office,	b which means that they often have to continue working in the evenings and at weekends.
3 Governments could build new high-speed railway connections between the capital and other big cities,	c which means that people generally have to use their cars to get around.
4 There are very few bus services in rural areas,	d which enables everyone to have access to them, regardless of their income.

2 Complete the sentences below with the relative clause phrases in the box.

> which enables them to • which is a negative development •
> which is a positive development • which means that •
> which would encourage more people to • which would help them realise •
> which would lead to • which would make it easier

1 The cost of rail travel is very high in some countries, ____ many people cannot afford to travel by train and have to drive instead.

2 Over-70s are given free rail travel in the UK, ____ visit other places in the country and see friends, even if they are not very well-off.

3 Governments should cut the tax paid by organic farmers, ____ for people to set up organic farms.

4 Schools should increase the amount of time pupils spend doing sport at school, ____ better fitness and health among children.

5 Some governments have stopped invested in renewable energy, ____ because it means that the country has to use more energy from fossil fuels.

6 Parents could take their children along to a local beach clean, ____ the importance of recycling and cutting down on plastic.

7 Governments could subsidise the cost of having solar panels on the roof of your house, ____ install them.

8 Some coffee companies have recently started charging people if they use a disposable cup, ____ because it will encourage people to bring a reusable cup when they buy a coffee.

3 Complete these sentences with a suitable relative clause phrase.

1 Tuition fees for university now cost over £9,000 a year in the UK, ...

2 There is much more choice of organic food and vegetables in supermarkets than there used to be, ...

3 Governments could offer cheap business loans to people who want to start green businesses, ...

4 Supermarkets now charge people if they want a plastic bag for their shopping, ...

4 Discuss these questions relating to some of the issues in Exercises 1–3.

1 Do you think rail travel should be free for people over 70? Why? / Why not?

2 Do you think governments should subsidise the cost of solar panels on people's houses?

3 Do you think governments should make it easier for farmers to grow organic food?

4 Do you think governments should invest more in renewable energy, and less in energy from fossil fuels?

5 Would you like to see more high-speed rail links built between cities in your country?

6 Do you think schoolchildren should spend more time doing sport at school? Or is it better for them to concentrate on studying, and do more sport in their free time?

Language for key topics

i The first five units of the book have looked at a range of topic areas (living home and away, education, health, media and technology and the environment).
This section helps you build up vocabulary and ideas for two other common topics – crime and the 'good society' – so that you have a wider range of language to use in the exam. This language will be useful in the Speaking Test as well as the Writing Test.

Crime

1 Read this exam task, then discuss the questions below in pairs.

Some people believe that prison is the best way to punish criminals. Others think that other punishments which do not involve sending offenders to prison are a better alternative.

Discuss both these views and give your opinion.

1 What is your opinion about this discussion essay question?
2 For which crimes do you think prison is the most suitable punishment?
3 Are there some crimes where you think punishments in the community would be better than prison?

2 Quickly read the four interviews on page 68 and write a heading for each paragraph. Compare your answers in pairs.

3 🎯 Do this exam task about the interviews.

Which paragraph contains the following information?
You may use each letter (A–D) more than once.

1   Sending criminals to prison means that they mix with the wrong people.
2   Criminals need to get qualifications while they are in jail so that they can succeed when they leave prison.
3   More money should be allocated to giving criminals therapy.
4   Crime is a reflection of bigger problems in society.
5   Sending criminals to jail stops other people committing crime.
6   The age of the offender is important when we decide how to punish people.
7   Criminals should be sent to prison for longer periods of time.
8   The majority of offenders should be punished in the community, not in jail.

4 Find words or phrases in the interviews with a similar meaning.

1 Prison stops possible criminals from committing crime. (paragraph A)
2 The length of time people are in prison (paragraph A)
3 In prison (paragraph A)
4 Very serious, shocking crimes (paragraph B)
5 Put criminals in prison (paragraph B)
6 The deeper reason (paragraph B)
7 The reason I disagree with prison is … (paragraph C)
8 Someone who commits crime for the first time (paragraph C)
9 A punishment in the community where you work for free (paragraph C)

10 Repay society for their crime (paragraph C)
11 Prisons are not good at helping people back into society. (paragraph D)
12 Therapy (paragraph D)

5 Discuss in pairs these questions related to prison and crime.

1 Do you agree that the root cause of a lot of crime is poverty?
2 Do you think there is enough education and counselling in prison for criminals?
3 Do you think it is true that putting people in prison reduces crime in society?
4 Which of the four people's opinion in the text do you most agree with, and why?

6 ⊚ Write an answer for the discussion essay question in Exercise 1.

Prison: does it work?

Below are four short interviews with people who have different opinions about prison and different ways to punish criminals.

A As far as I'm concerned, prison works, because it is a deterrent to potential criminals. In other words, because everyone knows that if you commit a serious offence you'll go to jail, it makes most people think twice before committing a crime. For that reason, I would make prison sentences longer than they are now, so that it's more effective in deterring crime. I'm not saying all criminals should go to prison, but lots more than go to prison now should definitely be behind bars.

B My view is that prison is a blunt instrument, which doesn't really work in the majority of cases. I think that for really heinous crimes, like murder, then of course we should lock criminals up. But for most crime, we are not dealing with the root cause, which is generally poverty. Many offenders turn to crime because they have no money, no job and no future. To deal with this, we should tackle poverty in society first, and second we should make sure that education in prison is really good, so that criminals leave jail with a chance to get a job.

C My objection to prison for all but the most serious cases is that it makes things worse. Take a young first offender, for example, who is caught shoplifting. If you send him or her to jail, he or she will rub shoulders with other criminals, and in the end will come out and probably commit more serious crimes. For me, we'd be better off punishing most criminals by making them do community service, where they can give something back to society, make amends for their crimes and avoid going to jail and meeting hardened criminals. I think this is particularly true for young offenders.

D I think if you commit the crime, you should do the time. What I mean is that it is fair to punish criminals by sending them to jail – they knew the consequences and they deserve the punishment. I also think that society needs to be protected from dangerous and violent criminals, and the only way to do that is to put them behind bars. I do think that prisons don't do a very good job of rehabilitating criminals, and I'd like to see more money spent on counselling for drug and alcohol addiction in jails, but overall, I want people who commit offences like burglary, as well as more serious crimes like murder, to be in prison.

The 'good society'

Sometimes in the IELTS exam you have to write a discussion essay on a slightly more general theme about society. You can be asked what you think makes a 'good society', what governments should do to make sure that people are happy or something similar.

1   **Read this exam task, then discuss the questions below in pairs.**

Some people believe that the most important goal for society is economic progress and growth. Others believe that other types of change and improvements are as important as economic growth.

Discuss both these views and give your opinion.

1   Why do some people believe that economic growth is the most important goal for a society?
2   What other types of change and improvements do societies need?
3   What is your opinion?

2   **Quickly read the four interviews on page 70. Which two texts agree with the first statement in the essay question, and which two texts agree with the second statement?**

3   🎯 **Do this exam task about the interviews.**

Which paragraph contains the following information?
You may use each letter (A–D) more than once.

1   Even wealthy societies face problems of poverty.
2   Economic growth is important because it provides money for other things.
3   There should be equal rights between all groups of people.
4   The most important thing is to provide the basics of life to everyone.
5   People should be able to afford to study whenever they like.
6   People should have more or less the same amount of money.

4   **Find words or phrases in the texts with a similar meaning.**

1   Make poverty disappear (paragraph A)
2   Somewhere to live (paragraph A)
3   Living in poverty (paragraph A)
4   Receiving a basic amount of money given to you by the government (paragraph A)
5   Being able to get an education (paragraph B)
6   Education at any time of your life (paragraph B)
7   Money should be given to people equally. (paragraph C)
8   Women are still treated unequally. (paragraph C)
9   The government's money (paragraph D)

5   **Which of the opinions in the texts do you most agree with, and why?**
    Discuss in pairs.

6 Write an answer for the discussion essay in Exercise 1. Then compare your answer with the sample essay on pages 164–165.

What is the 'good society'?

Four people give their view on what the 'good society' is.

A For me, the primary goal of a society, and therefore of a government, is to eradicate poverty. There are many important things in life, but without the basic means of survival, without a roof over your head, food and clothing, running water, and enough money to have a reasonable life, nothing else matters. I think governments should have as their main target lifting all of their people out of poverty, and then providing a decent standard of living for everyone. Even in supposedly rich societies, there are still many people living on the breadline, on benefits or sleeping rough, unable to feed their families. This should be the main priority and everything else can come later.

B I think that it is certainly important to have economic growth, and governments should try to encourage business to thrive and to expand the resources available in the country for everyone. However, for me, other aspects of life are equally important. Access to education would be my priority if I were running the government. Education and access to learning is one of the things that makes us human, that makes life worth living. I think education should not only be free right up to university level, but there

should also be lifelong education available, so that people can study new things at any time in their life. Education opens the door to new ideas and ways of thinking. For me, economic growth and education are just as important as each other. It's no good having a rich country if a large proportion of the country can't afford to study and learn.

C My view is that the main aim of society and governments should be equality. First of all, the wealth should be shared out, so that everyone has a roughly equal chance in life. Secondly, there should be equality for different groups of people in society. We have made a lot of progress, but there is still a lot of discrimination against women, against ethnic minorities, against LGBT people. This goes against what it is to be human, and for me, this should be the number-one priority for a society – making sure everyone feels fairly treated, respected and part of the society.

D I would argue that economic progress and growth is the most important thing for society, but the reason I think that is that it allows you to spend the money on things which benefit everyone. If you don't run the economy properly, everyone will be poor, so what's really important is that the people in charge of the economy are competent and they create growth. If they do this, then we can use government resources to pay for things like education, health, access to culture, transport, entertainment – all the things that we need to have a good life. I think economics comes first, and then we can put the money to good use.

Reading: Note completion

Skills focus

A common IELTS Reading task is to complete notes about a text. This type of question asks you to complete a set of bullet-point notes, often broken up into sections of the text with headings. Use the following technique when dealing with tasks of this type:

1   Follow the headings and bullet points so you can locate the answer more quickly.
2   Decide which type of word you are looking for (noun, adjective, etc.).
3   Think of possible synonyms of the words in the question.
4   When you have found the sentence in the text that contains the answer, read it carefully because the word order may be different from the sentence in the question.

1   Discuss these questions in pairs.

1   What do you know about the problem of plastic in the oceans?
2   How much plastic do you think you use in a typical week?
3   When you buy a coffee, do you take your own cup or use a disposable one?
4   How serious do you think our overuse of plastic is?

2   Look at gaps 1 and 2 in the exam task below and read the first paragraph of the text on page 72. Follow the technique in the box above and answer questions 1 and 2. Choose NO MORE THAN THREE WORDS from the text for each answer.

Skills application

1   Answer questions 3–14 in the exam task below.

2   What do you think about the ideas in the text? Discuss in pairs.

Scale of the problem
*   12.7m tonnes of plastic in our oceans annually
*   Plastic even ¹____ in ice at the North Pole

Packaging
*   800,000 tonnes of plastic packaging used in UK supermarkets a year
*   Majority of it is not recycled, but is ²____
*   'Problem plastics': cannot be recycled easily or can be ³____ for the environment
*   ⁴____ and black plastic trays holding produce are common examples of problem plastic containers.

How plastic gets into our seas
*   Wind removes plastic from ⁵____ and into rivers/seas
*   Litter gets into rivers and streams
*   Items made from plastic are ⁶____ in the toilet

Impact on sea life
*   Turtles confuse jellyfish with ⁷____
*   Plastic will not disappear for approximately ⁸____
*   Seas now have massive ⁹____ of plastic, often as big as a large state or country.

Solutions
*   Majority of the half a million straws produced worldwide are ¹⁰____ – stop using straws?
*   2.5bn disposable coffee cups used globally – customers could replace disposable cups with ones made of ¹¹____ .

Larger-scale solutions
*   Ocean Clean-Up: 600m arc to catch plastic
*   Ship picks up the plastic at regular intervals to be recycled.
*   But: process is still at the ¹²____ stage of development

Public opinion
*   A number of films and documentaries have increased people's ¹³____ of the problem
*   ¹⁴____ offered by coffee companies if you bring a cup with you

Why plastic is not so fantastic

According to the World Economic Forum report of 2016, the world is set to have more plastic than fish in the oceans by 2050. This astonishing fact highlights the massive and urgent problem of our use and disposal of plastic. Every year, according to estimates by Greenpeace, 12.7m tonnes of plastic end up in the oceans. This problem affects seas everywhere, from Mediterranean beaches to uninhabited Pacific islands, and there is even plastic now trapped in Arctic ice. Plastic is all around us in every aspect of our daily life. It is estimated that supermarkets in the UK alone use over 800,000 tonnes of plastic packaging every year. Almost everything we buy is wrapped in packaging, most of it plastic, and most of it gets thrown away rather than recycled.

One problem related to packaging is what is known as 'problem plastics', which refers to the type of plastic items which are either non-recyclable, too expensive to recycle or toxic to the environment. Examples of these are the black plastic trays that we buy fruit or vegetables in from supermarkets or the styrofoam boxes that take-away food often comes in. Because these problem plastics are difficult or impossible to recycle, they often end up dumped in the ocean.

Plastic gets into our oceans in a variety of ways. One way is simply being illegally dumped; another is that plastic is put into the normal bin, instead of being separated out for recycling. When these items of plastic are then taken to landfill sites, they are often blown away by the wind, because they are so light, and end up in rivers and seas. Similarly, plastic which is left on the streets as litter also often makes its way to rivers and streams, and from there into the seas, as rainwater and wind carry the plastic into the nearest water source. A further problem is plastic-based items that are disposed of down the toilet. Many items which we use daily are flushed down the toilet, and microfibres from these items make their way to the sea, damaging marine life.

The effects on marine life are stark. Big pieces of plastic are choking turtles and seabirds, and it is now common to find seabirds with their stomachs full of plastic items. Turtles often mistake plastic bags for jellyfish and end up consuming them, and marine conservationists now commonly come across whales who have ingested over 500 plastic bags. As most plastic takes around 200 years to biodegrade, there is no hope of this problem going away.

Many of our oceans contain large garbage patches of plastic – huge areas of plastic waste which has formed together into a reef. The largest of these, the Pacific Garbage Patch, situated halfway between Hawaii and California, is currently estimated to be 1.6 million square metres, which is twice the size of Texas and three times the size of France.

Possible solutions to the plastic epidemic take various forms. One step that individuals can take is to reduce their plastic footprint, by making small lifestyle changes. For instance, it is estimated that over 500,000 plastic straws are produced globally every day, most of which are single-use and get thrown away. Ditching straws altogether, or replacing plastic ones with reusable ones, is one measure people could take. Similarly, over 2.5 billion disposable coffee cups are used globally every year, and only one in 400 are recycled. Taking a cup to the coffee shop and re-using it, and changing to bamboo cups instead of plastic, are small but important steps that individuals can take.

On a larger scale, there are several initiatives in the early stages of development. Plastic Oceans International is a company set up by a Dutch inventor, Boyan Slat, in 2013. His invention, known as the Ocean Clean-Up, is a 600m-long floating arc, which sits on the surface of the ocean and traps plastic debris. Every few months, a ship acting as a garbage truck takes away the plastic and brings it ashore to be recycled. Although the technology is still in the roll-out stage, Plastic Oceans International claim that they could remove over 50% of the Pacific Garbage Patch within five years with sufficient funding.

What is not in doubt is the seriousness of the problem, and the tide of public opinion appears to be turning. Recent documentaries and films have helped raise awareness of the plastic issue, and supermarkets and shops are starting to get the message. Some coffee chains now offer discounts to those who bring their own mugs, and people's awareness of the need to cut down on plastic and to carefully recycle the plastic they do use is growing. What is needed now is the political will to fund research into clean-up methods and alternatives to plastic, such as bamboo, seaweed and beeswax.

Listening Part 3: Multiple choice and sentence completion

Skills focus

> In Listening Part 3, you normally hear two or three people discussing a topic, often related to study or education. In this section, you will hear a student, James, talking to his university tutor about an essay he is writing about the social and environmental history of Glasgow.

1 Discuss these questions in pairs.

1 Apart from IELTS essays, have you ever written an essay in English?
2 Do you enjoy writing essays? Are you good at it?

2 Read these Part 3 Listening techniques, then discuss the exam task below in pairs.

> - For questions 1–3, underline the key words in each question and think about possible synonyms.
> - For questions 4–10, you should:
>   - think about what kind of word(s) you are looking for (e.g. noun, adjective)
>   - look at the key words before and after the gaps, and think of possible synonyms
>   - guess a possible answer.

Questions 1–3
*Choose the correct letter, **A**, **B** or **C**.*

1 James has
   A written all of his essay.
   B written half of it.
   C not started his essay.

2 The tutor says
   A the organisation is good, but the ideas are poor.
   B the ideas are good, but the organisation is poor.
   C both the ideas and the organisation are poor.

3 James
   A made a plan, but didn't stick to it.
   B made a plan which wasn't very good.
   C didn't plan his essay.

Questions 4 and 5
Complete the sentences below.
*Write no more than **ONE WORD** for each answer.*

4 The tutor says that next Friday is the ____ for submitting the essay.
5 The tutor asks James to give her an ____ copy of the second draft of the essay.

Questions 6–10
Complete the sentences below.
*Write no more than **THREE WORDS** for each answer.*

6 In the 19th century, Glasgow became a large ____ in Europe.
7 This development took place primarily due to the dramatic improvement in ____ .
8 The tutor suggests that James should investigate further the problem of ____ , which was a major cause of health problems among the population.
9 She advises James to read a book about Glasgow called ____ .
10 The tutor says that before the Clean Air Act, the air in Glasgow was full of smog caused by ____ .

3 🎧12 Listen and do the exam task.

4 Look at the audioscript on page 150 and check your answers.

5 Look at the audioscript again and highlight the sentences which gave you each answer, matching any synonyms in the question and script.

Example: 1 *Answer A says: 'James has written all of his essay.'*
The sentence in the script says: 'I've written a complete draft of the essay.'

Skills application

1 🎧13 You will hear two university politics students, Sarah and Faris, talking about essays they have written about the environment. Listen and do the exam task.

Questions 1–5
*Choose the correct letter, **A**, **B** or **C**.*

1 Faris's grade for his latest essay was
  A A
  B B
  C C

2 Faris
  A has spoken to his tutor about his essay.
  B will speak to his tutor next week about his essay.
  C hasn't had any feedback on his essay yet.

3 Sarah
  A has won an award for her essay.
  B was more pleased with her essay than her tutor.
  C has been shortlisted for an award for her essay.

4 The winner of the Green Essay award will
  A be able to keep the prize money for themselves.
  B split the prize money between themselves and a green organisation.
  C be able to choose a green charity to give the prize money to.

5 Sarah most enjoyed reading about a green politician from
  A Germany.
  B Sweden.
  C the UK.

Questions 6–10
Complete the sentences below.
*Write **NO MORE THAN TWO WORDS** for each answer.*

6 For his assignment, Faris researched _____ .
7 Around a third of Denmark's electricity comes from _____ .
8 Faris says that British politicians avoid wind power because of the high _____ .
9 However, the UK has spent a lot of money on _____ .
10 Faris says many people wrongly think that solar power can only work well in _____ .

---

2 Discuss these questions in pairs.

1 Does your country use a lot of renewable energy?
2 Do you think governments should invest more in renewables?
3 Is there a Green Party in your country, and if so, how successful are they?
4 When you were at school, did you have any lessons about environmental issues?

Speaking Parts 2 and 3

The environment

It is very common to be asked questions about environmental issues in Parts 2 and 3 of the Speaking exam. In this section, you will find some useful language and common speaking questions for you to practise with.

1   Match the sentence halves to form phrases for environmental actions people can take.

1	Go	a	pressure group.
2	Take a reusable	b	to work.
3	Join a green	c	cup to work.
4	Join a carpool	d	vegan or vegetarian.
5	Have a staycation	e	organic food.
6	Buy	f	instead of flying abroad on holiday.

2   Discuss these questions in pairs.

1	Do you take a reusable cup to work?	4	Do you buy organic food?
2	Would you go vegan or vegetarian?	5	Have you ever joined a green pressure group?
3	Have you ever taken a staycation?	6	Would you join a carpool to get to work?

3   Match the sentence halves to form phrases for more environmental actions.

1	Recycle	a	plastic straws.
2	Stop using	b	vegetables.
3	Cycle to university or work	c	all your plastic.
4	Buy	d	bamboo toothbrush.
5	Grow your own	e	instead of driving.
6	Use a	f	local produce.

4   Write questions including the language in Exercises 1 and 3, using *Do you …?*,
Have you (ever) …?, *Would you …?*. Then ask and answer your questions in pairs.

5   ⊘ Make notes about this Speaking Part 2 task, then talk for two minutes
about it, using your notes.

Talk about an area of natural beauty that you enjoyed visiting (e.g. river, sea, countryside, forest).

You should say
which place it was
when you went there and for how long
what you did there
and why you enjoyed visiting it.

If you think it might be difficult to keep speaking about one idea for the whole two minutes, you can talk about another one. For example, you can talk about a second place of natural beauty in the last 30 seconds or so of the task if you find that you run out of things to say about the first one.

6   Discuss these Speaking Part 3 questions in pairs.

1   Do you think governments should increase taxes on flying, to try to reduce the number of flights?
2   Do you think governments should encourage people to take staycations?
3   Do you think governments should encourage carpooling?

Pulling it all together

Review

1   Rewrite these sentences for introducing ideas in a discussion essay using the impersonal passive.

1   People often say that governments should tax older cars which pollute the environment more than newer, cleaner ones.
2   People often put forward the argument that any environmental change has to start locally.
3   People generally think that there is too much packaging on the goods we buy.

2   Complete these phrases for introducing ideas in a discussion essay.

1   There is an a____ that …
2   One r____ that people b____ X is that …
3   There are m____ people w____ think that …
4   There are t____ who say that …
5   One l____ of argument is that …
6   There is a p____ of v____ that …

3   What steps should you follow when you are answering the following?

1   Listening Part 3 questions
2   Note-completion Reading questions

4   Complete the definitions of these vocabulary items about the environment.

1   Energy from the sun, wind and sea: s____ , wind and t____ power
2   Types of energy which don't deplete the planet's resources: r____ energy
3   Coal, oil and gas: f____ f____
4   Remove rubbish that people have left lying around: p____ up l____
5   Try to persuade the government to do something: l____ the government
6   Make people recycle by law: make recycling c____
7   A system where people leave their cars outside the city, and then take a cheap/free bus into the city centre: a p____-and-r____ scheme
8   Straws and cups which are used once and then thrown away: s____-u____ straws and cups
9   A holiday in your own country, without flying: a s____
10 A green organisation which tries to change government policy: a green p____ g____
11 Food which is grown in your area or region: l____ p____
12 Make people understand that a problem exists: r____ a____ of a problem

Final practice essay

> *Some people believe that governments should make laws about environmental issues and then strictly enforce those laws. Others say that it is better for governments to encourage and educate the population to make environmental changes.*
>
> *Discuss both views and then give your opinion.*

1   Write an essay for the exam task above.

2   Compare your essay with the sample answer on page 165.

Writing Task 1: Graphs with a trend

Model essay

> For Writing Task 1, you should describe data that you see in a graph, chart or diagram. You have to write a minimum of **150 words** and you have **20 minutes** to write your answer in the exam.
> One of the most common types of Writing Task 1 questions is a **graph with a trend**. This means information where there are changes over time (in the graph below, between 2008 and 2018).

1 Look at the exam task below and answer these questions.

1 How many years does the graph describe?
2 What information does the graph show about the cities?
3 Which city had more visitors in 2008?
4 Which city had more visitors in 2018?
5 What is the main trend over the period for the number of visitors to London and New York?
6 What happened to the number of visitors to London and New York between 2014 and 2015?

The graph shows information about visitors to London and New York, 2008–2018.
Summarise the information by selecting and reporting the main features and make comparisons where relevant.

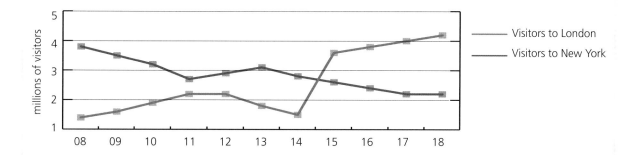

The graph shows information about how many people visited London and New York, over a ten-year period between 2008 and 2018.

Overall, what stands out from the graph is that there was an upward trend in the number of visitors to London, but the number of visitors to New York saw a significant decrease over the period. Another interesting point is that New York had more visitors in 2008, but in 2018, London was much more popular than New York.

In detail, the number of visitors to London started at around 1.5m in 2008 and then the figure rose steadily to 2.2m in 2011. After that, the figure levelled off and stayed at 2.2m until 2012. Having fallen slightly to approximately 1.6m in 2014, the number then soared, rising sharply to just under 4m in 2015. Finally, there was a gradual increase, with the figure finishing at 4.1m in 2018.

However, if we look at visitors to New York, the trend was very different. The number began at about 3.9m in 2008, after which there was a considerable drop to 2.8m in 2011. After going up slightly to 3.1m in 2013, the figure then declined steadily to just over 2m in 2017. Finally, the figure remained stable for the last 12 months of the period.

(217 words)

2 **Analyse the model answer by answering these questions.**

1 How many paragraphs are there in the model answer?
2 Does paragraph 2 talk about the graph in detail or in general?
3 How many ideas are there in paragraph 2?
4 What tense is mostly used to describe changes in paragraphs 3 and 4?
5 Which two verbs are used in paragraphs 3 and 4 to describe the first numbers of a line?
6 Which five phrases in paragraphs 3 and 4 are used to say 'more or less' about numbers?
7 Which verb in paragraph 3 means 'increased a lot, and quickly'?
8 Which phrase in paragraph 4 means 'stayed the same'?
9 Which linking phrase is used to start paragraph 3?
10 Why does paragraph 4 start with *However*?

Verbs and adverbs to describe changes

One way to describe changes in the main body of line graph is with a **verb + adverb** phrase:

*The number of visitors **rose steadily** to 2.2.m in 2011.*
*The number of visitors **fell considerably** to 2.8m in 2010.*

You will need to use a range of different verbs and adverbs to do this well.

1 **Complete the table below with the verbs for describing changes in the box.**

decrease ▪ decline ▪ drop ▪ fall ▪ go down ▪ go up ▪ grow ▪
increase ▪ jump ▪ plunge ▪ rise ▪ rocket ▪ shoot up ▪ soar ▪ surge

Increases	Big increases	Decreases	Big decreases

2 **The graph on page 77 describes a finished period of time in the past (2008–2018).**
  Look at these three sentences and answer the questions below.

a The number of visitors to London has increased between 2008 and 2018.
b The number of visitors to London increased between 2008 and 2018.
c The number of visitors to London increases between 2008 and 2018.

1 Which three tenses are used in sentences a–c?
2 Which sentence do you think is correct and why?

3 Complete this table with the past simple forms of the verbs. Be careful, they are not all regular! Use a dictionary to help you if necessary.

Verb	Past simple	Verb	Past simple
decline	declined	jump	
decrease		plummet	
drop		plunge	
fall		rise	
go down		rocket	
go up		shoot up	
grow		soar	
increase		surge	

When you describe increases or decreases, you need an adverb to say what kind of change it is. For example, for a small increase, you can write *The number of visitors increased **slightly** from 1.5m to 1.7m.*
For verbs like *soared* or *plummeted*, whose meaning includes an idea of a big change, you don't need an adverb: *The number of visitors to London **soared** to 3m.*

4 Match the adverbs in the box with their meanings.

> considerably · dramatically · rapidly · gradually ·
> sharply · significantly · ~~slightly~~ · steadily

1 A small change: slightly
2 Quite a big change: ____ and ____
3 A very big change: ____
4 A very fast change: ____ and ____
5 A small and slow change: ____
6 The same kind of change over a period of time: ____

5 Look again at the graph on page 77 and complete these sentences with a suitable adverb.

1 The number of visitors to London increased ____ between 2008 and 2011.
2 The figure for London rose ____ between 2014 and 2015.
3 The number of visitors to New York fell ____ between 2008 and 2011.
4 The figure for New York went up ____ between 2011 and 2013.
5 The number for New York decreased ____ between 2013 and 2017.

6 Write sentences with verb + adverb phrases about each of these changes.

1 New York, 2008–2011: The number of visitors to New York went down considerably to 2.8m in 2011.
2 New York, 2011–2013
3 London, 2008–2011
4 London, 2014–2015
5 London, 2015–2018

Adjectives and nouns to describe changes

Another way to describe changes in the main body of your essay is to use a sentence with an **adjective + noun** combination:
*There was a **slight increase** in the number of visitors to London.*
*There was a **considerable rise** in the number of visitors to New York.*

1 Complete the table with the noun forms of the verbs. Use a dictionary if you need to.

Verb	Noun	Verb	Noun
decline	a decline	increase	
decrease		jump	
drop		level off	
fall		plunge	
fluctuate		rise	
improve		surge	

2 Complete the table with the adjective forms of the adverbs. Check the spelling carefully.

Adverb	Adjective	Adverb	Adjective
considerably	considerable	sharply	
dramatically		significantly	
gradually		slightly	
rapidly		steadily	

3 Rewrite these verb + adverb sentences using an adjective + noun combination.

1 The number of visitors to London increased sharply.
   There was a sharp increase in the number of visitors to London.
2 The number of visitors to Cairo fell dramatically.
3 The number of travellers in South America rose steadily.
4 The number of tourists in Italy dropped gradually.
5 The number of visitors to Milan decreased considerably.
6 The number of people visiting Dubai declined significantly.

Introductions for Task 1 essays

To write a good introduction for a Task 1 answer, you need to rewrite the question in your own words. One way of doing this is to take the topic of the graph (e.g. *visitors to London and New York*) and change the grammar of the sentence.

1 The first step is to decide if the topic of the graph is countable or uncountable
(i.e. whether the words have a plural form or not). Complete the table below with
the common topic words in the box.

> cars · chocolate · coffee · DVDs · electricity · employees · gas · money ·
> oil · people · profit · smokers · spending · tourists · visitors · water

Countable	Uncountable

2 If the topic word is countable, you can rewrite the question in two specific ways.
Complete these sentences about visitors to New York and London.

1 The graph shows information about h____ m____ people v____ London and New York.
2 The graph shows information about the n____ of people w____ v____ London and New York.

3 Complete these two sentences about an uncountable topic: 'Chocolate production in Brazil'.

1 The graph shows information about how m____ chocolate w____ produced in Brazil.
2 The graph shows information about the a____ of chocolate w____ was produced in Brazil.

4 Rewrite these introduction sentences using the words in brackets.

1 The graph shows information about how much coffee was produced in Kenya.
 The graph shows information about ____ in Kenya. (*amount*)
2 The graph shows information about the amount of gas which was used in Kuwait.
 The graph shows information about ____ in Kuwait. (*how*)
3 The graph shows information about how many cars were sold in Oman.
 The graph shows information about ____ in Oman. (*number*)
4 The graph shows information about the number of people who worked for
 the government in Saudi Arabia.
 The graph shows information about ____ for the government in Saudi Arabia. (*how*)

5 Write two introduction sentences for each of these topics, using different grammar
in each one.

1 electricity use, UK
2 World Cup final viewers, UK

6 Complete the example introduction below with the words in the box.

> and · between · information · many · over

The graph shows ¹____ about how ²____ people visited London and New York, ³____ a
ten-year period, ⁴____ 1999 ⁵____ 2009.

7 Write an introductory sentence for each of these topics.

1 Car sales, UK and USA, 2000–2015
2 Coffee production, Brazil, 2010–2018

Overviews for Task 1 essays

 In the second paragraph, you need to write an overview, describing what happens in general in the graph. You shouldn't write any numbers or detail in this paragraph.

1 Look again at the overview from the model essay and discuss the questions below in pairs.

Overall, what stands out from the graph is that there was an upward trend in the number of visitors to London, but the number of visitors to New York saw a significant decrease over the period. Another interesting point is that New York was had more visitors than London in 2008, but in 2018, London was much more popular than New York.

1 What linking word is used to start the paragraph?
2 What two phrases are used in the first sentence to describe the overall trends?
3 What linking phrase is used to introduce the second change?
4 Which grammar structure is used in the second sentence to compare New York and London in 2008 and 2018?

> Note these key phrases that can be used in the overview:
>
> **There was an upward/downward trend in** the number of visitors to X.
> The number of visitors to X **saw a significant rise/fall over the period.**
> X **had more** visitors **than** Y in 2008.
> X **was more popular than** Y in 2018.

2 Rewrite these overview sentences using the words in brackets.

1 In general, the number of visitors to London went up.
  There was ____ the number of visitors to London. (*trend*)
2 In general, the number of visitors to New York went down.
  There was ____ the number of visitors to New York. (*downward*)
3 In general, car sales rose significantly.
  Car sales ____ the period. (*saw*)
4 In general, electricity use fell considerably.
  Electricity use ____ the period. (*saw*)
5 In 2008, there were more visitors to New York than London.
  In 2008, New York ____ London. (*more*)
6 In 2018, there were more visitors to London than New York.
  In 2018, London ____ New York. (*popular*)

3 Add the words in the box in the correct places in the example overview below, about visitors to Paris and Barcelona between 2005 and 2015.

> had · interesting · out · period · saw · than · trend · what · while

Overall, stands from the graph is that there was an upward in the number of visitors to Paris, the number of people who visited Barcelona a slight fall over the. Another point is that in 2005, Barcelona more visitors than Paris, but in 2015, Paris was more popular Barcelona.

Writing a main-body paragraph

When you write the main body of the essay, you need to:
• choose the main points of the graph to write about
• use linking words
• use suitable prepositions when you describe the changes
• use a range of grammatical structures.

1   Look at this main body paragraph and <u>underline</u> all the linking words.

In detail, the number of visitors to Paris started at just under 4m in 2005, <u>and then</u> there was a steady fall to approximately 2.8m in 2008. At this point, the number went up slightly to just over 3m in 2010. Subsequently, there was a considerable decrease to around 2.1m in 2013, and following this, the figure levelled off at 2.1m in 2014, finishing at the same number.

2   Complete these linking words you can use in main-body paragraphs.

• In the first sentence of the paragraph:
  ¹*To b____ with,* ²*To s____ with,*
• Linking stages together:
  ³*... and t____ ,* ⁴*At this p____ ,* ⁵*Sub____ ,* ⁶*... and f____ this,* ⁷*Th____ ,*
  ⁸*A____ that,* ⁹*Ne____ ,* ¹⁰*Afterw____ ,*
• In the last sentence of the paragraph:
  ¹¹*Fin____ ,* ¹²*... and fin____ at ,* ¹³*... with the figure f____ at*

3   Write down all the words or phrases in Exercise 1 which mean 'more or less'. Add any others that you know.

Example: *just under 4m*

4   Complete these phrases for describing trends with *at* or *to*.

1   The number of visitors **started** ____ just under 4m.
2   There was **a steady fall** ____ approximately 2.2m.
3   The number **went up slightly** ____ just over 3m.

4   The figure **levelled off** ____ 2.1m.
5   The figure **finished** ____ 2.1m.
6   The figure **stayed** ____ 2.2m until 2003.

5   Complete these rules about the use of prepositions for describing trends.

1   To talk about increases or decreases, use ____ .
2   To talk about the first or last number, use ____ .
3   When the number doesn't change, use ____ .

6   Complete this paragraph about visitors to Barcelona with *at* or *to*.

If we look at the number of visitors to Barcelona, the figure began ¹*____ around 2.2m in 2005, and then there was a significant rise* ²*____ approximately 2.9m in 2008. At this point, the figure levelled off* ³*____ 2.9m until 2011, and after that the number dropped considerably* ⁴*____ 1.6m in 2012. After rising dramatically* ⁵*____ 3.8m in 2013, the figure then stabilised, finishing* ⁶*____ 4.1m in 2015.*

Grammar: Describing changes

As you saw earlier, you can use linking phrases like *and then* to join together your sentences describing trends in the main body. To make your Task 1 answer more interesting, you can also use different grammatical structures to write about changes.

1 Read this sentence, then complete the two alternative ways of expressing it below.

The number of visitors fell considerably to 1.5m in 2004, and then it rose dramatically to 3.6m in 2006.

1 **After f____** considerably to 1.5m in 2004, the number of visitors then rose dramatically to 3.6m in 2006.
2 **Having f____** considerably to 1.5m in 2004, the number of visitors then rose dramatically to 3.6m in 2006.

2 With the structure *Having ...* , you need to use the past participle of the verb. Write the past participles of these common verbs.

1 fall   2 grow   3 rise   4 go up

3 Rewrite these sentences using either *After + -ing* or *Having + past participle*.

1 The number of visitors to Paris increased slightly to 2.2m in 2005, and then it rose sharply to 4.5m in 2007. (*After*)
2 The number of visitors to Barcelona fell slightly to 2.4m in 2008, and then it went up gradually to 2.8m in 2012. (*Having*)
3 The number of visitors to Paris remained stable at 4.7m between 2008 and 2011, and then the figure rose steadily to 5.5m in 2015. (*After*)
4 The number of visitors to Barcelona grew considerably between 2005 and 2010, from 2.1m to 4.2m, and then the figure levelled off until 2012. (*Having*)

You can also join two changes together by adding *after which* or *at which point* plus another clause:

The number of visitors to London dropped slightly to 1.5m in 2005, **after which/at which point** *there was a sharp rise to 3.6m in 2006.*

4 Join these sentences by adding *after which* or *at which point*. Make any other necessary changes.

1 There was a steady rise in the number of cars sold in the UK to 4.2m in 2015. Then the figure went up gradually to 4.6m in 2018.
2 The number of cars sold in the USA fell significantly to 21.5m in 2008. After that, there was a steady rise to 28.1m in 2012.
3 There was a sharp increase in the unemployment rate in the EU to 6.2% in 2011. Subsequently, the figure recovered to 4.1% in 2015.
4 The employment rate in the public sector in the UK decreased considerably to 8.3m people in 2015. After that, the figure went up gradually to 8.7m in 2017.

5 Look again at the graph on page 77 and write about these changes, using the phrase in brackets.

1 New York: 2011–13 and then 2013–17 (*After ...*)
2 London: 2008–11 and then 2011–12 (*Having ...*)
3 London: 2012–14 and then 2014–15 (*after which*)
4 London: 2014–15 and then 2015–18 (*at which point*)

Reading: Matching

Skills focus

A common Reading question type is **matching**, where you generally have to match a series of statements to a list of different people (or possibly dates).

Here are some techniques for answering this type of question:
1   Underline the names of the people in the text, so you can find them faster.
2   Before you start, read **all** the statements and underline the key words in each one.
3   Quickly think of some synonyms of the key words in the statements.
4   The questions are **not** in order, so as you read person A, you will need to think about more than just question 1.
5   Match the grammar of the question and the answer in the text – are the sentences in the present, past or future?

1   **You are going to read a text called 'Holiday disasters'. Before you read, discuss these questions in pairs.**

1   What disasters can happen to people when they go on holiday?
2   Have you ever had a holiday where something went wrong? What happened?

2   **Before you read the text, <u>underline</u> the key words in questions 1–4 and think of possible synonyms.**

Which person
1   stayed in accommodation which wasn't finished?
2   didn't get to their holiday destination?
3   had a meal that wasn't what they expected?
4   went on holiday at the same time as a big local event?

3   **Read this text and answer questions 1–4 in Exercise 2. When you find each answer, underline it in the text. You can use each letter (A and B) more than once.**

Holiday disasters

A   John

'When I finished university, my girlfriend and I decided to go to Paris for a romantic weekend. We had been studying for months for our final exams, and it was going to be a treat to celebrate finishing our studies. We got to the airport in London, and as we were in the queue to board the plane, suddenly an airport security guard came over and asked us to go with him to a little room. They searched our bags and kept asking lots of questions about who we were meeting in Paris and what we were going to do on holiday. We spent hours and hours in this room, with police and armed guards, and missed our plane. It turned out that someone with the exact same name as me was on a wanted list for drug smuggling and they thought it was me. By the time I managed to convince them that I was innocent, we had missed the plane and lost our hotel reservation. We had to go back home again and we ended up having a take-away from the local fish-and-chip shop for dinner. It just wasn't very romantic!'

B   Dave

'About ten years ago, my wife and I booked a week in Spain by the beach. We had been working a lot, and all we really wanted to do was sit by the pool and relax with some peace and quiet. So, when we saw an all-inclusive week on the coast, which looked good and was pretty cheap, we went for it. However, when we got there, it was a catalogue of disasters. The hotel was only half-built and some workmen were still building rooms on the back of the hotel. We could hear drilling and loud noises all day, it was impossible to relax. It also turned out that it was the week of the local rock festival, so everywhere we went, there was loud music blaring out. And to top it all off, I lost my passport. I had to spend two whole days in the British embassy filling in application forms to get a new passport. When we got back to England, it felt like we needed another holiday!'

4   **Which of these two holiday disaster stories do you think is the worst? Why?**

Skills application

1 🎯 Read the text below and match these statements to one of the people (A–D). You may use the same answer more than once.

List of people

A   Dr Roger Roberts
B   Adria Sacrest
C   Svetoslava Todorov
D   Renzo Rossetti

1   Tourism is a positive thing, but only up to a certain point.
2   Tourism has influenced people to visit other countries.
3   The city is less interesting than it used to be.
4   With this type of tourism, it is easy to interact with local people.
5   Tourism has made people more liberal in their mentality.
6   People want to see the country as the locals really live.
7   Tourism has made accommodation more expensive.
8   The local language is spoken less by tourists than in the past.
9   Tourism has had economic benefits.
10 Tourists do not get to know the local culture.

Can you have too many tourists?

These days, with the advent of cheap flights, visa-free travel and higher disposable incomes, more and more people are travelling abroad on holiday, whether for a city break in a capital city, a beach holiday or an exotic long-haul holiday to a far-flung destination. The growth of tourism seems a win–win situation for all concerned – tourists get to see new places, and locals make money from tourism. However, some experts are beginning to question whether tourism is such a good thing. One such expert is Dr Roger Roberts, a professor in urban geography and tourism at the University of London. According to Dr Roberts, there is a certain level of tourism which brings benefits to a city or resort, but once the numbers cross that threshold, the impact on the place concerned becomes more negative. A case in point is Venice, where, as a result of the massive influx of tourists, the price of an apartment has gone up ten-fold in the last 20 years, and locals find themselves priced out and having to move to the mainland. The result is, Dr Roberts says, that Venice by day is like a film set full of tourists, but by night is virtually empty.

Another problem is the lack of interaction with the local culture. Adria Sacrest, a local historian from Barcelona, bemoans the fact that tourists who come to his city often leave with little or no idea about the Catalonian language or culture. The centre of Barcelona, he says, has become a kind of international tourist island, where mainly English is spoken, and the restaurants, bars and tourist attractions could really be anywhere in the world. 'Everything is becoming standardised in Barcelona,' says Sacrest. 'Twenty years ago, central Barcelona was a really interesting place to visit and if you went into a local bar, you could well be the only tourist there. People used to be able to interact with locals and enjoy the hospitality of the Catalan culture, even learn a few words of the language, but now it is more about bus tours, organised visits to the football stadium and a drink in an Irish pub.'

However, not everyone sees tourism as a negative force. Svetoslava Todorov is head of the Bulgarian tourist board, and she believes that tourism in her country has opened people's minds to new ways of doing things. 'I believe Bulgaria has become a much more broad-minded and tolerant country in the last decade, and at least part of that is due to the influx of tourists,' she says. 'By coming into contact with people from other cultures, we Bulgarians have become far more European and cosmopolitan, and I think it has also encouraged us to travel abroad more.' In addition to that, she notes, the impact of the tourist dollar on the economy has been profound, bringing in much-needed revenue.

Another advocate of tourism, albeit of a specific kind, is Renzo Rossetti, a farm owner from Tuscany, who has benefitted from what the Italians call *agriturismo* – in other words, the kind of tourism where people stay with local people on farms, vineyards and country estates, and as such get to know the region and the locals. Agriturismo is booming in Italy, partly, Rossetti thinks, as a result of people's desire to see more of the 'real' country. 'The great benefit of what we do,' he says, 'is that people get to talk to locals, sit down to dinner with them, get to know their customs, habits and food, and therefore go away with at least a little appreciation of what our culture is all about.

So there you have it. Is tourism a curse or a blessing? Does the answer to that question depend on the type of tourism? There are no signs that tourism is going to do anything but increase in the future, but it is an open question as to what type of tourist experience the travellers of the future will be looking for, and how this will impact on tourist destinations around the world.

2   What do you think about the ideas in this text? Which speaker do you most agree with?

Listening Part 4: Sentence completion

Skills focus 1

> Part 4 of the IELTS Listening test is generally a lecture or talk by one person on a single topic.
> One key skill that you need for this part is focusing on the key word or words **before each gap**
> for the answer and trying to predict how the speaker will say those words.
> The speaker will not normally use the same words as in the question, so you need to practise thinking
> about and anticipating how they might say it differently.

1   You are going to listen to the first part of a talk about taking a gap year. Before you listen, discuss in
    pairs these questions about taking a gap year.

    1   What is a gap year, and what do people normally do when they take one?
    2   What do you know about the history of people taking a gap year?
    3   Have you taken / Are you planning to take a gap year?
    4   Do you know anyone (e.g. your parents, friends) who have taken a gap year?
        If so, what did they do? Did they enjoy it?

2   Look at the words in bold in questions 1–6. Work in pairs and write down as
    many synonyms or way to rephrase these words as you can.

    History of the gap year

    1   Many people think of the gap year as a kind of holiday, but the **initial idea** of the gap year was
        to **increase** _____ .

    2   Project Trust sent volunteers to Africa with **the main goal of** _____ between different cultures.

    3   In the 1970s, **organisations** wanting to make money from gap-year trips **started to** _____ .

    4   Some **parents who were concerned** about their children taking a gap year liked the idea of **organising a
        trip** with a _____ and _____ gap-year company.

    5   There was **a massive growth** in gap years in the 1980s, and companies started to have a positive view of
        people who had taken a gap year, **believing them to be more** _____ .

    6   Therefore, when applying for a job, if you hadn't taken a gap year, it was sometimes **viewed** as **a big** _____ .

3   ⏴14 🎯 Listen and answer questions 1–6 in Exercise 2. Write NO MORE THAN TWO WORDS for each
    answer.

4   Check your answers in the audioscript on page 151.

5   Compare the synonyms that you wrote down in Exercise 2 with what the speaker
    says in the audioscript. Were any of them the same?

Skills focus 2

1 **Before you listen to the second part of the talk, look at questions 7–13 below and do the following. When you finish, compare your answers in pairs.**

1 <u>Underline</u> what you think are the key words in the question before the gap.
2 Think of ways in which the speaker might express the key words in a different way.

7 The best-known person to take a gap year is believed to be _____ .

8 In the 2000s, not so many people took a gap year, mainly because of _____ .

9 Many students worked for a year to put money aside for university, particularly students from _____ backgrounds.

10 A new trend that has appeared in recent years is of more mature people taking a long break – this is often referred to as _____ .

11 Many employers think that workers who take a gap year will return to work feeling enthusiastic and _____ .

12 Many retired gappers have paid off their mortgage and their children have left home; therefore extended travel is easily _____ .

13 In the future, experts predict that gap years will get _____ .

2 🎧15 🎯 **Listen and answer questions 7–13.**

3 **Check your answers in the audioscript on page 151. For each question, identify the synonyms of the key words that the speaker uses.**

4 **Discuss these questions in pairs.**

1 What do you think are the benefits for young people of taking a gap year?
2 Do you there are any possible drawbacks?
3 How do employers in your country see doing a gap year? Is it good thing to have on your CV when you apply for a job?
4 Would you like to take a gap year, or 'career break', when you are older? Why?/Why not?
5 Do you think people in your country work too much? Should workers in your country have more holidays and time off work?
6 How many hours per week do you think people should work?
7 Do you think it is important to have at least two days off work a week (e.g. at the weekend)?

Speaking Part 3

Tourism

1 Discuss these Part 3 questions in pairs.

1 What do you think are the main advantages of tourism?
2 What do you think are the possible disadvantages of tourism?

2 🎧16 Listen to a student answering the two questions in Exercise 1 and make notes about what she says.

3 🎧16 Read the audioscript and try to complete the missing words. Then listen again and check.

Examiner: What do you think are the main advantages of tourism?
Student: One of the ¹k____ b____ of tourism for the city or resort is that tourism ²b____ in lots of money, and therefore ³c____ lots of jobs. In ⁴p____ , in tourist destinations, there tend to be lots of job ⁵o____ in sectors like hospitality – for instance, people working in restaurants, bars and hotels. Not ⁶o____ that, but another ⁷u____ of tourism is that it often has a positive ⁸e____ on the local culture. What I mean is that because lots of people from foreign countries come to the destination, local people end up ⁹m____ with people from all over the world, which can make them more ¹⁰o____-m____ and tolerant.
Examiner: What are the possible disadvantages of tourism?
Student: One of the ¹¹m____ d____ of tourism is that if there are too many tourists, it can have a negative ¹²i____ on local people and the environment. A ¹³g____ e____ is in a city like Venice, where because the city is overrun with tourists, many local people can't ¹⁴a____ to buy or rent a house in the city, and they are forced to move out to the surrounding area. As ¹⁵w____ as ¹⁶t____ , if there are too many tourists, it can ¹⁷r____ in higher levels of pollution, litter and noise, and this is bad for everyone.

4 Find words / phrases in Exercise 3 with a similar meaning.

Question 1
1 one of the biggest advantages *one of the key benefits*
2 gives people more jobs
3 areas of the economy which serve people
4 in addition
5 another advantage
6 It is usually good for the local culture.
7 spending time and talking with

Question 2
8 one of the biggest disadvantages
9 It is bad for local people.
10 for instance
11 It's too expensive to find somewhere to live.
12 in addition
13 It can cause
14 rubbish thrown in the street

5 🎯 Practise the language from this page by discussing these Part 3 questions in pairs.

1 Do you think it's possible for a tourist destination to have too many tourists? If so, what could the government or council do to limit the number of tourists?
2 Do you think it is true that tourism makes both tourists and local people more open-minded?
3 Is there a lot of tourism where you live? Do you see it more as a positive or a negative thing? Would you like more tourists to visit your home town?

Pulling it all together

Review

1 Write an introductory sentence for each of these Task 1 essays.

1 The graph shows the number of students of French and Spanish in UK universities, 2010–2016.
2 The graph shows data about electricity usage in the UK and the USA between 2000 and 2015.

2 Complete these overview phrases.

1 Overall, w____ s____ o____ from the graph is that …
2 T____ was an up____ t____ in the number of visitors to Paris …
3 … but the number of visitors to Barcelona s____ a significant decrease over the p____ .
4 A____ interesting p____ is …
5 Barcelona h____ m____ visitors t____ in 2005 …
6 … but Paris was m____ p____ t____ Barcelona at the end of the period.

3 Rewrite these sentences using either a verb + adverb sentence or an adjective + noun sentence.

1 Prices of mobile phone contracts increased sharply.
2 There was a substantial increase in exports of cheese from the UK to France.

4 Join these changes using *After* … or *Having* …

1 Sales of sports watches increased considerably to 600,000 in 2016, and then the figure went up slightly to 650,000 in 2018. (*After*)
2 The number of people participating in park runs soared to 1.4m a year in 2015, and then levelled off until 2016. (*Having*)

5 Work in pairs. Write as many linking words or phrases for the main body of a trends answer as you can.

6 What techniques should you apply when doing a Matching questions task in the Reading exam?

Final practice essay

The graph highlights data about travellers to Thailand and the Philippines, 2010–2018. Summarise the information by selecting and reporting the main features and make comparisons where relevant.

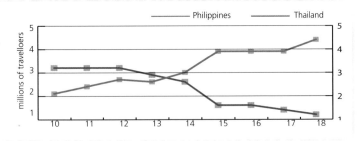

1 🎯 Write an essay for the exam task above. You should:

- include some verb + adverb phrases (e.g. *the number increased sharply*)
- include some adjective + noun phrases (e.g. *there was a steady fall*)
- include a sentence with *After -ing* …
- include a sentence with *Having* …
- include a sentence with *after which / at which point*

- use accurate prepositions
- use a range of linking words
- include a sentence at the start of paragraphs 3 and 4 to explain what the paragraph is about (e.g. *In New York, the trend was very different* …)
- check your spelling and grammar
- count the number of words (minimum 150).

2 Compare your essay with the sample answer on page 168.

Writing Task 1: Comparative graphs

Model essay

> Comparative graphs are where data is given about just one time period (e.g. 2018) and you have to use comparative language to describe the key features of the graph or chart.
> As for all Writing Task 1 essays, you have **20 minutes** to write an answer in the exam, and you have to write **a minimum of 150 words**.

1 **Look at the exam task below, then discuss these questions in pairs.**

1 What were the most popular professions for men and women?
2 Which profession had the biggest difference between men and women?
3 How many of the professions were more popular among men? And how many among women?
4 What does the graph show about the number of men and women working in law?
5 Which of these professions would you most like to work in? Why?
6 Are there any of these professions that you *wouldn't* like to work in? Why?

The bar chart shows the breakdown of employment by profession of men and women in the UK in 2018. The numbers are shown in percentages.
Summarise the information by selecting and reporting the main features and make comparisons where relevant.

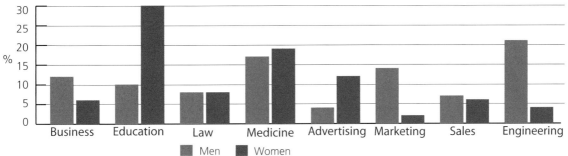

Breakdown of employment by profession, men and women, UK, 2018

The bar graph shows information about the percentage of men and women who worked in eight selected fields of work in the UK in 2018.

Overall, what stands out from the graph is that education was by far the most common sector for women, while engineering was more popular than the other jobs for men. Another interesting point is that the biggest difference between the genders related to education.

As regards the details, there were several areas of employment in which men outnumbered women. Engineering was far more popular for men than women, with figures of 21% and 4%. Similarly, a considerably higher percentage of men than women worked in marketing, the figures being 14% and 2% respectively. In terms of business, twice as many men as women were employed in this sector, at 12% compared to 6%.

By contrast, there were three sectors which were more popular among women. The percentage of women who were employed in medicine was slightly higher than that of men. The figures were 19% and 17%. Regarding advertising, it was significantly more common among women, at 12% as opposed to 4%. Far more women than men had jobs in education. The former figure was 30%, while the latter was 10%. Finally, law was equally popular for men and women, at 8% each.

(218 words)

2 Analyse the model essay by answering these questions.

1 How many paragraphs are there in the model answer, and what is the function of each paragraph?
2 How many sectors of employment are mentioned in paragraph 3? And in paragraph 4?
3 What is the purpose of the first sentence of paragraphs 3 and 4?
4 What structure is used when the two numbers are the same?
5 In the introduction, the writer says *the percentage of men and women who* **worked in** *eight selected fields of work.* How many synonyms of *worked in* can you find in the model essay?

Grammar: Comparative structures

 To write a good answer for a Task 1 comparative graph, you need to be able to use a good range of comparative language accurately.

> Paragraph 3 of the model essay on page 91 contains these three comparative structures:
> A *This sector was* **far more popular** *for men* **than** *women.*
> B ***A considerably higher percentage*** *of men* **than** *women worked in this sector.*
> C ***Twice as many*** *men as women were employed in this sector.*

1 In structure A above, the adverb *far* is used to show that there is a very big difference between the numbers of men and women. Answer the questions below with the adverbs in the box.

> considerably · much · significantly · slightly

1 What adverb could you use to describe a small difference?
2 Which two adverbs could you use to describe a medium-sized difference?
3 Which adverb is a synonym of *far* and describes big differences?

2 Write sentences about these professions from the graph on page 91, using comparative structure A and a suitable adverb.

1 Sales
   Sales was slightly more common for men than women.
2 Marketing
3 Medicine
4 Business

3 Write sentences about these professions from the graph on page 91, using comparative structure B and a suitable adverb.

1 Engineering
2 Sales
3 Advertising

4   Write a numerical comparative sentence for these professions from the graph on page 91, using comparative structure C. Don't forget that *twice* is an exception – with other numbers, you need to use the word *times* (*three times, four times,* etc.).

1   Advertising
2   Education
3   Marketing

5   Paragraph 4 of the model essay on page 91 contains three more comparative structures (D–F). Complete them.

D   The p____ of women who were employed in medicine was slightly h____ t____ t____ of men.
E   Far m____ women t____ men h____ jobs in education.
F   Law was e____ p____ for men and women.

6   Write sentences about the graph on page 91 using the structure indicated and an appropriate adverb.

1   Advertising (structure D)
    The percentage of women who were employed in advertising was significantly higher than that of men.
2   Engineering (structure E)
3   Education (structure D)
4   Business (structure E)

7   Write comparative sentences using the structures indicated about the table in the exam task below.

1   Spanish (structure C)
2   French (structure A)
3   Russian (structure E)
4   Mandarin (structure F)
5   Cantonese (structure B)
6   Korean (structure D)

The table shows a breakdown of the most popular foreign languages studied by English native speakers at the London School of Foreign Language Studies in 2018.

	Men	Women
Spanish	28%	14%
Mandarin	20%	20%
French	11%	23%
Arabic	10%	5%
Cantonese	4%	5%
Japanese	8%	16%
Italian	12%	3%
Russian	5%	6%
Korean	2%	9%

Language for writing about numbers

  The easiest way to describe the numbers in the main body of a Task 1 comparative essay is to write **with/at** *12% and 6%*. However, you can make your Task 1 answer more interesting by using a wider range of vocabulary and appropriate linking phrases.

1 Look again at the model answer on page 91. Find all the phrases for describing numbers.

with figures of 21% and 4%, ...

2 Rewrite these sentences with numbers and a suitable phrase, using the words in brackets. Use the figures from the graph on page 91.

1 Twice as many men as women worked in business. (*with* | *figures*)
Twice as many men as women worked in business, with figures of 12% and 6%.
2 A slightly higher percentage of women than men worked in medicine. (*opposed*)
3 Far more men worked in marketing than women. (*former* | *latter*)
4 Engineering was much more common among men than women. (*figures* | *being*)
5 The percentage of men who worked in sales was slightly higher than that of women. (*compared* | *respectively*)
6 Far more women had jobs in the education sector than men. (*figures* | *were*)

3 Look again at the sentences you wrote for Exercise 7 on page 93. Add the relevant percentages and a phrase from this page to each one.

4 Match these linking phrases from paragraphs 3 and 4 of the main body of the essay on page 91 with what they do.

1 As regards the details, …
2 Similarly, …
3 Finally, …
4 By contrast, …
5 In terms of (business), …
6 Regarding (advertising), …

a To show that two sets of figures are almost the same
b To talk about the last number
c To say that the next thing is very different from the one before
d To introduce the main body
e To introduce a new section of the graph (*two phrases*)

Other comparative language

You will need to learn and practise some additional grammar and vocabulary for writing comparative essays. In particular:
- more comparative structures (e.g. *X is not as expensive as Y*)
- language for ranking data, such as superlatives.

1 Look at the exam task below and write a sentence to compare each of these items from the table.

1 A one-bedroom flat in country A and country C
2 A man's haircut in country A and country B
3 A woman's haircut in country A and country B
4 A burger and fries in country C and country A
5 A double espresso in country C and country D

The table shows a comparison of the prices of five common items in four selected countries, in 2017. Summarise the information by selecting and reporting the main features and make comparisons where relevant.

International price comparison index (£), 2017					
	Average monthly rent of a one-bedroom flat	A man's haircut	A woman's haircut	A burger and fries	A double espresso from a coffee shop
Country A	£600	£20	£45	£6	£3
Country B	£585	£21	£45	£5.50	£3.10
Country C	£300	£6	£15	£2.50	£2
Country D	£450	£12	£15	£3	£4

2 Complete the sentences below about the table with the words in the box. Compare them with the sentences you wrote in Exercise 1.

> as (x4) ▪ half ▪ nearly ▪ quite ▪ twice

1 A one-bedroom flat is _____ as expensive in country A _____ in country C, at £600 and £300.
2 A man's haircut in country A is not _____ as expensive as in country B, at £20 and £21.
3 A woman's haircut is _____ expensive in country A _____ in country B, at £45 each.
4 A burger and fries is not _____ as expensive in country C as in country A, at £2.50 and £6.
5 A double espresso is _____ as expensive in country C _____ in country D, at £2 and £4.

3 Match the sentences in Exercise 2 with their meanings (a–e).

a slightly less expensive
b much less expensive
c the same price
d double the price
e 50% of the price

4 Write sentences comparing these items using the words in brackets and the language in Exercise 2. Add the prices from the table in Exercise 1.

1 A burger and fries in country C and country D (*not*)
2 A one-bedroom flat in country C and country A (*half*)
3 A man's haircut in country C and country B (*not*)
4 A burger and fries in country A and country D (*twice*)
5 A woman's haircut in country C and country D (*as*)

> You can also compare items like this:
>
> A one-bedroom flat is **slightly more expensive** in country A **than** in country B, at £600 and £585.

5 Compare these items using the structure above. Change the adverb as necessary.

1 A woman's haircut in country B and country C
2 A double espresso in country B and country C
3 A double espresso in country B and country A
4 A burger and fries in country A and country C

6 How do the prices of the items in the table compare with your country? Discuss in pairs.

7 🎯 Write a full essay for the table in Exercise 2. Then compare it with the sample answer on page 169.

Vocabulary for pie charts and ratios

1 Look at the exam task on page 97, then complete these sentences about the men's chart with the words in the box.

> bottom ▪ equally ▪ followed ▪ highest ▪ least ▪ lowest ▪ most ▪ place ▪ ranked ▪ second ▪ top

1 The ____ popular sector for internships for men was IT, at 25%.
2 The sector with the ____ percentage for men was IT, at 25%.
3 The ____ popular sector for internships for men was publishing, at 3%.
4 The ____ most common field for internships for men was law, at 14%.
5 The field with the ____ percentage for men was publishing, at 3%.
6 IT came ____ of the chart, with 25%.
7 Engineering ____ third in the chart, at 12%.
8 Journalism and science were ranked ____ , at 10%.
9 Publishing came ____ of the chart, with 3%.
10 Banking was in fifth ____ with 9%, closely ____ by PR with 7%.

The pie charts show a breakdown of the top nine industries in which male and female graduates did internships in the UK in 2018. The numbers are shown in percentages.

Summarise the information by selecting and reporting the main features and make comparisons where relevant.

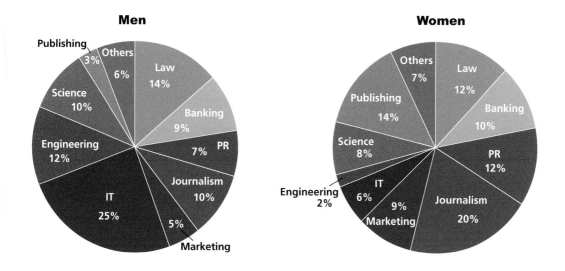

2 Use the prompts to write similar sentences about the women's chart.

1 came | top
   Journalism came top of the chart for women, with 20%.
2 least popular
3 third place | followed
4 highest
5 ranked second
6 bottom
7 equally

3 You can also express *10%* as *a tenth* or *one in ten*. Express these percentages with similar phrases.

1 20% = _____ or _____   4 50% = _____ or _____
2 25% = _____ or _____   5 66% = around _____
3 33% = about _____ or _____   6 75% = _____

4 Complete these sentences about the pie charts with phrases from Exercise 3.

1 _____ men did internships in IT.
2 Just over _____ men worked in engineering, at 12%.
3 _____ ten men did internships in journalism.
4 Exactly _____ women worked in journalism.
5 Just under _____ women worked in marketing, at 9%.
6 Approximately _____ ten women did work experience in PR, at 12%.

5 Complete this paragraph about the men's chart.

As regards internships for men, the ¹m____ popular sector was IT, with exactly a ²q____ , ³f____ by law in second ⁴p____ with 14%. Engineering ⁵r____ third, with 12%, and then science and journalism were ⁶e____ popular, with a ⁷t____ each. Just under one in ⁸t____ men did work experience in banking, while PR came ⁹s____ with 7%. The sector with the ¹⁰l____ percentage was publishing, at 3%.

6 Write a similar paragraph about the women's chart.

7 Write a full essay for this exam task. Then compare it with the sample answer on page 169.

> *The table shows a breakdown of the top ten sectors of employment entered into by recent graduates in the UK in 2018.*
> *Summarise the information by selecting and reporting the main features and make comparisons where relevant.*

	Men	Women
Marketing and sales	14%	13%
Law	9%	5%
Teaching	6%	12%
Human resources	10%	20%
Banking and insurance	3%	11%
IT	24%	6%
Engineering	11%	2%
Science	9%	8%
Medicine	2%	14%
Graphic design	4%	3%

Introductions and overviews for comparative essays

> The introduction to a Task 1 comparative essay is similar to the introduction to a trends graph (see Unit 6). You can use the structures on page 81 (*how much / many, the number of / the amount of*) to change the grammar of the question and rewrite it in your own words.
> For the overview, you should choose two key features of the graph that stand out and use good linking phrases to write about them.

1 Write an introduction for these comparative questions using the words in brackets.

1 Part-time university students, UK, 2018 (*how many*)
2 Sales of concert tickets, O² stadium, 2018 (*the number of*)
3 Production of solar energy, Chile and Argentina, 2017 (*how much*)
4 Water use in Spain and Italy, 2018 (*the amount of*)

2 Look again at the model essay on page 91 and discuss these questions in pairs.

1 Which two features of the graph are described in the overview?
2 Which linking phrases does the writer use to introduce the two key features?

3 Write an introduction and overview for the table on page 93. Then compare what you wrote with a sample answer on page 169.

Listening Part 3: Sentence completion

Skills focus

In Listening Part 3, you generally listen to a discussion based around students, university or education. There are often two students, or a student and a university lecturer.
This page practises a key question type for Listening Part 3: sentence completion.

1 **Discuss these questions in pairs.**

1   Have you ever done an internship in a company?
2   Is it common in your country for people to do internships?
3   What can you learn from doing an internship?
4   Do you think you will do one in the future?

2   🎧17 🎯 **Listen to two students, Brian and Sophie, discussing internships and complete the sentences below. Write NO MORE THAN TWO WORDS OR A NUMBER for each answer.**

Brian and Sophie's internships

1   Sophie was told in the beginning that she would be paid a ____ .
2   Sophie is now hoping to receive at least her ____ .
3   Although Sophie's mum thinks she should not do the internship, Sophie is attracted by the possibility of working with the ____ .
4   Brian has recently been interviewed for a work placement at a ____ .
5   If the internship is successful, Brian hopes it will result in a ____ .
6   Sophie doesn't think her brother will complete his university studies because he is now ____ .

3   **Discuss these questions in pairs.**

1   Do you think Sophie should take the internship, even though it is unpaid? Why?
2   Would you drop out of university if you had the chance to do an internship in something you were really interested in?

4   🎧18 🎯 **Listen to the rest of the conversation about internships in general and complete the sentences below. Write NO MORE THAN TWO WORDS for each answer.**

1   Sophie mentions that the article she read says that internships favour people from ____ .
2   Brian says it's difficult for less well-off young people to do internships in employment fields like ____ .
3   Sophie says that the government should introduce a law to make it ____ to pay people who are doing internships.
4   Brian disagrees with Sophie, because he thinks that if companies have to pay interns, they will ____ employing them.

5   **Do you think interns should be paid? Why? / Why not? Discuss in pairs.**

Reading: Summary completion with a wordlist

Skills focus

> A common question type in IELTS Reading is completing a summary of the text, or of part of it. Sometimes you have a list of words to choose from to complete the summary, and sometimes you have to complete the summary using words in the text.
> This section will look at the technique for summaries with a wordlist.

1 **Discuss these questions in pairs.**

1 Look at the title of the text on page 101. Do you know what the Universal Basic Income is?
2 Does the government of your country give people money when they are sick, old or unemployed?
3 Do you think the government should spend more money to helping people who can't work?
4 What do you think about the idea of the government giving a regular sum of money to everyone, regardless of their income?

2 **Look at the exam task below and discuss these questions in pairs.**

1 What kind of word do you think should go in each gap (e.g. noun, adjective, verb)?
2 What are the key word(s) before each gap?
3 Can you think of any synonyms of the key word(s) near each gap?
4 Which words in the box do you think are possible answers?

> benefits · citizens · food · men · money · poor · poverty ·
> tax · time · unemployment · women

The UBI is seen by some as the answer to the age-old issue of ¹____ . The essential idea of the UBI is that it ensures that all ²____ are given enough money to live on throughout their life. Everyone would have a place to live, would be able to afford to clothe themselves and their family, and would have sufficient ³____ . The UBI would be given throughout one's lifetime, no matter how much ⁴____ people have or what their circumstances are.

3 📌 **Read the first paragraph of the text on page 101 and complete the summary in the exam task in Exercise 2 with the words in the box.**

4 **Work in pairs. Compare your answers to Exercise 3 and discuss why you chose them.**

5 **Repeat steps 1–4 in Exercise 2 for this summary of the rest of the reading text.**

> benefits · considered · fluctuations · government · huge · income ·
> permanent · private · slight · tax · temporary · tried · universal laws

Making the UBI possible would mean considerable increases in ¹____ among more affluent members of society. It could also be paid for by eliminating a very costly system of ²____ , and saving money by not employing thousands of ³____ workers to implement those benefits. Another issue is the psychological and health problems such as stress and depression caused by ⁴____ contracts and job insecurity. Supporters of UBI believe that the security of knowing you had the basics in life taken care of would result in ⁵____ falls in the cost of healthcare. Would it work? Some local authorities, like Glasgow, have ⁶____ pilot schemes, but no one has done it across a whole country yet.

6 🎯 Complete the summary in the exam task in Exercise 5 with the words in the box. Then check your answers on page 169.

Universal Basic Income – the way forward?

Is the Universal Basic Income (UBI) the solution to a problem that has plagued the world since time began – the problem of people being too poor to live comfortably? The basic idea of the UBI is that every single person in society is given a sum of money each month, from birth to death, to cover their basic needs, such as housing, clothing and nutrition. This is given regardless of their income, so in other words if they are working and earning a significant salary, they still receive the UBI each month, just the same as someone who is unemployed, a child or unable to work for other reasons, like ill health.

The obvious question is how can a society afford a UBI? It would seem to go against common sense – if everyone is given a lump sum of money throughout their life, the money has to come from somewhere. The short answer to this is that the UBI does require substantial tax rises among richer members of society to pay for it. What supporters argue is that although the rich would lose out in one way, by paying more tax, they and everyone else would gain by the lifetime security of knowing that you never had to worry about the future.

Another potential benefit of the UBI is that it would get rid of an expensive system of benefits that every country has developed in the last 100 years. What is known as 'means-testing', in which people who need money from the state have to have their income tested, to see if they qualify, is extraordinarily costly. There are hundreds of thousands of state-employed workers whose job it is to check if someone is entitled to a certain benefit or not. Often mistakes are made, and in addition to that, many people feel the stigma of means-tested benefits and do not apply for

them, even though they are entitled. Contrast that with a universal benefit like child benefit in the UK. This is money given to every mother with children, every week, from birth until the age of 16. Because it applies to everyone equally, the take-up is high and it is easy and quick to administer. When a woman has a child, it is a simple procedure to apply for child benefit and it does not require any regular checks. Supporters of the UBI point to child benefit as an example of how universal benefits are cost-effective and cheap to run.

A further possible upside of the UBI is psychological. In a modern capitalist society, the stress of job insecurity for many people is immense. Not knowing if you will keep your job in the long term, because of short-term contracts, zero-hours contracts and frequent dramatic changes in the labour market, often leads to stress, illness and depression. On top of that, many people similarly worry about their accommodation – will they have enough money to pay the rent or mortgage, and as well as that, will they be able to feed their children? The UBI takes away all this insecurity, say its supporters, and as a result, as well as the improvements to human life, the savings to the healthcare and mental health services would be astronomical.

So, has it been tried? Some local councils, such as Glasgow in Scotland, and even the country of Finland have experimented with pilot schemes, but no country has launched a full-blown UBI scheme yet. Would it work? It would require a radical shift in our thinking about work, the state and the world, but in societies where the current benefit systems are not really fit for purpose, it is an idea certainly worth trying.

7 Discuss these questions in pairs.

1 What do you think about the UBI? Do you think it's a good idea?
2 Do you think it's possible to increase tax on rich people enough to pay for it?
3 Do you agree that it would make life less stressful and insecure?
4 Would you like to see your government try to introduce it?

Speaking Parts 1, 2 and 3

Talking about jobs

> A common topic in Part 1 of the Speaking exam is jobs and work. You may be asked about your job or your future work plans, and also about what aspects of a job are most important to you.

1   **Discuss these questions in pairs.**

1   Have you ever worked? If so, what jobs have you done?
2   Have you ever had a part-time job?
3   What job would you like to do in the future?
4   What qualifications will you need to get the job you want?
5   What are you looking for in a job? What things make a job attractive to you?

2   **Look at these aspects of a job and rank them in order (1 = most important, 6 = least important).**

Aspect of a job	Salary	Feeling of working in a team	New challenges	Autonomy/ freedom to be creative	Distance between the job and home	Possibilities of promotion
Rank						

3   **Discuss your answers in pairs and compare your ideas. Is there anything else you would add to the list of what makes a good job?**

Grammar: Cleft sentences

> Cleft sentences are used in speaking to give emphasise what you are saying. You have to change the structure of the sentence in order to do this.
>
> *I like working from home because I don't have to travel.* →
> **What I like about working from home is that** *I don't have to travel*
> *I like being a teacher mainly because you can help people learn and achieve their goals.* →
> **The thing I like most about being a teacher is that** *you can help people learn and achieve their goals.*
>
> Cleft sentences will help you sound more natural in all parts of the Speaking test.

1   **Rewrite these sentences about jobs using cleft sentences.**

1   I would like to work as a doctor so that I can help people.
    The reason I …
2   I think the most important thing in a job is the possibility of promotion.
    What I think …
3   I think the least important aspect of a job is flexible working hours.
    The aspect of a job that I think …
4   I need to get a good Master's degree in order to become a lawyer.
    What I …
5   I worked as a customer assistant, and I really enjoyed dealing with people.
    I worked as a customer assistant, and what I …
6   I worked in a factory, and I found it was really boring and repetitive.
    I worked in a factory, and what I …

2   **Practise the questions in Exercises 1 and 2 at the top of this page again.**
    Use as many cleft sentences as you can.

Grammar: Using comparatives

In Speaking Parts 2 and 3, you can improve your grammar by using some common comparatives.

1 ☉ Make notes for one minute about this Speaking Part 2 question, then speak for two minutes about it.

> **Talk about a business you might like to set up one day.**
>
> > **You should say**
> > > **what type of business it would be**
> > > **where and when you would set it up**
> > > **why you would choose this type of business**
> > **and if you think you** will **set up this business one day.**

2 🎧 19 Listen to a teacher answering the same question and make notes about what he says.

3 🎧 19 Read the audioscript and try to remember the word or phrase that goes in each gap. Then listen again and check your answers.

I'm going to talk about a business I would like to set up one day, which is a language school. The main reason I would like to do that is that it would be great to have the freedom to make the decisions and to run the school in the way that I want. I think in terms of the place, I would set up a school in Malta, because although I'm English, the weather is ¹____ in England ²____ in Malta, and it would be great to work in a sunny climate.

I think I would set up the school in the next two or three years. First, I would have to borrow some money, because I'm a teacher and so I'm ³____ people in some jobs, so I would have to take out a loan or find an investor. What I would do is to be the academic manager, so I would train the teachers and organise the classes, and then I'm thinking of hiring my sister as the financial and marketing manager, because she's ⁴____ , and she has ⁵____ of marketing as well.

If I think about whether I will do it or not, well, I'm ⁶____ I was a couple of years ago, as the world economy is having a few problems, but I'm sure in a few years you will see my school opening up in Malta.

4 ☉ Try the Speaking Part 2 task from Exercise 1 again, adding in some comparatives.

5 Read these common Speaking Part 3 questions and write some comparative sentences you could use to answer them.

1 What are the advantages of running your own business, compared to working for a company?
I think if you run your own company, you can earn <u>much more money than</u> if you work for a company if the business is successful. Also, if you're working for a company, it's not <u>nearly as flexible as</u> working for yourself, because you have to follow the company's rules and do what your line manager tells you.

2 What are the pros and cons of working at home, compared to travelling to work every day?

3 What are the pros and cons of working in a small company, compared to a big multinational with lots of branches?

4 Do you prefer working alone or working in a team? What are the advantages and disadvantages of both of these ways of working?

5 Do you think it is better to do work experience while you are studying for a degree at university, or is it better just to concentrate on your studies?

6 What do you think has been the impact on technology on the way people work?

Pulling it all together

Review

1 Write five more phrases for describing numbers.

Spanish was considerably more popular for women than men, <u>the figures being</u> 11% and 3%.

2 Write sentences with suitable comparative structures using this information.

1 A meal for two in country A = £30, in country B = £35
   A meal for two in country A <u>is not quite as expensive as</u> in country B, at £30 and £35.
2 A packet of cigarettes: country A = £3, country B = £9
3 A litre of petrol: country A = £1, country B = £2
4 A cheese sandwich: country A = £2, country B = £2
5 A loaf of bread: country A: £2, country B = £1

3 Complete these synonyms for ranking information.

1 Journalism was the most popular job. = Journalism was in ____ ____ .
2 Publishing was the least popular job. = Publishing came ____ of the chart.
3 Human resources ranked second in the chart. = HR was the ____ ____ popular job.
4 Law was in first place. = Law was the sector with the ____ percentage in the chart.

4 Write these figures in as many different ways as you can.

1 10%   2 one in four   3 half   4 75%   5 33%

5 Rewrite these sentences as cleft sentences.

1 The feeling of helping others is the best thing about being a nurse.
   What I like …
2 Knowing that I'm making a difference to a child's life is what motivates me to be a primary school teacher.
   What …

Final practice essay

The bar graph shows a breakdown of the top nine university subjects of men and women in the UK in 2018. The numbers are shown in percentages.
Summarise the information by selecting and reporting the main features and make comparisons where relevant.

Breakdown of university majors of men and women in the UK, 2018

1 Write an essay for the exam task above.

2 Compare your essay with the sample answer on page 170.

Writing Task 1: Maps

Model essay

A common Task 1 question is where you have to describe the changes you see in two maps. The question shows two diagrams of a city or a place in different time periods, and you have to write about the most important changes that you see.

As with other Task 1 essays, you have **20 minutes** to write a minimum of **150 words**.

1 **Discuss these questions in pairs.**

1 How has your home town changed in recent years? Think about these things:
  - shopping
  - restaurants
  - transport
  - parks and green areas
  - places to visit
  - prices

2 In general, do you think your home town is a better place to live than ten years ago?

2 **Look at this exam task and answer the questions on page 106.**

The maps below describe the main changes which have happened in the city of Westville between 2000 and today.
Summarise the information by selecting and reporting the main features and make comparisons where relevant.

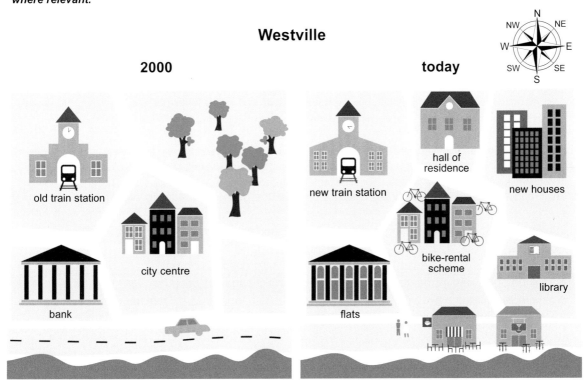

1 How do you think Westville has changed in general? Do you think it's more modern? Is it a more interesting place to live?
2 What has happened to the trees in the north-east of the city?
3 What has happened to the bank in the south-west of the city?
4 What has changed in the city centre in the last few years?
5 How could you compare accommodation in 2000 and now?
6 What has changed in the area near the sea?
7 What do you think are the biggest changes that have taken place? Circle the most important ones.

3 Discuss the biggest changes in the maps in pairs. When you finish, think about what language you needed to use to describe the changes.

4 Discuss these questions in pairs.

1 How many paragraphs would you write for this Task 1 question, and what would you write in each paragraph?
2 What grammar and vocabulary do you think you will need to answer this question?

5 Read the model essay and answer the questions below.

These two maps highlight the main developments which have taken place in the coastal city of Westville, over the period between 2000 and today.

Overall, what stands out from the maps is that Westville has become much more modern and developed, with more accommodation and entertainment facilities, and fewer trees and green areas.

In detail, if we look at the north of the city, one change has been that the trees in the north-east have been cut down and new houses have been constructed in their place. In 2000, there did not use to be a student hall of residence, but a new one has been built north of the city centre. As regards the city centre, the last few years have seen the introduction of a new bike-rental scheme, making it easier for people to get around the city centre by bike.

Regarding the south of the city, a significant change is the conversion of the bank in the south-west into flats. There used to be trees in the south-east too, but they have been cut down and a new library has been built. A further important development is the pedestrianisation of the road near the beach. Cafés and bars have also been opened along the seafront, meaning that the beach area is now a nicer and more interesting place to go out.

(224 words)

1 How many paragraphs are there, and what happens in each one?
2 Which adjectives are used in the overview to describe the general changes in Westville?
3 In the overview, what does the writer say there are more of and fewer of?
4 In paragraph 3, how many changes are mentioned? And in paragraph 4?
5 In paragraphs 3 and 4, find and highlight:
    a any examples of the present perfect passive (e.g. *have been cut down*)
    b linking phrases to introduce new changes (e.g. *one change has been ...*)
    c examples of where the writer is commenting on the changes (e.g. *... making it easier to get around the city by bike*)
    d examples of *used to*.

Language for describing changes in maps

> To answer a Task 1 maps question, you will need some common verbs which describe different types of changes.

1 Complete the table below with the words in the box according to their meaning.

> build · construct · convert · cut down · demolish · enlarge · erect · expand ·
> extend · introduce · knock down · make into · modernise · open ·
> pedestrianise · pull down · redevelop · remove · replace · turn into

Make bigger	Add something new	Take away something	Change one thing into something different

2 Discuss these questions about some of the verbs in Exercise 1 in pairs.

1 What can you *cut down*? Can you cut down a building?
2 What is the difference between *enlarge/expand* and *extend*?
3 What do you *pedestrianise*?
4 Can you *introduce* a new building? What can you introduce?

> You can see from the model answer on page 106 that when you describe changes between the past and now, you need to use the **present perfect passive**.
>
> To make the present perfect passive, use:
> object + *have/has* + *been* + past participle of the verb
> *The trees in the north-east* **have been cut down.**

3 Rewrite these sentences using the present perfect passive.

1 They have built a new hall of residence in the north of the city.
   A new hall of residence has been built in the north of the city.
2 They have opened new bars and cafés near the beach.
   New bars and cafés _____ near the beach.
3 The government has introduced a bike-rental scheme in the city centre.
   A bike-rental scheme _____ in the city centre.
4 They have converted the bank in the south-west into new flats.
   The bank in the south-west _____ .
5 They have pedestrianised the road near the seafront.
   The road _____
6 They have cut down the trees in the south-east and they have built a new library.
   The trees near the city centre _____ and a new library _____ .

4 Write about these changes using present perfect passive sentences.

1 The old train station | new train station in the north-west
2 The trees | new houses in the north-east

A useful grammar structure for describing things that were one way in the past but have now changed is *used to*:
There used to / did not use to be … , but …

A   *There **used to be** trees to the east of the city centre, but they have been cut down, and a new library has been built.*
B   *There **did not use to be** a hall of residence in Westville, but a new one has been built in the north of the city.*

Remember that the negative form does not have a *d* at the end!

5   Discuss these questions in pairs.

1   What is the difference in meaning between sentences A and B in the box above?
2   If you want to write about something new in the second map, which sentence should you use?
3   If you want to write about something in the first map which isn't in the second, which sentence should you use?

6   Write about these changes in the maps on page 105 using *There used to be / did not use to be … , but …*

1   The bike-rental scheme
2   The bank / flats in the south-west
3   The trees / new houses in the north-east
4   The new bars and cafés near the beach

Another way to describe changes in maps is to use noun phrases with this structure:
the + noun + *of* + noun
A new hall of residence has been built. → ***the building of a new hall of residence***

7   Complete the table with the noun forms of the verbs.

Verb	Noun	Verb	Noun
build	*building*	introduce	
construct		knock down	
convert		modernise	
cut down		open	
demolish		pedestrianise	
enlarge		pull down	
erect		redevelop	
expand		remove	
extend		replace	

8 Rewrite these sentence with suitable noun phrases.

1 A new hall of residence has been built in the north of the city.
   One change has been *the building of a new hall of residence* in the north of the city.
2 A new tower has been erected near the beach.
   Another change has been _____ .
3 A bike-rental scheme has been introduced in the city centre.
   An interesting development is _____ .
4 New bars and cafés have been opened along the seafront.
   A further change is _____ .
5 The trees in the north-east have been cut down, and new houses have been built in their place.
   One significant development is the _____ in the north-east, and the _____ in their place.
6 The bank in the south-west has been converted into flats.
   A striking change is _____ .
7 The road near the seafront has been pedestrianised.
   One noticeable improvement is _____ .
8 Over the last few years, the trees to the east of the city centre have been removed, and a new library has been opened.
   The last few years have seen the _____ and the _____ .

When you write about maps, you will need some linking phrases to introduce the changes.
If you are using a noun phrase, you must use a linking phrase to make the sentence complete:
One change has been *the building of a new hall of residence in the north of the city.*

9 Cover the sentences in Exercise 8 and try to complete the linking phrases from memory.
   Then check your answers.

1 One c_____ has b_____ …
2 A_____ change has been …
3 An in_____ d_____ is …
4 A f_____ change is …
5 One s_____ development is …
6 A s_____ change is …
7 One n_____ im_____ is …
8 The last f_____ years have s_____ …

When you are writing the main body of your answer for a maps question, you should:

1 circle the main changes in the maps question that you are going to write
   about. You should choose between six and eight changes that you think are
   the most important and interesting to write about;

2 decide which changes you are going to write about in each paragraph of the
   main body. The easiest way to do this is to divide the city into different
   areas. For example, paragraph 3 could describe the changes in the north of
   the city and the city centre, and paragraph 4 could describe the changes in
   the south of the city;

3 use a linking phrase to introduce each separate area of the city. If you look
   at the model essay on page 106, the writer has used these three linking
   phrases to show which part of the city is being written about:
   If we look at the north of the city, …
   As regards the city centre, …
   Regarding the south of the city, …

Introductions and overviews for map essays

ℹ When you write an introduction for a maps question, it's important to rephrase the question using your own words. To do this, learn some common synonyms of words which are often in the question.

1 Look at this sentence from the exam task and write down as many synonyms of the underlined words as you can think of.

The maps below <u>describe</u> <u>the</u> <u>main</u> <u>changes</u> which have <u>happened</u> in the city of Westville <u>between</u> 2000 <u>and</u> today.

2 Write an introduction for the exam task in Exercise 1, using the synonyms you thought of.

ℹ When you write an overview for a maps essay, think about these questions:
1 What has happened to the city in general? Has it become more modern? More urban? More industrialised? Better for tourists?
2 Generally speaking, what does the city have more of (e.g. shopping or entertainment facilities) and fewer of (e.g. trees or parks)?
Then write two sentences to describe the general changes in the city over the period.

3 Complete the overview from the model essay below with the words in the box.

> become ▪ developed ▪ fewer ▪ modern ▪ more ▪ stands ▪ what

Overall, ¹____ ____ out from the maps is that Westville has ²____ much more ³____ and ⁴____ , with ⁵____ accommodation and entertainment facilities, and ⁶____ trees and green areas.

ℹ One way to try to get a higher score with maps is to make one or two interpretations of key changes, saying what effect these changes would have on people living in the city.

4 Discuss these questions in pairs.

1 If there are more bars and clubs near the beach, how will life be better for people in the city?
2 If there is a new bike-rental scheme, how will life be easier for people travelling in the city centre?

5 Complete these sentences from the model essay.

1 The last few years have seen the introduction of a new bike-rental scheme, m____ i____ e____ for people to get around the city centre by bike.
2 Cafés and bars have also been opened along the seafront, m____ t____ the beach area is now a n____ and m____ i____ place to go out.

6 Complete these sentences with a comment, using the words in brackets.

1 One change is the pedestrianisation of the road near the beach, … (*make | safe*)
2 Another development is the building of a new hall of residence, … (*mean | cheap for students to live*)
3 A significant change is that new houses have been built in the north-east of the town, … (*make | easy for young families to find a place to live*)
4 An interesting development is that the old train station has been demolished, and a new one has been constructed in the same place, … (*mean | more trains to London every day*)

Two maps in the past

In the IELTS exam, it is also possible to have to write about two maps in the past (e.g. 2008 and 2018), instead of one map in the past and one map in the present. Write your answer in the same way, but you will need to change the grammar slightly.

1 Discuss these questions in pairs.

1 Is it possible to write present perfect sentences like *A hall of residence has been built*? If not, why not?
2 How do you think you should change the grammar in your answer?

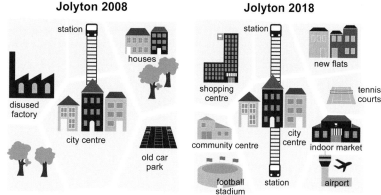

Jolyton 2008   **Jolyton 2018**

The maps on the right show changes which took place in the town of Jolyton between 2008 and 2018. Summarise the information by selecting and reporting the main features and make comparisons where relevant.

- Use the past simple passive:
  *A new shopping centre **was built** in the city centre.*
  *The trees in the south of the city **were cut down** and a library **was opened** in their place.*

- Use *by* + date + past perfect passive in the second part of the sentence:
  *In 2000, there were trees in the south of the city, but **by 2015**, they **had been cut down**, and a library **had been opened** in their place.*

2 Complete these sentences with a suitable verb in the past simple passive.

1 One change is that a new shopping centre _____ in the north-west of the city.
2 Another change is that the trees in the south-west _____ and a football stadium _____ .

3 Write about these changes using the past simple passive.

1 the trees | tennis courts   2 the old car park | an indoor market

4 Complete these sentences with the past perfect passive of the verbs in brackets.

1 In 2008, there were trees in the south-east of the city, but by 2018 _____ (*cut down*) and a football stadium _____ (*build*).
2 There did not use to be a shopping centre in Jolyton, but by 2018, _____ (*build*) in the north-west.
3 In 2008, there was a disused factory in the west of the city, but _____ (*knock down*) and replaced by a community centre.
4 There did not use to be tennis courts in the city, but _____ (*construct*).

5 ⊙ Write an essay for the exam task in Exercise 1. Make sure you include:

- past simple passive
- *by* + date + past perfect passive
- *there used to / there did not use to*
- noun phrases
- linking phrases
- comment / interpretation.

When you finish, compare your work with the sample answer on page 171.

Listening Part 4: Predicting answers

Skills focus

> **i** Listening Part 4 is usually a section of a university lecture. Although some of the vocabulary in Part 4 can be complicated, if you use the following techniques, you can tackle it with confidence and do well.
> 1   Lectures have a very clear structure. Try to follow the speaker when they change topic (e.g. when they talk about a different aspect of London).
> 2   If you need to complete a sequence of gaps, then you should decide what kind of word (adjective, noun, verb, adverb, etc.) will go in each gap.
> 3   Think of synonyms of one or two of the key words next to each gap and listen for them.
> 4   If you miss an answer, don't worry – just keep following the lecture and try to get the next one. Remember that you have ten minutes to check your answers and write them on the answer sheet at the end of the Listening test, so you can go back and think about any answers you have missed.

1 🎧 20 **Listen to the introduction to a lecture about London in the 21st century and write the four topics the speaker is going to talk about.**

2 **Look at sentences 1–4 in this exam task, then discuss the questions below in pairs and note your ideas.**

Contemporary London

Rising costs

1   A generation ago, it was possible for a normal worker to ＿＿ the rent and bills.

2   As a result, areas of London like Hackney were very ＿＿ in terms of the population.

3   However, today, due to the process of ＿＿ , less well-off people have had to move out of areas like Hackney.

4   One answer to this issue might be for governments to fix a ＿＿ amount that much people pay for their accommodation each month or year.

Question 1
1   What type of word do you think the answer is?
2   Do you think London was cheaper or more expensive a generation ago?
    What is your guess for question 1?

Question 2
3   What type of word is the answer? How do you know what kind of word it is?
4   Can you think of any synonyms of *very*?
5   What do you think the answer could be?

Question 3
6   What kind of word do you think the answer is?
7   What's a synonym of *less well-off*?
8   How would you describe this process in your own words?

Question 4
9   What kind of word is it?
10 Can you think of a synonym of *fix*?
11 What do you think the answer is?

3 🎧21 **Listen to the first part of the lecture and complete the gaps in the exam task in Exercise 1.**

4 **Look at the audioscript on pages 152–153 and check your answers.**

Skills application

1 🎧22 **Listen to the rest of the lecture and complete sentences 5–13. Use the techniques from the Skills focus section above.**

Transport	5	Tourists who come to London can be surprised by the ____ in the quality of transport.
	6	Many Tube lines on the outskirts of London can be ____ and old.
	7	Season tickets on London transport are ____ as expensive as in Paris.
Leisure opportunities	8	The Labour government in the 1990s decided to ____ entrance fees for museums.
	9	This is an initiative which has been ____ by other world cities.
	10	London has lots of green spaces, including Hyde Park, neighbourhood parks and children's ____ .
Multi-culturalism	11	According to the census in 2011, there were more than ____ nationalities living in London.
	12	Around 25% of the people living in London were born ____ .
	13	When there are problems, the fact that English is a ____ makes things a lot easier.

2 **Check your answers in the audioscript on page 153.**

3 **Discuss these questions in pairs.**

1 Did anything you heard about London in the Listening surprise you?
2 Have you ever visited London? Would you like to?
3 When you visit a capital city like London for a day trip, what do you normally do?
4 Do you like to spend your holidays in big cities?
5 What do you think is the best thing about living in a large city like London?
6 How do you think London compares to the capital city of your country?
7 Why do you think people enjoy spending time in big cities like London?
8 How much do you know about the history of the capital city of your country?

Reading: Table completion
Skills focus

> **i** A common question type in IELTS Reading is completing a table with information taken from the text. To answer this type of question more effectively you should:
> • use the headings and categories of the table to help you
> • decide which word form is required in each gap
> • think of synonyms of the words around the gaps
> • make predictions about possible answers.

1 Discuss these questions in pairs.

1 Have you ever been to London or Dubai?
2 Which of these cities would you most like to visit, and why?
3 What would the pros and cons of going on holiday to these cities?

2 Decide if the words in the box are synonyms of *advantage*, *disadvantage* or *verdict*.

> benefit · bonus · conclusion · cons · downside · drawback · negative
> point · opinion · plus point · pros · view

3 Work in pairs. Decide which word form is required in each gap of this exam task.

Example: 1 *The answer should be a plural noun because it follows* <u>many</u>.

City holidays – the verdict

City	Advantage	Disadvantage	Verdict
London	Many ¹____	²____ may be poor	Very good for ³____
Dubai	Outstanding ⁴____	Often ⁵____ in summer	Suitable for a holiday in ⁶____

4 Brainstorm possible synonyms of the key words in each section of the exam task in Exercise 3.

Example: 1 Many = a lot of / a large number of

5 Quickly predict what you think each answer might be.

6 Read the text below and complete the table in Exercise 3 with NO MORE THAN THREE WORDS from the text for each answer.

City holidays – the verdict

This survey looks at two popular holiday destinations and compares their main advantages and disadvantages. First of all, London. The best part about taking a holiday in London is that there are a large number of monuments. You can visit places like Buckingham Palace, the Tower of London and many more. However, one downside of going to London is that the weather can be changeable. Sunny weather is not guaranteed, even in the summer, so bring an umbrella. Overall, though, we think London is excellent when it comes to historical places.

Now let's look at Dubai. Dubai is well-known for its amazing shopping malls, in particular the Mall of the Emirates, which is one of the largest and best shopping malls in the world. However, one problem in Dubai is that in June, July and August, the weather can be unbearable. There are often temperatures of up to 50˚C, which even the locals struggle to cope with. Therefore, our view that Dubai is best for travellers in winter and spring. The holiday you choose, therefore, depends a lot on what type of holiday, and what type of weather, you are looking for.

Skills application

1 ⊙ Complete the table below. Choose NO MORE THAN THREE WORDS from the passage for each answer.

London	The underground in London was an immediate [1]____ with people in the capital.
Paris	The Paris metro has featured in many [2]____ .
New York	The New York metro is unusual because passengers can use it [3]____ a day.
Singapore	With the aid of up-to-date technology, the Singapore metro can transport a higher [4]____ each day than older underground systems.
Seoul	Underground passengers in Seoul can enjoy rapid and [5]____ internet connections while travelling.
Kobe and Osaka	[6]____ were first introduced in Kobe and Osaka in 1981. In the beginning, many metro users were [7]____ to travel in the first carriage of the train, but this did not last long.
Moscow	The Moscow metro is known all over the world because of its [8]____ .

Going Underground

A brief look at metro systems around the world

The world's first underground system was built in London in the 19th century and was an instant success with Londoners. It was not long before other capital cities around the world wanted their own underground systems. The Paris metro, which is one of the most attractive and distinctive metro systems in the world, mainly due to the Art Nouveau signs and station architecture, opened in 1900. Today, over half a billion people a year use the Paris metro, and its stations have appeared in numerous films and advertisements. Across the Atlantic, the New York underground, known as the subway, opened four years later, in 1904. Today, it is one of the few metro systems which is open 24 hours a day, seven days a week.

In the later 20th century, rapidly developing cities such as Singapore and Seoul built their own metro systems, and with the benefit of modern technology were able to construct more sophisticated and up-to-date metro networks. In Singapore, they were able to construct deeper and larger tunnels, and therefore carry a greater volume of passengers through the network every day. In addition, more modern systems have included interconnectivity into their metro systems. Visitors to Seoul, for instance, are often surprised at the availability of reliable and rapid internet connections during their journey underground. A ground-breaking step forward in metro technology was the introduction of the first driverless trains. In 1981, two Japanese cities, Kobe and Osaka, opened metro systems simultaneously, both with driverless trains. At first, worried passengers were reluctant to travel in the front coach of a fully automated metro train, but it did not take long for the travelling public to become accustomed to it.

Whether the system is modern or old, driverless or driven, internet-connected or not, all metro systems in the world share one thing which explains their enduring popularity – the ability to shift people at great speed from one part of a city to another. Some metro systems, like Moscow, are famed worldwide for their beauty; others, like Singapore, for their efficiency; but it is clear that modern cities simply could not function effectively without the presence of the thousands of miles of track and stations sitting right beneath us in every major city on Earth.

2 Check your answers on page 172.

Speaking Part 2

A city you enjoyed visiting

> One way to improve your performance in Speaking Part 2 is to use good linking phrases and accurate past tenses if you are talking about a past event.

1   🎯 Make notes about this Speaking Part 2 task for one minute, then practise in pairs.

Talk about a city you enjoyed visiting.

    You should say:
           why you went there
           when you went there and how long for
           what you did there
      and why you enjoyed visiting it

---

2   🎧23 Listen to a student talking about a holiday to Barcelona. Make notes about what he says about the four points in the exam task in Exercise 1.

3   🎧23 Listen again and complete the linking phrases the speaker uses. Then check your answers in the audioscript on page 153.

1   I'm g____ to t____ you about …
2   The r____ I chose to go to Barcelona was …
3   One t____ I really liked about Barcelona was …
4   A____ great thing about Barcelona was …
5   One of the h____ of my trip was …
6   As w____ as seeing the sights, I a____ …
7   If I h____ to choose one thing I enjoyed most, though, it w____ be …

> Most of the time you need to use the **past simple** in Part 2, because you are describing a past experience. However, there are some cases where you can use the **past perfect** or the **past continuous**.

4   Complete these paragraphs with a suitable past tense of the verbs in brackets.

Last year, I ¹____ (*take*) three months off work and I ²____ (*go*) travelling in South America by myself. When I ³____ (*arrive*) in Argentina, I was really nervous, because I ⁴____ (*not travel*) alone for such a long time before. But it was fantastic and I ⁵____ (*meet*) lots of interesting people.

Two years ago, I ⁶____ (*work*) in a boring office job in London, and I ⁷____ (*hate*) it, so one day I ⁸____ (*decide*) to give up my job and go backpacking in Australia. I ⁹____ (*have*) a great time – it was amazing! I remember when I was 21, I ¹⁰____ (*go*) to France for a month to pick grapes on a vineyard. I ¹¹____ (*just finish*) university and I ¹²____ (*not have*) anything to do. A few weeks earlier, a friend ¹³____ (*tell*) me that it was easy to find work, so I ¹⁴____ (*buy*) a ticket to France and did it. It was such a great adventure.

5   🎯 Take a few minutes to prepare an improved answer to the Part 2 in Exercise 1. Then practise in pairs.

Speaking Part 3

Talking about improvements

> A common type of question in Speaking Part 3 is to be asked your opinion about how to improve things. You might be asked questions like:
> - *How could the education system in your country be improved?*
> - *What could governments do to reduce air pollution?*
> - *How can cities be improved for people who live there?*
> You can use a range of grammar structures to do this effectively.

1 Complete these answers to the question *How could the education system in your country be improved?*.

1 It w____ be good if the government i____ more money in school sports facilities, because it would allow more children to keep fit and enjoy sport from an early age.
2 I w____ the government w____ reduce university tuition fees, so that more people could afford to go.
3 If it w____ up to me, I w____ increase teachers' pay, in order to attract more people into teaching.

2 Find the phrase in each sentence in Exercise 1 used to introduce a reason.

1 *because it would*

3 Make notes about the question *How can cities be improved for people who live there?*. Think about these aspects:

- Transport
- The cost of living
- Housing
- Air quality
- Noise
- Access to culture

4 Work in pairs. Using the topics in Exercise 3, discuss ways to improve life in cities with the grammar structures from Exercise 1 and making sure you give reasons for your opinions.

If it was up to me, I would create more cycle lanes in big cities, because it would make it easier and safer to get around by bike, instead of having to drive or take public transport.

5 🎯 Discuss these questions related to cities in pairs.

1 Do you know any cities that have a bike-rental scheme? Do you think it is a good idea?
2 What are the advantages of living in a multi-cultural city? Are there any possible drawbacks?
3 Do you think that governments should set a limit on how much rent people can pay, in order to try to make cities less expensive?
4 Do you think charging car drivers to enter the city centre is a good way to reduce traffic and air pollution?

Pulling it all together

Review

1   Rewrite these sentences using the present perfect passive.

1   They have built a new football stadium on the outskirts of the city.
2   They have knocked down the old factory in the south of the city, and they have constructed a science park.

2   Rewrite these sentences using *used to / did not use to*.

1   There is a new Lebanese restaurant in the city centre.
2   The pub near the beach has closed down, and now it is an art gallery.

3   Rewrite these sentences using a linking phrase and a noun phrase.

1   A new library has been opened in the middle of town
2   The trees in the north-east of the city have been cut down, and a new shopping centre has been built.
3   A new recycling scheme has been introduced in the city.
4   The village hall has been converted into a café.

4   What are the two different ways you can comment on maps?

5   Complete these sentences with a suitable comment.

1   Three new restaurants have been opened in the city centre, meaning that …
2   A new railway line has been built in the south of the city, making it easier for people in the south …

6   Complete these sentences for two maps in the past using the past perfect passive of the verbs in brackets.

1   In 2000, there was not an airport in the city, but by 2015 _____ (*build*).
2   In 2000, there were old flats near the beach, but by 2015 they _____ (*knock down*) and a new tower _____ (*erect*).

7   Add the missing words to these Speaking Part 3 phrases for talking about improvements.

1   It be good if the government more money in healthcare.
2   I the government invest more money in education.
3   If it up me, I would increase tax on petrol.

Final practice essay

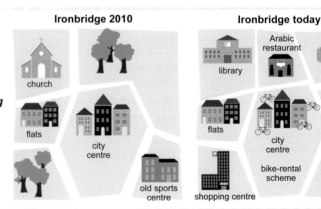

The maps on the right show changes in the town of Ironbridge between 2010 and today.

Summarise the information by selecting and reporting the main features, and make comparisons where relevant.

1   🎯 Write an essay for the exam task above.

2   Compare your essay with the sample answer on page 172.

Writing Task 1: Future trends graphs and maps

Model essay 1

> In the majority of cases, when you write about a trends graph for Task 1, the time period is in the past. However, sometimes you can be asked to write about trends in the future.
> You should organise your answer in the same way as the model essay in Unit 6, but you need to use future tenses and expressions instead of past tenses.

1 Discuss these questions in pairs.

1 Do you speak any languages apart from English and your native language?
2 Do you think you will learn another language in the future?
3 Which languages do you think are going to become more popular in the future?

2 Look at the exam task below and discuss these questions in pairs.

1 Which language will be the most widely studied in 2030 and in 2040?
2 What will happen with Arabic between 2038 and 2040?
3 What is going to happen to the number of students of Spanish in the last four years of the graph?
4 How could you describe what will happen to the number of students of Arabic between 2030 and 2038?
5 What is going to happen to the number of students of English between 2036 and 2040?
6 What future tenses and expressions could you use to write about this graph?

The graph highlights data about predictions about the number of students of three languages, 2030–2040.
Summarise the information by selecting and reporting the main features and make comparisons where necessary.

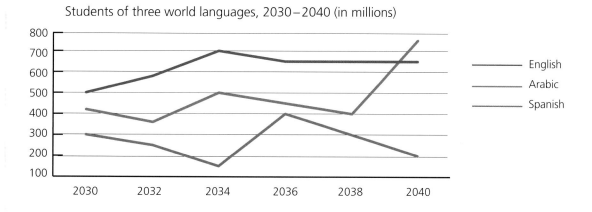

Students of three world languages, 2030–2040 (in millions)

The graph shows information about how many students will study three languages, English, Spanish and Arabic, over a ten-year period between 2030 and 2040.

Overall, what stands out from the graph is that there will be upward trends in English and Arabic, while the number of people studying Spanish will see a slight fall over the period. Another interesting point is that by 2040, Arabic will have become the most popular language.

In details, regarding English, the number is set to begin at 500m, and then there will be a steady increase to 700m in 2034. At this point, the figure will drop slightly, to approximately 650m in 2036, and then it looks set to remain stable until 2040. As regards Arabic, the figure is estimated to fluctuate between around 360m and 500m until 2038, at which point there will be a sharp rise to 750m in 2040.

Finally, if we look at Spanish, according to predictions, 300m people will be learning it in 2030, and then the figure is likely to fall considerably to around 150m in 2034. The figure is then going to recover to 400m in 2036, after which predictions show that it will decline significantly to just 200m at the end of the decade.

(208 words)

3   **Read the model essay above and answer these questions.**

1   The first line of the introduction includes the phrase *how many students will study three languages.* How could you rewrite this using *the number of*?
2   What are the two points mentioned in the overview?
3   Which linking phrases are used to introduce these two points?
4   Which tense is used in the second sentence of the overview after the phrase *by 2040*?
5   Which languages are discussed in paragraph 3? And paragraph 4?
6   Which linking expressions are used to introduce each line of the graph?
7   Which two synonyms of *about* are used in the main body?
8   In paragraph 3, the model essay uses *at which point* to join two parts of a sentence together. Find a synonym of this phrase in the fourth paragraph.
9   Which phrase in the last sentence of the model essay is a synonym of *in 2040*?
10 How many different future tenses and expressions are used in paragraphs 3 and 4?

Language for future trends graphs

> When you write about a future graph, the verbs, adverbs, adjectives and nouns that you use to describe changes are the same as the ones studied in Unit 6 (pages 78–80). However, you need to use different tenses to write about the graph, and you also need some vocabulary to talk about the future.
>
> For future graphs, you should:
> • use *will* and *be going to* instead of the past simple
> • learn and practise a range of future expressions (e.g. *looks set to*)
> • use the future continuous tense.

1   **Rewrite these sentences using *will* or *be going to*.**

1   There was a sharp fall in the number of students of Spanish. (*will*)
   There will be a sharp fall in the number of students of Spanish.
2   The number of students of Arabic dropped considerably. (*be going to*)
3   There was a dramatic increase in the number of students of English. (*will*)
4   The figure for Spanish decreased gradually. (*will*)
5   There was a steady increase in the number of students of Arabic. (*be going to*)

2 Complete these sentences about the graph on page 119 using *will* or *be going to*.
Include data from the graph in your answer.

1 English, 2030–2034 (*will*)
The number of students of English …
2 Arabic, 2030–2032 (*be going to*)
There …
3 Spanish, 2034–2036 (*be going to*)
The number of students of Spanish …
4 Arabic, 2038–2040 (*will*)
There …

3 Write a sentence about each of these sections of the graph on page 119.
Use either *will* or *be going to* and either a verb / adverb phrase or an adjective / noun phrase.

1 English, 2034–2036
2 Arabic, 2034–2038
3 Spanish, 2036–2040

4 Complete these future expressions.

1 *A____ to predictions*, the number of students will increase sharply.
2 The number of students *I____ set to* rise considerably.
3 *There is I____ to be* a gradual drop in the number of students.
4 *P____ show that* the figure is going to increase considerably.
5 *It is e____ that* the number of students will go up sharply.
6 The figure *is s____* to remain stable for the rest of the period.

5 Rewrite these sentences with the same meaning, using the words in brackets.

1 The number of students of English will rise considerably to 700m in 2034. (*likely*)
The number of students of English is likely to rise considerably to 700m in 2034.
2 There will be a slight fall in the number of students of Arabic to 360m in 2032. (*show*)
3 The figure for Spanish is going to rise sharply to 400m in 2036. (*looks*)
4 The number of people learning English will drop gradually to 650m in 2036. (*estimated*)
5 There is going to be a steady decline in the number of students of Spanish to around
150m in 2034. (*predictions*)
6 The figure for Arabic will go up sharply to 750m in 2040. (*set*)

You can use the future continuous (*will + be + -ing*) to talk about things happening at a specific time in the future:

*If we look at Spanish, predictions show that 300m people **will be learning** it in 2030. There will be a sharp rise in the number of students of Arabic in 2040, when 750m people **will be studying** it.*

6 Complete these sentences with a number from the graph and the future continuous.

1 If we look at English, the graph shows that _____ in 2030.
2 There will be a slight drop in the figure for English in 2036, when _____ .
3 Regarding Arabic, according to predictions, _____ in 2030.
4 The number of speakers of Spanish will decline sharply in 2040, when _____ .

7 ⊙ Practise the language from this section by writing an essay for this exam task. Then compare your work with the sample answer on page 173.

The table shows estimates about the number of speakers of three languages, 2030–2040, in millions. Summarise the information by selecting and reporting the main features and make comparisons where necessary.

	2030	2032	2034	2036	2038	2040
Welsh	1.2m	1m	0.7m	0.5m	0.5m	0.9m
Breton	0.6m	0.8m	1m	1m	1.4m	1.8m
Gaelic	0.2m	0.4m	0.6m	0.5m	0.9m	1.2m

Model essay 2

i As well as future graphs, you may also be asked to write about future maps for Writing Task 1. A typical question will ask you to compare two maps, one relating to the present and one which describes planned developments in the future.

1 Look at the exam task on the next page and discuss these questions in pairs.

1 How many planned changes are there for the university campus in 2035?
2 How will the university campus change in general?
3 What is going to happen to the library? And the lecture hall in the south of the campus?
4 How could you describe what is going to happen to the trees in the south-west of the campus?
5 What new things will be built by 2035?
6 How will the campus be better for cyclists in 2035?

The two maps below show a university campus today and the planned developments for 2035.

Summarise the information by selecting and reporting the main features and make comparisons where necessary.

University campus today

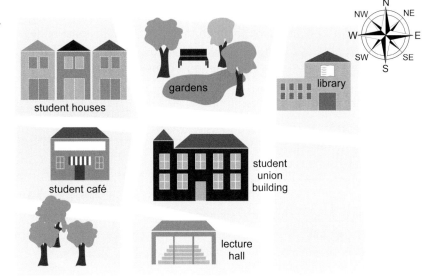

Planned development of University campus, 2035

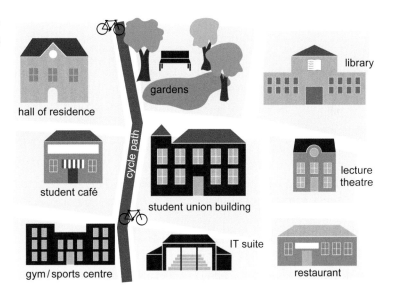

The two maps highlight information about the main changes which will take place on the campus of a university, between the present day and 2035.

Overall, what stands out from the maps is that the campus is going to become much more developed, with more facilities for studying and sport, and fewer trees and green areas.

In detail, one change will be that the houses in the north-west of the campus are going to be knocked down, and a new hall of residence will be built in their place. Another important development is that the library is set to be expanded, meaning that there will be more space for students to study. It is also planned that a new lecture theatre will be constructed in the east of the campus.

If we look at the south part of the campus, by 2035 the lecture hall will have been converted into a new IT suite. Another striking change is the creation of a cycle path running from the south to the north, making it easier to cycle around the university. Finally, the trees in the south-west are due to be cut down and replaced by a new gym and sports centre.

(200 words)

2 **Analyse the model essay on page 123 by answering these questions.**

1 How many changes are described in the main body of the model answer?
2 Write down all the uses of *will*/*going to* + passive in the model answer.
3 Which tense is used with *by 2035*?
4 Find an example of change in the main body which is described using a noun phrase.
5 Find two examples of interpretation of the maps.
6 What other future expressions or structures are used in the main body?
7 What linking phrases to introduce changes are used in the main body?
8 How does the writer explain what the topic of paragraph 4 is?

3 **Discuss these questions in pairs.**

1 Would you prefer to study at a university which is in the city centre, or one which is on a separate campus outside the city?
2 Do you prefer to study in a library or at home? Why?
3 Have you ever lived in student accommodation? If so, what was it like?
4 What additional facilities could the university build to make the campus better?

Language for future maps

> When you write about future maps, you can use most of the language from Unit 8, such as the verbs and nouns to describe changes and many of the linking phrases. You can also follow the same structure for the introduction and overview; all you need to do is to change the tense to the future.
>
> Other language that you can use specifically for future maps:
> * *will*/*going to* + passive
> * *by* + future time + future perfect passive:
>   **By 2035**, *the lecture hall* **will have been converted** *into an IT suite*.
> * some additional future phrases (e.g. *is due to be* + past participle).

1 **Rewrite these sentences in the passive form.**

1 They are going to build an IT suite in the south of the campus.
2 The university will cut down the trees in the south-west and build a gym.
3 They are going to create a cycle path running across the university.
4 The university will turn the lecture hall into an IT suite.
5 They are going to open a new restaurant in the south-east of the campus.
6 The university will expand the library in the north-east of the campus.

2 **Look at these future perfect passive sentences, then write similar sentences using the prompts below.**

One development is that **by 2035** *the library in the north-east* **will have been expanded**.
Another change is that **by 2035** *the trees in the south-west* **will have been cut down**, *and a new gym* **will have been built** *in its place*.

1 The new restaurant in the south-east of the campus
2 The student houses | new hall of residence in the north-west
3 The new lecture theatre in the east of the campus
4 The new cycle path in the middle of the campus

3 **Rewrite these sentences using the words in brackets.**

1 A new supermarket will be opened in the north of the campus. (*due*)

2 A new student nightclub is going to be built on the edge of the campus. (*set*)

3 More computer facilities are going to be built. (*planned*)

4 A new car park is going to be constructed. (*scheduled*)

5 New tennis courts are going to be built next to the university gardens. (*due*)

6 They are going to open a brand new doctor's surgery. (*set*)

Model essay 3

Sometimes you may have to write a Task 1 answer for a graph which requires **a combination of trend and comparative language**.

This is often the case when you have chart which contains just two time periods (e.g. 2010 and 2018). In this case, you need to use language from both Units 6 and 7 to write about the graph.

1 **Look at this exam task and read the model essay on page 126. Then answer the questions below it.**

The pie charts provide data about the 10 most popular university subjects for undergraduates at London University in 2010 and 2018.

Summarise the charts by selecting and reporting the main features and make comparisons where relevant.

Top ten subjects at London University, 2010

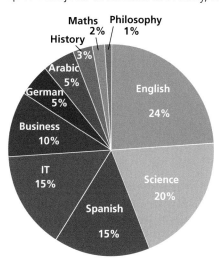

Top ten subjects at London University, 2018

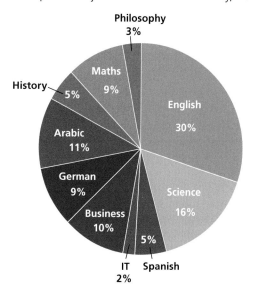

The pie charts show information about the percentage of people who studied ten selected subjects at the University of London, in two time periods, 2010 and 2018.

Overall, what stands out from the pie charts is that the most popular subject in both 2010 and 2018 was English. Another interesting point is that the biggest change related to IT, which fell dramatically over the period.

If we look at 2010, English was considerably more popular than science, with figures of 24% and 20%. Spanish and IT were equally popular, at 15%.

Twice as many people studied business as German. The former figure was 10%, while the latter was 5%. Finally, a slightly higher percentage of people studied maths than philosophy, with 2% and 1% respectively.

As regards the changes in 2018, English went up considerably from 24% to 30%. By contrast, the number of students of science dropped slightly from 20% to 16% in 2018. Business remained at the same percentage in both years, at 10%. Finally, in 2010, 15% of students studied IT, but by 2018 the figure had gone down dramatically to just 2%.

(186 words)

1 The introduction rewrites the question like this: *the percentage of people who studied ...*
   How could you write this in another way?
2 What are the two key points in the overview?
3 Is the language in paragraph 3 comparative language or trend language?
4 What is the function of paragraph 4? Does it use comparative language or trend language?
5 Which two linking expressions are used at the start of paragraphs 3 and 4?
6 Which tense is used in the last sentence of paragraph 4, and why is it used?

2 **Complete these sentences comparing the changes between 2010 and 2018 in the graph with *by 2018* + a suitable past perfect verb.**

1 In 2010, 15% of students studied IT, but by 2018, the figure had gone down dramatically to just 2%.
2 In 2010, 20% of students chose science, but ...
3 In 2010, 5% of undergraduates studied Arabic, but ...
4 In the first graph, 15% of students were enrolled in Spanish, but ...

3 Practise mixed-graph language and organisation by writing an essay for this exam task. Then compare your work with the sample answer on page 173.

The table below gives data about the number of schoolchildren in an English-speaking country aged 18 who took an Advanced Level exam in a range of optional foreign languages in 2012 and 2017. Summarise the information by selecting and reporting the key information and make comparisons where relevant.

Subject	2012	2017
French	50,000	34,000
Spanish	32,000	68,000
Mandarin	10,000	22,000
German	11,000	4,000
Latin	8,000	4,000
Portuguese	8,000	2,000
Arabic	4,000	10,000
Japanese	1,000	4,000
Polish	2,000	3,000
Cantonese	2,000	6,000

Listening Part 3: Matching information

Skills application

1 ♪24 ⊚ You will hear the first part of a talk by a local politician about proposed changes to the city centre. For questions 1–5, choose the correct option A–G from the box.

A   It will be used for a different purpose.
B   It will be closed down.
C   It will be enlarged.
D   A new one will be built.
E   It will be sold to a private company.
F   The price of entry will be cut.
G   The price of entry will be increased.

1   Sports centre
2   City museum
3   Underground car park
4   City offices
5   Swimming pool

2 ♪25 ⊚ In the second part of the talk, the politician gives more details about the future plans for the city. Complete these sentences. Write NO MORE THAN ONE WORD OR A NUMBER for each answer.

1   The city aims to complete all the changes within a maximum of ____ years.
2   The politician promises that they will not increase ____ to pay for the changes.
3   If members of the public do not agree with the changes, they should ____ their local councillor before May.
4   Once the changes have been introduced, the city hopes to attract a minimum of ____ new visitors a year.
5   The city hopes to create 5,000 new ____ as a result of the changes.

3 Check your answers in the audioscript on page 154.

4 Find words or phrases in the audioscript on page 154 with a similar meaning.

1 Expensive (track 24)
2 New and super-modern (track 24)
3 Cut the ticket prices significantly (track 24)
4 The area just outside a city (track 24)
5 A lack of housing (track 24)
6 Modernised and improved (track 24)
7 Organise a sports event in your city (track 24)
8 The latest time something should be done (track 25)
9 Strong disagreements (track 25)
10 A large number of something coming (e.g. tourists to a city) (track 25)

5 Practise some of the vocabulary from Exercise 4 by discussing these questions in pairs.

1 Are you good at meeting deadlines?
2 Would you prefer to live in the city centre or in the outskirts of a city?
3 Would you like your city/country to host a major sporting event?
4 Is there a shortage of housing where you live?
5 If there was an influx of tourists into your city, would you think it was a good thing?

Reading: Matching headings and multiple-choice questions

Skills application

1 🎯 Read the text on page 129 and choose the correct heading for paragraphs A–E from the list of headings.

> **List of Headings**
> i   An area of life which will be more expensive than in the past
> ii   A shift from isolated to collective provision
> iii A collection of opinions about future trends
> iv Ignoring the traditional providers
> v   The end of permanent contracts at work
> vi A fundamental change in the relationship between provider and recipient
> vii A trend which will affect people in radically different ways

Paragraph A _____
Paragraph B _____
Paragraph C _____
Paragraph D _____
Paragraph E _____

2 Answer these multiple-choice questions about the text. When you finish, discuss in pairs why you chose each answer, and why you think the other options are incorrect.

1 Twenty years ago
  A people did not have mobile phones.
  B only a small number of people had the internet on their phones.
  C only a small number of people had mobile phones.

2 The 'gig economy' is
  A unlikely to grow.
  B likely to have a mixed impact on the workforce.
  C likely to be beneficial for most workers.

3 Home schooling is
  A less popular than it used to be.
  B going to be the dominant model of education.
  C likely to expand.

4 In terms of travel and holidays,
  A there are far more holiday choices for consumers than in the past.
  B the period of low-cost air travel is over.
  C people are set to use travel websites more than they do now.

3 Discuss these questions in pairs.

1 Do you think the future changes predicted in the text will happen?
2 Do you think these changes are positive or negative?

Tomorrow's World

*A recent report by the Future Foundation think tank tries to predict
how we will be living in 20 years' time.*

A Think back 20 years. How different life was – the internet was in its infancy, very few people had mobile phones, and if they did, they certainly did not have access to emails and images on them. Think back another 20 years. It is almost unimaginable now to think about life 40 years ago, without all the modern technological aspects we take for granted. But it is not just technology which has changed – every element of life has been transformed in a short period of time. The way people lived in the 1970s and 1980s is like another world. So, how will things be different 20 years in the future? The Future Foundation has collated the views of several experts in different fields to try to come to some conclusions about where we are headed.

B The first area the report touches on is work. We have already seen massive changes in working conditions and practices in the last few years, the biggest being the shift from permanent, fixed jobs that people tended to do for their whole careers to a flexible labour market, in which people move from job to job, from career to career throughout their lifetimes. This trend looks set to continue and deepen, as the so-called 'gig economy', in which people work on short-term and flexible contracts, is predicted to expand. The picture is of a world in which people now train themselves to do a variety of different jobs and work for different employers. This is predicted to have positive and negative impacts – for those with sought-after skills, the financial rewards will be significant. For those left behind in unskilled, low-paid jobs, there will be more insecurity and poverty, the report suggests.

C Another area expected to see massive changes is education. The typical educational model of uniform provision by the state is likely to continue, and the vast majority of children will attend normal schools, but there will be greater diversity in education. Home schooling, for instance, is already rising in popularity, and this is set to grow dramatically. In the past, home schooling tended to be individual; in other words, one parent would stay at home and educate his or her child. However, the trend for the future is for groups of parents to club together and provide education for their children in local hubs.

D In relation to education, the shift is already underway from a passive consumer of education provided by the state to a customer–seller relationship. The post-war baby boom generation benefitted from free higher education, but the downside of this was that education was handed down to them from universities, with very little say on the part of students, and any feedback from students was essentially ignored. The future is likely to see university students acting as consumers, shopping around for the best university course, demanding a change of lecturer if they are not happy with the service, and writing reviews of their university courses online.

E Finally, travel. The revolution in travel that has taken place over the last 30 years is set to continue, but in potentially different forms. The rise of low-cost air travel, starting from the early 1990s, has shattered the cartels of expensive holiday providers. These days, travellers have a much bigger variety of flights, hotels and holiday types to choose from, and perhaps the greatest change has been the springing up of sites which give feedback on holidays. Booking a holiday is one of the biggest single outlays customers will undertake every year, and travel websites which give feedback from thousands of customers have become a trusted way of choosing a holiday. In the future, the report predicts that more and more holidaymakers will try to book directly with each other – renting rooms from each other, for example, without going through accommodation websites and exchanging houses for a fortnight, for example – in order to have a cheap holiday.

Speaking Part 3

Future predictions

> In Part 3 of the Speaking exam, you often have to answer questions where you need to make predictions about future events and trends, on a range of different topics.

1 **Discuss these questions about the future in pairs.**

1 Do you think English will continue to be the international language in the future?
2 Do you think more people will work from home in the future?
3 Do you think the population of cities will continue to grow?
4 Do you think smoking will be made illegal?

2 🎧26 **Listen to two students talking about the questions in Exercise 1 and make notes about what they say.**

3 🎧26 **Listen again and complete these phrases for making future predictions.**

Question1

1 I think it's ____ ____ that English will continue as the international language.
2 There's a really ____ ____ that English will stay as number one.

Question 2

3 I think that more people will ____ work from home in the future.
4 I can definitely ____ more people ____ from home in the future.

Question 3

5 I think there's no ____ that cities will continue to grow in the future.
6 I ____ that cities will keep growing.

Question 4

7 I think there's ____ ____ chance that smoking will become illegal.
8 I think it's very ____ that smoking will become illegal.

4 **Which phrases in Exercise 3 can you use to talk about things you think will/won't happen?**

5 **Complete the phrases below for when you are not sure what will happen with the words in the box.**

> 50-50 · impossible · know · wait

1 I don't really ____ what will happen, but I guess …
2 I think it's ____ as to whether it will happen or not.
3 I think we will have to ____ and see.
4 It's ____ to predict what will happen.

6 🎯 **Practise the language from Exercises 3–5 by discussing these questions in pairs.**

1 Do you think cars will be banned completely from cities in the future?
2 Do you think more people will become vegetarian and vegan?
3 Do you think printed newspapers will disappear in the future?
4 Do you think people will have to pay for healthcare in countries where it is now free?

Speaking Part 1

Your future plans

In Part 1 of the Speaking Test, you will have the opportunity to talk about your future plans. You can learn and practise a range of grammar and vocabulary for doing this more fluently.

1 Discuss these questions about your future plans in pairs.

1 What are you going to do in the next few months?
2 What are your longer-term plans?
3 What would you like to be doing in ten years' time?

2 🎧 27 Listen to a student answering the questions from Exercise 1 and make notes about what she says.

3 🎧 27 Listen again and complete the phrases she uses to talk about her future plans.

Question 1
1 I'm waiting for my final exam results, but hopefully I _____ a good grade overall.
2 In the _____-_____ , I'm going to take a break and have a month off.
3 I have a work placement in a fashion company _____ in September.

Question 2
4 If all goes to _____ , I'll start a Master's degree in fashion design next year.
5 My dream _____ set up my own fashion company in the long-term.
6 Hopefully, by the time I'm 30, I _____ my own company.

Question 3
7 In ten years' time, I'd like _____ my own company.
8 Hopefully, I'll _____ the right person and settled down.
9 I'd love to start a family _____ .

4 Match the phrases in italics from Exercise 3 (1–4) with their meanings (a–d).

1 I have a work placement *lined up.*
2 *If all goes to plan,* …
3 Hopefully I'll have *settled down.*
4 I'd love to *start a family*.

a have children
b If everything works the way I want, …
c already organised
d a stage of life where you get married, buy a house and so on

5 🎯 Practise the language in Exercises 3 and 4 by discussing these questions in pairs.

1 Do you have anything lined up in the near future?
2 If all goes to plan, what would you like to be doing in five years' time?
3 How do you feel about settling down?
4 How do you feel about starting a family?

Pulling it all together

Review

1   Rewrite these sentences expressing future trends using the words in brackets.

1   The number of students of Turkish will rise significantly to 120 million. (*looks*)
2   There will be a sharp rise in the number of students of Japanese to 60 million. (*according*)

2   Complete these sentences for future maps using the prompts.

1   A new shopping centre | due | build | city centre
2   One change is that by 2040 | a new swimming pool | construct | on campus
3   A new IT suite | set | build | campus
4   One development is that by 2040 | cut down trees | in the south of the city | build new flats

3   Complete the sentences below about future predictions with the words in the box.

> chance ▪ highly ▪ much ▪ see

1   It's ____ likely that Arabic will become more popular.
2   There's a really good ____ that Spanish will increase in popularity.
3   I can definitely ____ more people working part-time in the future.
4   I think there's not ____ chance that people will stop reading newspapers.

Final practice essays

The table below shows data concerning the expected number of students of three languages in millions between 2034 and 2050.
Summarise the information by selecting and reporting the main features.

	2034	2036	2038	2040	2042	2044	2046	2048	2050
Korean	50m	60m	70m	140m	140m	140m	130m	200m	270m
Italian	100m	80m	65m	65m	65m	80m	110m	150m	160m
Turkish	110m	130m	150m	170m	140m	135m	130m	200m	200m

The two maps on the right show the centre of a city today and the planned developments for 2040.
Summarise the information by selecting and reporting the main features and make comparisons where necessary.

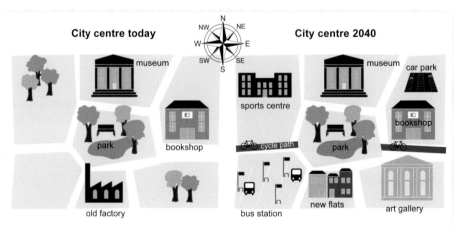

1   🎯 Write essays for the two exam tasks above.

2   Compare your essays with the sample answers on page 174.

Food and drink

Writing Task 1: Describing a process
Model essay

 Another common type of Task 1 question is **describing a process**. You will be given a diagram which shows steps in either a natural process (e.g. the life cycle of an animal or insect) or the process of producing something (e.g. coffee). There may also be some key words included in the diagram, but you will generally have to change the grammar of these words in your answer.

1 Discuss these questions in pairs.

1 Do you drink coffee? If so, what is your favourite type of coffee and how often do you drink it?
2 If you don't drink coffee, what is your favourite drink?
3 Do you make coffee at home? How do you make it?
4 What is your favourite café near your home? How often do you go there?
5 When was the last time you had a really good coffee?

2 Look at the diagram below showing the process of producing coffee and complete it with the verbs in the box. Use a dictionary if you need to. The first four have been done for you.

> add ▪ buy ▪ ~~clean~~ ▪ deliver ▪ drink ▪ ~~dry~~ ▪ fill ▪ grind ▪ heat ▪
> label ▪ pack ▪ ~~pick~~ ▪ pour ▪ ~~put~~ ▪ put ▪ ~~roast~~ ▪ take

1

Pick the beans, then _put_ them in baskets.

2

Clean the beans.

3

Dry the beans.

4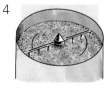

Roast the beans.

5

____ the beans.

6

____ in packets and ____ them.

7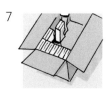

____ into boxes.

8

____ to supermarkets.

9

____ packets of coffee and ____ them home.

10

____ with water and ____ coffee.

11

____ the coffee pot.

12

____ into a cup and ____ the coffee.

3 Read the model essay and answer the questions below.

The diagram shows information about the process of growing coffee and the steps involved in making a cup of coffee. There are 12 stages in the process, starting with picking coffee beans and finishing with drinking a cup of coffee.

In the first stage, coffee beans are picked from the trees and put into a basket. Once the coffee beans have been cleaned in a machine, they are dried in the sun. Having been dried, the beans are then roasted and ground. Subsequently, the ground coffee is put into packets and labelled. Finally, the packets of coffee are packed into boxes, and then they are delivered to supermarkets.

If we look at the process of making a cup of coffee, to begin with coffee is bought by customers from supermarkets, after which it is taken home. After the coffee pot has been filled with water, coffee is added into the top part, and then the coffee pot is heated. When the coffee is ready, it is poured into a cup. The final stage is that the coffee can be drunk and enjoyed. This completes the process of making a cup of coffee.

(192 words)

1 How many paragraphs are there in the model answer? How is this different from the Task 1 model answers in Units 7, 8 and 9?
2 Why are there two paragraphs in the main body?
3 Circle all the linking words in paragraphs 2 and 3 (e.g. *In the first stage*).
4 What is the main grammar used in the main body?
5 Which linking phrase is used to start paragraph 3, and what is it used for?
6 What does the last sentence of the model answer do?

4 Look at the diagram in Exercise 2 again. Cover the model essay and try to describe the process to a partner.

5 Do you make coffee in the same way as in stages 10–12? If not, work in pairs and explain how you make coffee.

Grammar: Present simple passive

1 Which sentence in each of these pairs is better for describing a process, and why?

1 a A lorry delivers the boxes of coffee to a supermarket.
  b The boxes of coffee are delivered to a supermarket.
2 a Someone picks the coffee beans.
  b The coffee beans are picked.

To form the present simple passive:
object of the sentence + *is / are* + *past participle of the verb*

*The boxes of coffee **are delivered** to supermarkets.*
*The coffee pot **is heated**.*

If you think it's necessary to mention the person/agent who does the action, you can add *by* + person/agent at the end of the sentence:
*The boxes of coffee are bought and taken home **by customers.***

2 Change these active sentences into a passive ones. All the verbs are regular, but some need slight spelling changes.

1 Someone roasts the coffee beans .
  The coffee beans are roasted.
2 A worker picks the coffee beans from the trees.
3 Someone dries the coffee beans in the sun.
4 A machine roasts the beans.
5 A worker labels the coffee packets.

6 A machine cleans the coffee beans.
7 Someone packs the coffee into boxes.
8 You fill the bottom part of the coffee pot with water.
9 You heat the coffee pot.

3 Most past participles are regular (verb + *-ed*), but there are some common irregular ones which you need to learn. Complete the table.

Verb	Past participle	Verb	Past participle
grind	*ground*	buy	
sell		grow	
put		cut	
throw away		take	
sow		choose	
hold		leave	

4 Rewrite these sentences with present simple passives. They all have irregular past participles.

1 They grow coffee in Brazil.
2 A machine grinds the coffee beans.
3 Someone puts the coffee into packets.
4 They throw away the bad coffee beans.
5 Customers buy the coffee.
6 Customers take the coffee home.

Grammar: Present perfect passive and participle structures

You can the present perfect passive to write about two stages of a process together:

*Once the coffee beans **have been cleaned** in a machine, they are dried in the sun.*

You use *Once / When / After* + present perfect passive in the first part of the sentence. The second half of the sentence uses the present simple passive.

1 Rewrite these sentences using the present perfect passive.

1 The coffee beans are picked and placed in a basket.
  Once the coffee beans have been picked, they are placed in a basket.
2 The bad beans are thrown away, and then the good beans are cleaned.
  When …
3 The beans are roasted, and then they are ground.
  After …
4 The coffee pot is filled with water, and then it is heated.
  Once …
5 The boxes of coffee are delivered to supermarkets, and then put onto the supermarket shelves.
  When …

6 The packets of coffee are packed into boxes, and then delivered to supermarkets.
  After …

You can also link two stages together by replacing the present simple passive with one of these participle structures:

Having been + past participle + subject + second part of the sentence
After being + past participle + subject + second part of the sentence

The coffee beans are cleaned in a machine, and then they are dried in the sun. →
Having been cleaned *in a machine, the coffee beans are then dried in the sun.*
After being cleaned *in a machine, the coffee beans are then dried in the sun.*

Note: You can only use these structures if the subject (here, *coffee beans*) is the same in both parts of the sentence.

2 Rewrite these sentences with *Having been* … or *After being* …

1 The coffee beans are picked and placed in a basket.
  Having been …
2 The beans are roasted, and then they are ground.
  After being …
3 The coffee pot is filled with water, and then it is heated.
  Having been …
4 The packets of coffee are packed into boxes, and then they are delivered to supermarkets.
  After being …
5 The boxes of coffee are delivered to supermarkets, and then they are put onto the shelves so that customers can buy them.
  Having been …
6 The coffee beans are dried in the sun, and then they are roasted.
  After being …

Linking phrases

1 Decide whether each of these linking phrases describes the start, the next stage or the end of a process.

> After that, … ▪ …, after which … ▪ … and then … ▪ At this point, … ▪ Finally, … ▪ Next, … ▪ Following this, … ▪ In the first stage, … ▪ In the final stage, … ▪ In the next stage, … ▪ Subsequently, … ▪ The final stage is that … ▪ The first stage is that … ▪ Initially, … ▪ The following step is that … ▪ The next step is that … ▪ Then … ▪ To begin with, …

2 Put these stages of making a cup of tea in order, then use linking phrases from Exercise 1 to write a paragraph.

a Milk and sugar are added to the tea. ☐
b The kettle is filled with water. [1]
c The tea is drunk. ☐
d The kettle is boiled. ☐
e A tea bag is put into a cup. ☐
f Hot water is poured into the cup. ☐
g The tea, milk and sugar are stirred with a spoon. ☐
h The tea bag is removed. ☐

Example: The first step is that the kettle is filled with water.

Introductions and overviews for process essays

> As you can see from the model essay on page 134, you do not need to write two different
> paragraphs for the introduction and the overview – you can join them together.

**1 Look again at the first paragraph of the model essay on page 134 and discuss
these questions in pairs.**

1 How does the model essay rewrite *how coffee is grown*?
2 How does the model essay rewrite *how a cup of coffee is made*?
3 Which two stages of the process are mentioned in the second sentence?
4 What follows *starting with* and *finishing with*?

**2 Complete these ways of rewriting the essay question, using the verbs in brackets where necessary. The
first letter of some of the words has been given to help you.**

The diagram shows information about …
1 how _____ grow coffee.
2 how a cup of coffee is _____ (*make*).
3 the process of _____ (*grow*) coffee.
4 the process by w_____ coffee is grown.
5 the steps in_____ _____ growing coffee
6 the stages of _____ (*make*) a cup of coffee.

3 Rewrite these introduction sentences using the phrases from Exercise 2 in brackets.

1 The diagram shows information about how to grow coffee. (*the process of*)
2 The diagram highlights information about how to grow coffee. (*the steps*)
3 The pictures illustrate information about how to grow coffee. (*the stages of*)
4 The pictures show information about how to grow coffee. (*the process by*)

4 Look again at Exercise 3. How can you say *diagram* and *shows* in different ways?

5 Rewrite these introduction sentences in a suitable way.

1 The diagram highlights information about how to make tea.
2 The pictures show information about how tomato ketchup is produced.
3 The illustration gives information about the process of making a tennis racket.
4 The diagram shows information about the steps involved in producing mobile phones.

**6 Complete the second sentence of the introduction / overview from the model essay,
using the correct information and grammar.**

There are 12 [1]s_____ in the process, [2]s_____ with [3]p_____ coffee beans and [4]f_____ with [5]d_____ a cup of coffee.

7 Write introductions and overviews for these two questions.

1 The pictures below show how chocolate bars are produced.
   10 stages: first stage: plant cocoa seeds; last stage: eat chocolate
2 The diagram below highlights how to make potato crisps.
   12 stages: first stage: harvest potatoes; last stage: eat crisps

**8 Think about these processes and make notes about all the stages. Then work in pairs and describe them,
using as much language as possible from this unit.**

1 The process of learning to drive and getting a driving licence
2 How to make your favourite dish
3 What happens between going on a first date and getting married
4 The process of buying your own house

Reading: Completing a flowchart

Skills focus

> **i** Another common reading task is complete a flowchart with words from the reading passage. There are three important techniques for completing a flowchart:
> - Decide what type of word (verb, noun, adjective, past participle, etc.) goes in each gap.
> - Use the linking and sequence words in the text to follow the order of the flowchart correctly.
> - Identify the key words near the gaps in the flowchart and think about synonyms of them.

1   Look at the first part of the exam task below showing the process of opening a restaurant, then discuss these questions in pairs.

1   In question 1, what kind of word follows *become*, and what do you think the answer could be? What are synonyms of *deciding* and *getting rich*?
2   In question 2, can you think of a synonym for the linking phrase *First of all*?
3   In question 3, what kind of word follows pronouns like *your*?
4   In question 4, what kind of word follows *an*? And what letter could the answer start with? What phrase means *good-quality but inexpensive*? And would you expect the answer to question 4 to be similar to *inexpensive* or different? Why?
5   In question 5, what is another way to say *find*? From the rest of the question, what do you think answer could be?

Complete the flowchart below. Choose NO MORE THAN TWO WORDS from the text for each answer.

How to open a restaurant (part 1)

It is common to want to open a restaurant because you can become ¹____, as well as deciding on the menu and getting rich.

↓

First of all, you need to take the ²____ to open a restaurant.

↓

And then you should identify your ³____ of what type of restaurant you want it to be.

↓

You need to decide between an ⁴____ restaurant and one that serves good-quality but inexpensive meals.

↓

If there are lots of restaurants which are similar to your idea, then your restaurant will not be successful. You need to find a ⁵____ in the market.

2   ⌖ Read the first part of the text. Complete the flowchart in Exercise 1 and check your answers to the questions.

How to open a restaurant (part 1)

Many people dream of giving up their day job and opening a restaurant. It's an attractive idea – you get to be the boss, you get to choose the menu and the décor, and if it's successful, you can make a lot of money, not to mention the perk of being able to eat good food every night. But how realistic is it? I just opened my new restaurant a month ago, and it took three years of hard work to make it happen. Here's my advice on how to do it.

To begin with, once you have made the decision to open a restaurant, your next step is the concept. What type of restaurant is it? What kind of food do you want to serve? Is it going to be cheap and cheerful, or is it going to be an upmarket restaurant catering for people with lots of money? Then, when you have decided that, you have to see if there is a gap in the market in the area you want to open. If there are already three pizzerias in the area, opening a fourth doesn't make much sense.

Skills application

1 🎯 Follow the techniques on page 138 to complete this exam task.

*Complete the flowchart below. Choose **NO MORE THAN TWO WORDS** from the text for each answer.*

How to open a restaurant (part 2)

He advises that you should only design your own restaurant if you have ¹____ .

↓

The writer advises employing a ²____ to create the interior of the restaurant.

↓

Make sure that the design of your restaurant feels ³____ and ⁴____ inside.

↓

Next, you should employ ⁵____ .

↓

The number-one thing to look for when hiring a chef is ⁶____ .

↓

⁷____ is the stage that comes after you have hired your staff.

↓

Giving an ⁸____ to the local media is also useful.

↓

Get your chef to make some ⁹____ of the food for the public to try.

How to open a restaurant (part 2)

Having spotted a gap in the market, what follows is that you need to find premises for hire. This is a key step, because in the restaurant business, location is very important. Some people will come to your restaurant because they have been before and liked it, others will come due to a recommendation from friends, but the majority of people will be customers passing by who are hungry and like the look of your restaurant.

So, when you have found and rented premises, the next step is the interior. How do you want the restaurant to look? A tip here from someone who knows – whatever you do, do not design the interior of your own restaurant unless you have experience. It may seem costly to hire a professional designer, but it will be worth it in the long run. Invest now, because so much of what attracts people to a restaurant is how it looks and, more importantly, how it feels. If it doesn't feel warm and welcoming, people won't come. So, find yourself a good designer, tell them what you want, but let them be creative.

Recruiting quality staff is the subsequent step. Start from the top, and when you're searching for a chef, make sure they have experience, qualifications and, above all, excellent references. It is worth going online to check out reviews of the applicants' previous restaurants. If you read lots of reviews saying the quality of the food is poor, then it's a warning sign. Take your time and interview a shortlist of at least three chefs before you make your final decision. And I would recommend setting them a blind challenge. When they come for interview, give them all the same ingredients and an hour to cook a dish that they would be happy to serve in the restaurant. The results of this will point you in the right direction as to who to hire.

Having got your team in place, now you need to turn your attention to marketing. You need to find a way to get people talking about your wonderful new restaurant that is about to open. One way is to flyer shopping centres and maybe student areas, to spread the word. Another thing you can do is try and get a radio interview with a local station. You could also get your chef to cook some samples of the food and go out into the streets and offer people a freebie. If they like the food, there's a good chance they'll give the restaurant a go, especially if you offer a significant discount for their first visit. So, you've got all that done – now it's just time to open the door, get ready, calm the nerves and make sure that your opening night goes with a bang. And good luck!

2 Discuss these questions in pairs.

1 Would you like to open a restaurant one day? If so, what type of restaurant would it be?
2 Would you take the advice in the text and hire a professional to design the interior of your restaurant?
3 What do you think the pros and cons of having your own restaurant?

Speaking Part 2

Grammar: Linking phrases

> One way to make your speaking flow better in Part 2 is to learn some linking phrases which allow you to change from one bullet point on the card to the next one. If you do this, it also gives you extra time to think while you're speaking.

1 🎧 28 **Read this Part 2 Speaking task and the transcript of a model answer below. Try to complete the linking phrases in pairs. Then listen and check your answers.**

> **Talk about a friend that you admire. You should say:**
> **how long you have known this friend**
> **where you met**
> **how often you meet this friend**
> **what your friend does in terms of studying or working**
> **and why you admire them.**

I'm going to talk about a friend I admire, which is my friend Paul. Paul is a friend from school, and in ¹t_e_r_m_o_f_f___ how long I've known him, it must be about 20 years now, because we met when we were 11, and now we have just turned 30.

As I said, ²r____ where we met, it was at primary school, in the last year, and the teacher made us sit next to each other that year. We hadn't really spoken before that, but we hit it off and became really good mates.

If I ³t_h_i_n_k_a_b_u_t___ how often we meet, well, unfortunately we don't meet so often these days, because we live in different countries, but we try to meet up at least once a year, for an evening or a weekend, and catch up on what we've been doing.

⁴T____ about Paul's job, so he's a teacher of kids with special needs, he works in a school in Scotland, and his job is to help those kids to learn, to socialise and to get as much out of school as possible.

⁵W____ I r_e_a_l_y___ admire about Paul is that he is so patient and kind with the kids. I know that for me I would find this kind of job really stressful, and I don't think I would be very good at it, but Paul never loses his temper and he's always positive and friendly with them.

⁶A____ t_l_i_n_k__ that I admire about him is that he always goes the extra mile with the kids – if they need extra help after school, he's always willing to stay late, and with a smile on his face, so that's amazing.

2 🎯 Make notes for your own answer to the Part 2 question in Exercise 1, then talk about the question for two minutes, using linking phrases from the model answer.

3 🎯 Make notes about this Part 2 question, then talk about the question for two minutes, using linking phrases.

> **Talk about a person who has had a big influence on your life.**
>
> **You should say**
> **who the person is**
> **when and where you met**
> **how often you meet this person now**
> **and why this person has had a big influence on you.**

Grammar: Modal verbs to talk about the past

Many Speaking Part 2 questions require you to talk about something that happened to you in the past. For example, you might have to talk about topics like this:
• a time when you were late for something
• a time when you got lost
• a great holiday you had
Make sure you use good past tenses for this type of question. You can also show your range of grammar by using past modal verbs to talk about when something happened or how old you were.

1　Read these short extracts from Part 2 questions. What do you think the missing past modal verb phrases are?

1　So, I'm going to talk about a time when I got lost. I can't remember exactly how old I was, but I think I m*ust* h*ave* b*een* around 11 or 12. Anyway, I was staying in the countryside with my grandparents, and what happened was …

2　I'm going to tell you around a great meal I had, which was for a friend's birthday at university, so I w*ould* h*ave* b*een* 19 or 20, something like that. So, we all went to an Italian restaurant, and …

3　I'm going to talk about I time I was late. It was in my final year at university, so it m*ust* h*ave* b*een* about 2011 or 2012, around then. One day, I woke up at 9 a.m. and I suddenly realised I had overslept …

4　So, I'm going to tell you about a great holiday I had. I was 11 or 12, I think, so it w*ould* h*ave* b*een* about 2008 or 2009, that kind of time. Anyway, my parents decided to take us on a round-the-world trip for a month and …

2　🎧 29　Listen to the four extracts and check. Then discuss these questions in pairs.

1　Why do we use these two phrases?
2　Are the speakers 100% sure about when these things happened, and how old they were?

3　Complete the rules by writing one word in each gap.

1　To talk about a year/time in the past: *So, _____ must/would have been 2008 or 2009 …*
2　To talk about how old you were: *So, _____ must/would have been about 11 or 12 …*

4　Discuss these topics in pairs, using the language from Exercise 1.

1　A great holiday you had when you were a child
2　A time you got lost as a child or teenager
3　The first time you spoke English to a native speaker
4　The first time you visited an English-speaking country

5　🎯 Practise the language from this section by doing this Speaking Part 2 question.

Talk about a time when you were late for something important.

　　You should say
　　　　why you were late
　　　　how late you were
　　　　what happened because you were late
　　and how you felt about being late.

Listening Part 2: Sentence completion

Skills focus

 Listening Part 2 often involves two types of task: matching statements to a list of options, and sentence-completion questions.
For the matching task, you will need to think of possible synonyms of the statements, and for the sentence-completion task, you should try to predict the answers that you will hear. You will be given the maximum number of words you can write in each gap, and you will hear the words in the recording.

1   **You are going to listen to a restaurant reviewer, Maria Jenkins, talking about some restaurants that she has visited recently. Look at these questions and write down synonyms of the key words in each question.**

Which restaurant has:
1   new owners? *a new boss*
2   a new menu? *a new dishes diuches*
3   new premises? *a new biulding, a new ~~Plase~~ ~~Pata~~ Plas*

2   🎧30 🎯 **Listen and choose a letter A–D for the questions in Exercise 1.**

List of Restaurants
Ⓐ A Taste of Italy *(2)*
B   The Taj Mahal
Ⓒ The Parisian Bistro *(3)*
Ⓓ The Tokyo House *(1)*

3   **Read the audioscript on pages 154–155 and check your answers. Did the synonyms you wrote down in Exercise 2 match what the speaker said?**

4   **Read this exam task and predict possible answers for the gaps.**

> **The Parisian Bistro**
>
> If you come for lunch with a friend between 12 and 2 from Monday to Friday, you will be
>
> entitled to a ¹_50_ discount.
>
> There is a great selection of wines and ²___ available. *craftbeers*
>
> The Parisian is famous for its cheese and mushroom ³_otet_ *omelette*
>
> All dishes are cooked to order and made with ⁴___ from the local area. *ingredients*
>
> The Parisian's most popular dessert is called 'Tarte Tatin', which is a pie made
>
> from pastry and ⁵___ *apples*
>
> On the first Saturday of every month, there is live music from a local ⁶ *Jazz band*

5   🎧31 🎯 **Listen and complete the sentences in Exercise 4. Write NO MORE THAN TWO WORDS for each answer.**

6   **Read the audioscript on page 155 and check your answers.**

[handwritten Arabic note]

Skills application

1 You're going to listen to restaurant critic Maria Jenkins talking about four more restaurants.
Read these questions and think of synonyms for the key words and phrases.

1 This restaurant does not sell alcohol. *[handwritten: soft drinks / offer]*
2 This restaurant has a separate menu for children. *[handwritten: kids menu menu/kiddie menu]*
3 This restaurant imports a key ingredient from abroad. *[handwritten: flown in from another country]*
4 This restaurant is open 365 days a year. *[handwritten: everyday / whole year / even on holidays]*
5 This restaurant has been open for less than a year.
6 This restaurant is suitable for people on a budget.

2 🎧32 Listen and match the statements in Exercise 1 with these restaurants (A–D).
You can use each letter more than once.

A The Pancake Palace *[handwritten: (2)]*
B Tang's Chinese *[handwritten: (3) (6)]*
C The Argentine Steakhouse *[handwritten: (4)(3) (6)]*
D The Thai Temple *[handwritten: (1), (6)]*

3 Check your answers in the audioscript on page 155.

4 Read this exam task and predict possible answers for the gaps.

The Thai Temple

The owners first visited Thailand when they went
¹_____ in Thailand during their gap year. *[handwritten: backpacking]*
They hired a Thai chef in order to try to make the
food as ²_____ as possible. *[handwritten: authentic]*
Their aim was for all their dishes to be simple,
cheap and ³_____ . *[handwritten: nutritious]*
The owners say that most customers who eat
in the restaurant are students, young people or
⁴_____ *[handwritten: tourists]*
Once a year, the restaurant holds a special ⁵_____ *[handwritten: chilli]*
event. *[handwritten: eating]*
The owners say the most popular dish is the ⁶_____ . *[handwritten: vegetarian and curry]*

5 🎧33 🎯 Listen and complete the sentences in Exercise 4. You may use up to THREE WORDS ONLY in
each gap.

6 Check your answers in the audioscript on page 155.

7 Which of the restaurants you have heard about in this section would you most like to go to, and why?
Discuss in pairs.

Pulling it all together

Review

1 Rewrite these process sentences using the present simple passive.

1 A worker plants the tea seeds. *The tea seeds are planted by a worker.*
2 Someone picks the tea leaves and puts them into a basket. *the tea leaves are picked and puts them into a basket by someone*
3 The farmer packs the tea leaves into boxes and puts the boxes onto a lorry.
4 Lorries deliver the tea boxes to supermarkets, where customers buy them.

2 Rewrite these process sentences using the word in brackets and the present perfect passive.

1 The coffee beans are washed and then dried in the sun. (*Once*)
2 The packets of coffee are filled and labelled. (*When*)
3 The coffee beans are roasted and ground. (*After*)

3 Rewrite these process sentences with *Having been ...* or *After + -ing.*

1 The coffee is unloaded from the lorry and put onto the shelves for customers to buy.
Having *been unloaded from the lorry the coffee is put onto the shelves custom to buy.*
2 The packets of coffee are loaded onto a lorry, and then delivered to supermarkets.
After *being loaded onto a lorry the packets of coffee are delivered to supermarkets*

4 Write down three more linking phrases that you can use in Speaking Part 2 to move to the next bullet point.

In terms of ...

5 Rewrite the part of each sentence in *italics* using a modal verb.

1 I can't remember how old I was when I first watched a film in English, *I think I was maybe 11 or 12 years old.*
2 I'm not sure exactly when I first cooked a proper meal for my parents. *I think it was maybe 2001 or 2002.*

6 Discuss these questions in pairs.

1 What techniques can you use to answer flowchart questions in the Reading exam?
2 Which of the exam tips on page 145 do you think are the most important and useful for you?

3: the tea leaves are packed into boxes and put onto a lorry,
4: The tea boxes are delivered to supermarkets and bought by customers.

Final practice essay

The diagram shows how to make potato crisps.

Summarise the information by selecting and reporting the main features and make comparisons where relevant.

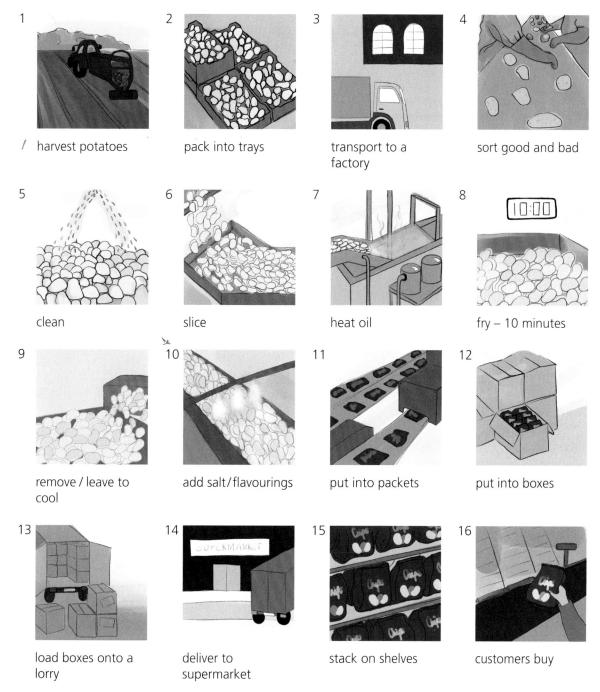

1 / harvest potatoes

2 pack into trays

3 transport to a factory

4 sort good and bad

5 clean

6 slice

7 heat oil

8 fry – 10 minutes

9 remove / leave to cool

10 add salt/flavourings

11 put into packets

12 put into boxes

13 load boxes onto a lorry

14 deliver to supermarket

15 stack on shelves

16 customers buy

1 🎯 Write an essay for the exam task above.

2 Compare your essay with the sample answer on page 176.

> **i** This page contains some advice about the exam and things to remember when you're doing it. Read through the information carefully before you take your IELTS exam. Good luck!

Writing

- Make sure you follow the correct structure and organisation for each type of Task 1 and Task 2. Have clear paragraphs and leave a blank line on the exam answer sheet between each paragraph.
- As your exam approaches, do plenty of timed writings. Make sure you can finish a Task 1 and a Task 2 answer in an hour. Ideally, try to finish two or three minutes early so that you can check your work.
- For Task 2 in particular, planning before you write is vital. Take three or four minutes to make a quick plan. It will make your essay more organised and easier to read.
- Make sure you finish your answers. Even if you rush a bit, you will have a much better chance of getting a good score if you finish everything.

Reading

- Don't spend a long time on one or two passages and then have to rush or guess the answers in the third passage. If you come across a question which is difficult, don't spend more than two minutes on it. Make a guess, and come back to it later.
- Always think about how you will do each type of reading task. Use the techniques in this book to approach the key question types.
- There isn't generally time to read each passage before you start looking at the questions. So focus on the questions first instead of skim-reading the whole text.
- Remember that you don't have extra time to write your answers on the answer sheet. You need to write your answers on the answer paper as you go along.

Listening

- Make sure you're aware of and practise listening for distractors. The listening test is full of distractors (much more than exist in real conversations!).
- You have time at the end to transfer your answers to the answer sheet, so write your answers on the question paper, then transfer them at the end.
- Remember what happens in each part of the listening. For example, Part 4 is always a lecture, so you know that the speaking will be organised and have lots of linking words that you can follow.

Speaking

- In Part 1, don't give really short answers, even if the question is quite simple.
- Plan Part 2 carefully with a mind map and have 'another one' in mind so that you always finish the two minutes.
- Remember that Part 3 is connected to the topic of Part 2, so you know what type of questions to expect.
- If you don't hear or you don't understand a question from the examiner, you can always ask them to repeat or explain. You will not be penalised for this.
- Try to relax and be yourself. If you speak normally, in a confident way, you'll come across better.

Audioscripts

🎧 01 Unit 1, Listening, Skills focus, Exercise 2 (p. 14)

Hi, everyone, and welcome to this talk about studying and working abroad. My name's James Stevens, and I'm the director of Overseas Opportunities. We're one of the oldest study and work agencies in the country – we've been sending people on work and educational placements abroad for over 40 years, since 1978. I've been with the company since 1992, and in that time, we've expanded greatly, especially after we got new premises in 2001.

So, let me tell you a bit about what we do and the opportunities that we can offer you. We normally post around 500 people abroad to work or study for up to a year, but the placements can be as short as a month, and the average stay is about four months.

🎧 02 Unit 1, Listening, Skills application, Exercise 1 (p. 14)

Around a third of our placements are for voluntary work, so what that means is that you'll be helping out with a charitable organisation overseas. For these, we pay your air fare and accommodation, but you'll need to cover your own food costs and any additional travel expenses, for example if you want to travel within the country at weekends or at the end of your stay.

You don't need any experience to do these charitable placements, but you have to be willing to live in fairly basic conditions, and to live without luxuries. However, we're sure you'll find it a fulfilling and rewarding experience, and if it goes well, there's often the option to extend the placement for an additional period of up to three months. We used to have a lot of projects in India, but recently our focus has shifted, and now the majority of our postings are in Sub-Saharan Africa, along with a few in South-East Asia.

We also offer an advisory service for those who wish to undertake a period of study overseas. We don't have our own schools abroad, but what we do have is a system where we offer impartial advice on a range of educational institutions in the area you want to study. For instance, if you're keen on studying Spanish, we have over 20 accredited language schools, both in Spain and South America, all of which have been inspected and approved by our overseas inspectors. What we offer is a specialised service based on your needs. If you want to study in a coastal area, for instance, we can narrow down the choices to two or three great schools near the sea, and then the final decision is up to you. Or if you want to study Spanish for Business, we would probably recommend a school in a large city like Madrid or one of the South American capitals, so that you're based in a city near the commercial heart of the country.

Now, we can also offer you a range of internships abroad, in companies across the world and in different fields. Some of these internships are unpaid, and you'll need to fund the travel, accommodation and living costs yourself. Others pay a basic monthly income which probably just covers the costs, and this is the main type of internship we have. A few will pay a full salary, but do be aware that the competition for these placements is fierce, and make sure your CV is up to date and shows you in your best light – we'll send your résumé to the company, but it's ultimately their decision, so my advice is to sell yourself. If you're interested in doing an internship abroad, it's worth coming in for a chat with us, to talk about your interests and future career prospects. This initial consultation is free of charge, but after that you'll need to pay a fee for any additional advisory sessions with us. If your placement is successful, we'll ask for a one-off fee, but we think it'll be worth it, in terms of saving you the time and money of finding a placement yourself.

Anyway, we think that whichever option you choose if you go ahead, it will be the experience of a lifetime. Not only will you be able to improve your CV, but more importantly you'll come into contact with new people and experiences. If you get a fully paid internship, you might even save a bit of money, but that's not really the main thing. If all of this sounds good, please stay for a complimentary drink, and three of our advisors will be around for the rest of the day if you want to have an informal chat. I'll leave our brochures on the table here, and our email address is on the back page, so do feel free to drop us a line if you want any further information after the end of today's session. So, best of luck, and we hope you have a great overseas opportunity in the future!

🎧 03 Unit 1, Speaking, Exercises 2 and 4 (p. 15)

Interviewer: Do you work or are you a student?
Man: So, at the moment, I'm studying English in a language school. I have great teachers, and I'm living with a great host family.
Interviewer: How long have you been studying?
Man: I've been studying English for about three months, and I've got one month left before I finish my course.
Interviewer: What do you enjoy most about what you do?
Man: What I really like about studying English is that I've met lots of interesting people. For example, I have classmates from Asia, from the Middle East and from South America, and it's been really interesting to get to know them.
Interviewer: What did you do before?
Man: Before I came here, I worked as a shop assistant in a supermarket, but I decided that I wanted to get a better job, so I quit and I came here. I want to improve my English and pass the IELTS exam with a good score.
Interviewer: What are your future plans?
Man: I'm planning to study at university in the UK. If I get good results in IELTS, I'll start an MBA in London in September.

🎧 04 Unit 1, Speaking, Exercises 3 and 4 (p. 15)

Interviewer: Do you work or are you a student?
Woman: I work as a nurse in a local hospital. I specialise in caring for young children who are in intensive care. It's a great job, I really love it!
Interviewer: How long have you been working?
Woman: I've been working as a nurse for nine years. I worked for six years in a hospital in another city, and I've been working in this job for three years.
Interviewer: What do you enjoy most about what you do?
Woman: What I really like about my job is that you can make a difference to people's lives. Obviously when people come to hospital, they feel very nervous and scared, especially children, and it's part of my job to reassure them that everything will be OK and that they will get better. It's quite a stressful job, because you're dealing with some difficult situations, but I feel really privileged to help people, and when they're discharged from hospital feeling better, it's a wonderful feeling.
Interviewer: What did you do before?
Woman: When I finished school, I took a gap year, and I travelled around Asia and Australia for about nine months. I worked for a few months on a farm in Australia, and I visited lots of different places. Then I spent three years training to be a nurse, and as I said, I've been working as a nurse now for nine years.
Interviewer: And what are your future plans?
Woman: Next year, I'm going to apply for a promotion to senior nurse. If I get it, I'll have more responsibility, and of course more money, which will be great.

🎧 05 Unit 2, Listening, Skills focus, Exercise 1 (p. 30)

Receptionist: Hello, StayFit Gym. How can I help you?
Man: Hi, I'm phoning to ask about joining the gym.
Receptionist: OK, what would you like to know?
Man: So, first of all, how much does it cost to sign up?
Receptionist: Well, we have three different levels of membership. If you sign up for the full membership, you have free access to all the gym classes, plus two free sessions with a personal trainer when you join, who will give you tips on your exercise programme.
Man: OK, that sounds great, but I'll probably only go to one or two classes a month, so I might not need the full membership. What are the other options?

Receptionist: OK, well, you can have our standard membership. With that, you get two classes per week included in the cost, but if you want a consultation with a personal trainer, you have to pay extra.

Man: OK, that sounds interesting.

Receptionist: And then finally there is the basic membership. It just gives you access to the gym, so if you want to go to any classes, you need to pay extra.

Man: OK, well, as I said, I think I'll probably only go to one or two classes a month, so I won't need the full membership. I think the standard membership is the one I'll go for. If I sign up for the basic, I'll end up paying for the classes anyway, so I might as well have them included in the price. By the way, how much is it?

Receptionist: Well, the standard membership is £215 per year. It was £200 last year, but we've had to raise the price by £15. But that still works out at less than £5 a week.

🎧 06 Unit 2, Listening, Skills focus, Exercise 3 (p. 30)

Man: OK, that sounds reasonable. And can I ask you about the classes? I'm really keen on yoga, do you have yoga classes?

Receptionist: We're currently not running yoga classes, but we're planning to add a class to the programme in the new year.

Man: OK, that's fine. And what about spinning?

Receptionist: We used to have spinning, but not many people booked it, so we stopped running it, I'm afraid. But of course we have lots of stationary bikes in the gym, so you can always use those.

Man: OK, well, that's not a problem.

Receptionist: We do have judo classes at the moment, but our most popular class is boxfit. It's a great workout, you get to burn lots of calories and it's always in demand. Previously, our number-one class was always pilates, but it's been overtaken this year.

Man: Well, that sounds great. So, how do I sign up?

Receptionist: OK, well, I can take a payment over the phone if you like, or you can come in and pay. But you'll also need to book an induction with one of our trainers, so that we can show you how to use all the equipment.

Man: That's fine. I'll pay now if that's OK.

Receptionist: Sure. So, what's your name?

Man: It's Geoff Stephenson. That's S-T-E-P-H-E-N-S-O-N.

Receptionist: OK, Geoff. And your date of birth?

Man: It's 17-6-74.

Receptionist: OK. And can I take a card number? I need the long number across the front of the card.

Man: Sure. It's 4453 3608 0987 1421.

Receptionist: And the expiry date?

Man: It's 11/26.

Receptionist: Great, and I just need the security code on the back.

Man: OK, I think it's 585. No, hang on, it's 588.

Receptionist: Great, that's all gone through for you. So, when would like to come in for the session with the trainer? We have a slot at two o'clock on Wednesday. Would that suit you?

Man: Wednesday … no, sorry, I can't do that, I'm working. How about Thursday? Would four o'clock work?

Receptionist: Let me have a look. Could you make it quarter past four on Thursday?

Man: Yes, that's fine.

Receptionist: OK, great. Is there anything else I can help you with?

Man: No, that's all good. You've been very helpful.

Receptionist: No problem. So we'll see you on Thursday.

Man: Thanks a lot.

Receptionist: Thank you, bye.

🎧 07 Unit 2, Listening, Skills application, Exercise 1 (p. 32)

Receptionist: Hello, South Coast School of English.

Woman: Hi, I'm phoning to ask about English courses.

Receptionist: Sure, what do you want to know?

Woman: So, I'm planning to go to university in London next year, but my English isn't good enough. What course would you recommend?

Receptionist: OK, well, if you just need to improve your level of English, then our General English courses are what you need, but if you need to pass an exam to prove that your English is good enough to study at university, then you'll need to take an IELTS course to prepare for the IELTS exam.

Woman: I do need to take the IELTS exam, but I think first I'd like to improve my grammar and vocabulary in general, so I won't do an IELTS course yet, I'll start with General English.

Receptionist: OK, great. Well, we have three different General English programmes … shall I tell you about them?

Woman: Yes, that would be great.

Receptionist: OK, so we have the intensive General English course: that's 25 hours a week of lessons, so five hours a day. That's the best option if you need to improve your English quickly, obviously.

Woman: OK.

Receptionist: And then we have what we call the part-time General English course, which is 15 hours a week, so three hours every morning. That's really suitable if you have other commitments, like if you have a part-time job, or other things to do in the afternoons. Our third option is the evening General English course. This is ten hours a week, two hours per day, from Monday to Friday. This is really designed for people who work full time and then come to study after work.

Woman: OK, well, I'm not working at the moment, so the evening course is not really for me. My daughter is at nursery in the mornings, and then I look after her in the afternoons, so I couldn't do the intensive course without paying for childcare all day, and the nursery is a bit expensive. It sounds like the part-time course is ideal for me, so I think I'll go for that. Can you give me some more details about it?

Receptionist: Yes, sure. For the part-time course, as I said, it's 15 hours a week. We used to run the classes from 8.30 to 11.30, but we found that it was a bit early, so it's now from 9.30 to 12.30. This helps people who have to drop off their kids at nursery or at school to make it to the class on time.

Woman: OK, that sounds perfect. And how much does it cost?

Receptionist: Well, for 15 hours a week, it's £150 per week, but if you book eight weeks, you get a discount of 10%, so that makes it £135 per week if you do that. There's also a registration fee of £50 when you make your booking.

Woman: OK, that all seems fine. And can I start any week?

Receptionist: Yes, sure. You can start your course any Monday. You'll need to do a placement test before you begin, so that we can assess your level of English and put you in the right class. Normally we do the test on a Monday morning, but if you live locally, you could pop in and do it this Friday, and that way you can go straight into the class on Monday morning, instead of Tuesday. Could you do that?

Woman: Yes, definitely. I could come in tomorrow morning and do the test. What time would be good?

Receptionist: Why not come in at ten? Oh, no, sorry, actually I've got a meeting at 9.30, and it'll probably last until about 10.30, so let's say 11. Is that all right with you?

Woman: Yes, 11 is absolutely fine. I just have one more question. If I want to study the IELTS preparation course later on, after a few weeks, how can I do that?

Receptionist: OK, well, it's very simple. You can change to the IELTS course on any Monday. So, for example, if you studied three weeks in the General English class, and then you wanted to change, you could come and see me on the Friday, and I could change your class for you. Do be aware, though, that it costs £15 extra per week for the IELTS class, so you would need to pay extra as well.

Woman: OK, that's fine.

Receptionist: So, can I take a few personal details from you before you go?

Woman: Yes, sure.

Receptionist: So, first of all, what's your name?

Woman: It's Jana, that's J-A-N-A, Kasatkina, that's K-A-S-A-T-K-I-N-A.

Receptionist: OK, Jana, that's great. And where are you from?

Woman: Well, I was born in Russia, but I've lived in Switzerland since I was eight, so my nationality is Swiss.

Receptionist: OK, and can I take your date of birth?

Woman: Yes, it's 21-4-82.

Receptionist: Great. OK, as you're Swiss, you must have an ID card – do you have it with you, and could you give me the number?

Woman: Yes, sure. Hold on … yes, it's KM154334 … no, sorry, let me start again … KM1453446791.

Receptionist: OK, great, I've got it. And can I have your phone number?

Woman: Sure, it's 07745 671239.

Receptionist: That's great. Do you have any other questions?

Woman: No, that's all clear.

Receptionist: Great. In that case, I'll see you on Friday morning.

Woman: Great, thanks for your help.

Receptionist: No problem. Bye.

Woman: Bye.

🎧 08 Unit 2, Speaking, Exercises 2 and 3 (p. 33)

Examiner: Do you think that it is a good idea to test children?

Student: Yes, I do, but only up to a point. As I see it, testing is a really good way to measure progress, and you can see how you're doing, and your strengths and weaknesses, by doing a test. Not only that, my view is that it motivates students to work harder if they know there is a test coming up. But it's important to strike a balance between having tests, and allowing children to enjoy learning without being tested all the time.

Examiner: Do you think children in your country are tested too much?

Student: Yes, I think so. In my case, for example, we had tests all the time, especially from the age of about 13 upwards, and I remember feeling stressed and under pressure most of the time between about 13 and 18. As far as I'm aware, it's even worse now, there are more and more tests, and I think sometimes they were just about learning by heart and memorising information, and not about really learning and thinking for yourself.

Examiner: How could the education system of your country be improved?

Student: Well, I think for one thing, it would be good if the government reduced the number of tests, as I said before, and maybe replaced some of those tests with coursework or a presentation or a project. And for another, I'd like to see the government scrap or at least cut tuition fees for university, because it's really expensive, and it means that poorer kids sometimes can't afford to go.

🎧 09 Unit 3, Listening, Skills focus, Exercise 2 (p. 45)

Sales assistant: Good morning, London Sports Tickets, how may I help you?

Customer: Hello, I'm going to be taking my son to London in a few weeks' time as a birthday treat, and I'm interested in getting some sports tickets as a present. What kind of events do you have tickets for?

Sales assistant: Well, we have lots of tickets for Premiership football matches, especially for the big teams like Chelsea or Arsenal. We also have tickets for a big athletics competition in July as well – that's quite popular and lots of big names are appearing. But we have lots of other sports, too. What sports is your son interested in?

Customer: Well, he is a big football fan, so maybe we could go and see a game. But his favourite sport is tennis. Do you have any Wimbledon tickets? He'd love to go and see that.

Sales assistant: Oh, unfortunately, we did have some tickets for the Wimbledon final on the 3rd of July, but I'm afraid they've all sold out.

Customer: Oh, that's a shame. OK, what else do you have?

Sales assistant: Well, we've got lots of tickets for the UK swimming championships at the Olympic pool at the end of June, and also we still have some tickets available for baseball as well.

Customer: And golf? My son loves golf, too. Are there any golf tournaments coming up in the London area?

Sales assistant: Oh, if you'd asked me last week, I'd have said yes, but I'm sorry, we don't have any golf tickets at the moment.

Customer: OK, then in that case, I think I'll go for the football tickets.

Sales assistant: OK, great. How many tickets are you looking for? I should say that we can only sell you up to six tickets in one order. Sometimes people are looking for 15 or 20 tickets, but we're not allowed to do that.

Customer: Well, there's my son and his friend, so that's two … and I need a ticket for myself, so that's three.

Sales assistant: OK, no problem. Which team would you like to see?

Customer: I'd like to watch Chelsea if possible.

Sales assistant: Hold on, let me check. Yes, I see we have some tickets for the match on June the 28th, that's against Liverpool … but we also have tickets for June the 14th, against Arsenal. Which would you prefer?

Customer: The 14th would be great. How much are the tickets?

Sales assistant: Well, we have tickets on sale for £30, £40 or £50. Which would you prefer?

Customer: Well, it's for his birthday, so I'll go for the £50 tickets.

Sales assistant: OK, so that's a total of £150 altogether. Can I take your details, please, Mr…?

Customer: It's John Wilkinson.

Sales assistant: Could you just spell your surname for me?

Customer: Of course. It's W-I-L-K-I-N-S-O-N.

Sales assistant: Great, thank you. And your address?

Customer: It's 34 Commercial Road, Manchester. 'Commercial' is spelled C-O-M-M-E-R-C-I-A-L.

Sales assistant: OK, and can I take your credit-card details? Could you give me the long number on the front of the card?

Customer: Of course. It's 4156 3245 2341 8875.

Sales assistant: Sorry, was that 8879?

Customer: No, 8875.

Sales assistant: Great, thank you.

Customer: Do you have any idea when the tickets will be delivered?

Sales assistant: Well, I'll send them off to you tomorrow, so that's Tuesday, so they should get to you by Thursday at the latest.

Customer: OK, fantastic.

Sales assistant: Just one thing to tell you is that if you have to cancel for any reason, I'm afraid we don't give refunds.

Customer: OK, fine, that's no problem.

Sales assistant: Thank you very much.

Customer: You're welcome. Goodbye.

Sales assistant: Goodbye.

🎧 10 Unit 4, Listening, Skills focus, Exercise 2 (p. 58)

Presenter: Hi, everyone, and welcome to the programme. Today's guest is Sally Jones, manager of the London Museum of Film and Television. As many people know, the museum was badly damaged in a fire three years ago, but after a lot of hard work, it's about to re-open next month. Welcome, Sally. Tell us about what's been happening with the museum.

Sally: Thanks for inviting me, it's a pleasure to be here. Well, the first thing to say is that we're really happy to be finally opening. We had originally planned to be closed for just 18 months, but it's taken us twice as long, so that's three years. However, we're really happy with the new museum, and we think people will like what's inside.

So, our main collection of exhibits is now a room which is considerably larger and brighter than the old space, which means we can include a lot more things for people to enjoy. There are beautiful views now of the river from the north side of the museum, so I think people will really enjoy that, too.

Something which is completely new is our interactive room for children. Once we got the go-ahead from the government to rebuild the museum after the fire, we had a six-month period of consultation with the public, where we asked people what they thought of the old museum, and how we could make it better. Something which came up a lot was making the museum more fun for kids, so we've built a whole new section of the museum for children. It's got all sorts of exhibits that they can touch, sit on and get involved with.

The highlight is a mock TV studio where children can pretend to be TV presenters. They can read a script from an autocue, and then have their news bulletin filmed and watch it back. We've tried it with some of the children of the staff, and the kids absolutely love it.

🎧 11 Unit 4, Listening, Skills application, Exercise 1 (p. 59)

Sally: Another new feature is the buffet restaurant. We felt our old restaurant was a bit too formal and stuffy, and it was never very popular, so now we've got a more informal and relaxed area, where people can have finger food, snacks, cheaper meals and sandwiches, as well as a wide range of drinks. The old museum bar has kept its original design – we've just changed the colour of the décor and lowered the prices a bit, since public feedback indicated that our old bar was a bit pricy.

Presenter: That all sounds wonderful. So, when are you re-opening?

Sally: Well, we had planned to open next Monday, the 7th of July, but we've got a few last-minute things to finish, so the new opening date is going to be Thursday the 17th. The grand opening will be attended by over 150 film and television stars – originally we planned for just 50 or 60 guests, but we kept getting more and more people writing to us and asking to be invited, so we've increased the numbers by about 100. We're open to the public from Friday the 18th, and we'll be open 363 days a year – that's every day except Christmas Day and New Year's Day.

Presenter: And what about the entrance fee? Have you decided how much to charge?

Sally: Well, this was a difficult decision. We wanted to keep the costs as low as possible, but of course we've got to pay the bills and salaries. Under-fives can enter for free, and then there's a child rate of £2, and then £3 for students, but only if you can produce a valid student card. The adult rate is £5, and it's also free for the over-70s.

Presenter: Great! Well, very best of luck with it, Sally, and do come back in a few months and let us know how it's all going.

Sally: Yes, of course, I will. Thanks very much.

🎧 12 Unit 5, Listening, Skills Focus, Exercise 3 (p. 74)

Tutor: Hi, James, come in, have a seat. How's it going?

Student: Well, I'm having a bit of trouble with my essay on the social and environmental history of Glasgow. I've written a complete draft of the essay, but I'm not happy with it. I don't think it's very good, and I want to get some advice about it. What do you think about it?

Tutor: OK, well, I've read it a couple of times, and while I think you have some really original ideas, the structure I find a bit confusing. I can't really follow the flow of the essay, and your conclusion is a bit unclear.

Student: Yes, I know what you mean. What do you think I could do about it?

Tutor: Did you make a detailed plan of the essay before you started?

Student: To be honest, I was going to make a plan, and I normally plan in a lot of detail, but I was a bit short of time, so this time I just wrote it. I guess that explains why it wasn't very clear to read.

Tutor: Yes, I'm sure that's the case. I'd advise you to start again with a detailed plan, and then rewrite it. Keep the ideas, but see if you can organise and write it in a way that makes it easier to read.

Student: OK, I'll do that. When do you want me to do the rewrite by?

Tutor: Well, as you know, the last day you can submit the essay is next Friday, so if you could get me a draft by Monday, I'll have time to give you feedback before the deadline. Is that manageable for you?

Student: It will mean a busy weekend, but yes, that's fine. Shall I email it to you, or would you rather have a hard copy?

Tutor: It would be a lot easier for me if you could email me an electronic copy, so that I can write some comments on it and send it back to you by the end of the day. That way you'll have time to take on board any feedback or comments before Friday.

Student: OK, great, that's really helpful, thank you.

Tutor: Now, we've talked about the organisation, so let's discuss the content. As I said, there are some really good ideas here, but I want to talk through some of your points and see if we can improve them.

Student: OK.

Tutor: So, firstly, you wrote about the development of Glasgow in the 19th century, from a small town to a major trading centre in Europe. I like what you wrote, but I think you should write more about how that process came about. I mean, the main reason seems to be the fact that shipbuilding techniques improved dramatically, but you haven't really mentioned this, so I think you should expand on that a bit more. What do you think?

Student: Yes, that's a fair point, I'll do that. What else would you change?

Tutor: Well, again, I thought your insights into 19th-century poverty in the East End of Glasgow were very interesting, but I would look more into the issue of poor housing, because I think that was the biggest cause of ill health at the time.

Student: OK, that's fair enough, I'll do that, too. Is there anything you think I should read to find out more about it?

Tutor: Yes, there's a great book called *The Working Poor*, which has a lot of excellent research into working-class housing in Glasgow at the time. I'd recommend Chapters 2 and 3 in particular. You can find it in the library.

Student: That's great, thank you. I'll look at that.

Tutor: Finally, no essay on the social history of Glasgow would be complete without a section on air pollution. You'll have seen the old films where the air was full of smog, and this was the result of factory pollution. It wasn't until the Clean Air Act was introduced in 1956 that Glasgow's air became cleaner, along with the rest of the country. I'd definitely look at that. There's a chapter on it in the same book.

Student: Brilliant. That's absolutely great. Many thanks for your help.

Tutor: Good luck with it, and I look forward to reading your next draft.

Student: Thanks.

🎧 13 Unit 5, Listening, Skills application, Exercise 1 (p. 74)

Sarah: So, Faris, how did you get on with your essay? Were you happy with the feedback?

Faris: Hmm, not really. I mean, I normally get at least a B in my essays, and in fact the last one I wrote I got an A for, but I haven't done so well this time – it's only a C. I'm not very happy about that.

Sarah: Do you know why? What did the tutor tell you?

Faris: Well, I've had written feedback, and he seems to think the organisation of my essay was a bit disjointed, but I haven't been able to talk with him face-to-face to find out more. I'd really like to know exactly what I did wrong so that I can improve for the next essay. I've got an appointment to see him on Monday, so I guess I'll find out more then. Anyway, what about you? How did you get on?

Sarah: Well, to tell you the truth, I was pretty nervous when I went to get my feedback, because I wasn't very happy with my essay, and I didn't think it was very good, but actually my tutor loved it and I got an A. He even says he's going to put me forward for the Green Essay prize.

Faris: What's the Green Essay prize? I mean, it sounds obvious, but what exactly is it?

Sarah: Well, apparently, every year the university has an awards ceremony where they give prizes to the best essays in different categories, so in science, in literature, in philosophy and so on, and there's an award for the best essay on environmental issues. If I win, I get a trophy and the university will donate £500 to an environmental cause of my choosing. It would be awesome to win, don't you think?

Faris: Sounds amazing, well done! So who will you give the money to if you win?

Sarah: Well, initially I thought about giving the money to Greenpeace, as I'm a member, and I know that last year's winner gave the money to a local recycling charity, but I realised that if I do win, I'd like to support the beach clean, as they really need the money to advertise for more volunteers.

Faris: Great, that's a really good cause. Fingers crossed! So, tell me a bit more about your essay. What was it about exactly?

Sarah: Well, I wrote about women in green politics. It was absolutely fascinating, I discovered so many interesting female green activists and politicians that I didn't know about before. I found out a lot more about Caroline Lucas, of course. She's the only British Green member of parliament at the moment – she's amazing – and I really enjoyed reading about green politicians in Sweden, as they have a long tradition of environmentalism over there. But the person I found most interesting was a women called Petra Kelly.

Faris: Who's she?

Sarah: She was one of the founders of the Green Party in Germany. I'd really recommend her autobiography, it's fascinating.

Faris: OK, I'll check it out. We can talk about it when I've read it!

Sarah: Cool! So, anyway, Faris, what about *your* essay? What did *you* write about?

Faris: Well, for my essay, I read up on green energy. It seems that here in the UK, we still lag quite a way behind some other countries in this area. For instance, in Denmark, around 30% of their electricity is generated from wind turbines, which compares to only about 2% in the UK. It's a shame, because we definitely have enough wind in this country to generate a lot of electricity.

Sarah: So, what's the reason for that, then?

Faris: Well, from what I read, many politicians in the UK are put off by the high start-up costs of wind power. It's expensive in the beginning to buy and install wind farms, but what they are missing is that once you have everything in place, it's virtually free.

Sarah: Yes, that's really true.

Faris: However, one area where we *have* invested money is in tidal power. Obviously the UK is an island, so we have a great opportunity to use the sea to generate some of our energy. And my reading suggests that we're ahead of other countries in this area. There are plans to open several tidal energy projects in the next few years, which is great.

Sarah: What about solar? I'm guessing it's not that relevant in the UK, with our weather?

Faris: You know, it's a common misconception that solar power is only effective in hot countries. It's not true. If we wanted to, research suggests that at least 10% of our energy could come from the sun. Obviously, we don't have as much sun as countries in Southern Europe or the Middle East, but we shouldn't rule it out. If politicians wanted to, they could generate a lot of energy from solar power.

Sarah: Well, that's all very interesting. I'd love to read your essay. Why don't we swap essays, and then meet up for a coffee and talk about them afterwards?

Faris: Yes, that's a great idea. Let's do that.

🎧 14 Unit 6, Listening, Skills focus 1, Exercise 3 (p. 87)

Hello and welcome to this talk about taking a gap year. My name is Rebecca Johnson, and I'm the manager of Gap Year Volunteers International, one of the oldest gap-year organisations in the world. I'm going to talk to you today about the history of the gap year and also about how it is evolving and changing these days into something quite different from when the idea started.

So let's start with the history of the gap year. Gap years today are often associated with young people having a fun year travelling or backpacking, but originally the gap year was designed as a way to enhance cultural understanding. In 1967, an organisation called Project Trust sent three volunteers to Ethiopia, with the primary aim of

sharing knowledge between cultures. The idea was that young people from the UK would work with local people and there would be a mutual exchange of skills and understanding. This approach was later mirrored by organisations like Raleigh International, a charity whose goal was to improve international co-operation.

However, it wasn't long before profit-making companies and individuals got in on the act. In the 1970s, gap-year companies began to spring up, and a whole industry was born. Worried parents saw that booking a gap-year trip through a well-known and trusted gap-year company might be safer way for their teenage child to enjoy the experiences and challenges of a gap year than simply saving up some money and hitch-hiking around the world. In the 1980s, the number of young people taking a gap year boomed and it became common for employers to favour young people who had taken a gap year because they saw them as more mature. As a result, a CV without an interesting gap year on it began to be seen as a significant disadvantage. In the 1980s and 90s, gap-year companies flourished. Universities started encouraging young people to defer their university course for a year and to start their undergraduate degrees a year later. In a moment, I'll move on to later developments concerning gap years, but first of all, does anyone have any questions?

🎧 15 Unit 6, Listening, Skills focus 2, Exercise 2 (p. 88)

So, as I was saying, the 20-year period from the 1980s onwards was the peak time for gap years in the UK, and it became the norm for young people. In fact, so common was it that many parents started saving up well in advance to put money towards their children's gap years. The most famous gap-year participant is thought to be Prince William, who took a gap year in 2000 and spent it working on various voluntary projects in different parts of the world.

However, everything changed in the 2000s. From 2005 onwards, fewer people took a gap year in the UK, essentially due to university fees. As students now had to pay to study at university, for many students, if they took a year off, it was to work and save to pay for their university course. This was particularly the case among poorer students, naturally. Those from wealthier backgrounds could still afford to take a gap year, but the numbers overall taking a gap year fell significantly.

Surprisingly, though, what has emerged in the last ten or 15 years or so is the phenomenon of older people taking an extended break, a trend generally known as 'late gapping'. This is the idea of people in their 30s, 40s or even older taking a long break from their jobs and doing all the things that teenage gap-year participants do. As employment has become more fragmented, many people change careers several times in their lifetime, and the opportunities to take long breaks between jobs are multiplying. Employers are also much happier to allow their employees to take time off, seeing it as an investment, because happy employees are more likely to come back from a break enthused and refreshed.

Finally, the other trend is the growth of the retired gapper. For those now of retirement age, it is common to have no mortgage to pay and no kids to support, and therefore taking a gap year is absolutely affordable. And why not? Shouldn't everyone have the opportunity to take a break from study or work, see the world, have new experiences and open their minds? I believe age is just a state of mind, and I think it is great that gap years are now increasingly available to people of all ages.

So what of the future? Most experts anticipate that gap years will become shorter. In fact the idea of a gap 'year' is not really the way to look at it any more. According to many gap-year organisations, people are more and more likely to take three-month or six-month breaks, as they are more affordable and can be done more often. Instead of the once-in-a-lifetime trip around the world for a year when you're 18, shorter periods taken more regularly is likely to be the norm. So, if you're thinking about taking an extended break of any kind and would like some advice, do feel free to get in contact. Now, are there any questions?

🎧 16 Unit 6, Speaking, Exercises 2 and 3 (p. 89)

Examiner: What do you think are the main advantages of tourism?

Student: One of the key benefits of tourism for the city or resort is that tourism brings in lots of money, and therefore creates lots of jobs. In particular, in tourist destinations, there tend to be lots of job opportunities in sectors like hospitality, for instance – people working in restaurants, bars and hotels. Not only that, but another upside of tourism is that it often has a positive effect on the local culture. What I mean is that because lots of people from foreign countries come to the destination, local people end up mixing with people from all over the world, which can make them more open-minded and tolerant.

Examiner: What are the possible disadvantages of tourism?

Student: One of the main disadvantages of tourism is that if there are too many tourists, it can have a negative impact on local people and the environment. A good example is in a city like Venice, where because the city is overrun with tourists, many local people can't afford to buy or rent a house in the city, and they are forced to move out to the surrounding area. As well as that, if there are too many tourists, it can result in higher levels of pollution, litter and noise, and this is bad for everyone.

🎧 17 Unit 7, Listening, Skills focus, Exercise 2 (p. 99)

Sophie: Hi, Brian! How are you doing?

Brian: Yes, good, how are you?

Sophie: Good, I'm just thinking about whether I should take up that internship that I've been offered in that marketing company or not. I can't decide.

Brian: Why can't you decide?

Sophie: Well, the thing is, initially they said they would pay me a full-time salary, but then they completely went back on their word, and the manager told me he'd made a mistake and it was unpaid. I'm hoping to change their mind and at least get paid my travel expenses, but as it stands, I'm not going to earn anything.

Brian: That's a shame. Still, do you think it would be worth it anyway, as it would be good for the experience?

Sophie: My mum thinks that I shouldn't do it, but I'm with you, I think it's too good to turn down. There's lots of opportunities to work with the marketing manager, and they've promised me that I can help design the new brochure, as well as the flyers they're making for a new dance studio. It sounds great.

Brian: Yes, that does sound great.

Sophie: Anyway, how about you?

Brian: Well, I went for an interview for a three-month work placement at a local newspaper, and I think I made a good impression. I've just found out that I've been given a second interview – there's a shortlist of four of us, so we'll see what happens.

Sophie: Wow, that's great! Well, good luck.

Brian: Thanks! The great thing about it is that if it all goes well, it might lead to a permanent job – if that did happen, I'd probably have to drop out of university, but I think I probably would take the chance if it came.

Sophie: Are you sure? Even though it's a good job, I wonder if you shouldn't finish your studies first. You know, my brother dropped out of uni half-way through, and he keeps saying he'll go back and finish his degree, but he never does. He's 30 now, and realistically, I don't think he'll ever do it.

Brian: Yes, it's a tough one. Maybe you're right. Anyway, I have to pass the interview first.

Sophie: Well, fingers crossed!

Brian: You too!

🎧 18 Unit 7, Listening, Skills focus, Exercise 4

Brian: Anyway, Sophie, what do you think about internships in general? I read a really interesting article recently saying that it's unfair that they are often not paid. What do you think?

Sophie: Yes, I think I read the same article, and it was saying that because you often only get travel expenses when you're doing work experience, it's an unfair advantage for people from wealthy

families, because the parents can afford to pay rent for their children and give them money to live on, whereas poorer kids can't afford to do that. And I think it's true.

Brian: Yes, I agree. It means that it's really difficult for poorer kids to get into professions like journalism, because all the newspaper offices are in London. If you don't have parents living in London, or rich parents who can afford to subsidise your rent while you're in London, it's impossible to do.

Sophie: Yes, it is. I think that the government should bring in a law to make it compulsory for firms to pay at least the minimum wage to interns. That way everyone would be able to afford it.

Brian: It's a great idea, and I agree in principle, but I think unfortunately if you did that, a lot of companies would stop employing interns, because it would be too expensive for them. I think bringing in a law wouldn't achieve what you want to achieve.

Sophie: Well, I think we'll have to agree to disagree there! Anyway, let's talk about this again another time. I have to dash now … see you soon!

Brian: See you.

🎧 19 Unit 7, Speaking, Using comparatives, Exercises 2 and 3 (p. 103)

I'm going to talk about a business I would like to set up one day, which is a language school. The main reason I'd like to do that is that it'd be great to have the freedom to make the decisions and to run the school in the way that I want. I think in terms of the place, I would like to set up a school in Malta, because although I'm English, the weather is not nearly as good in England as in Malta, and it would be great to work in a sunny climate.

I think I'd set up the school in the next two or three years. First, I would have to borrow some money, because I'm a teacher and so I'm not as well-paid as people in some jobs, so I would have to take out a loan or find an investor. What I would do is to be the academic manager, so I would train the teachers and organise the classes, and then I'm thinking of hiring my sister as the financial manager, because she's far better with money than I am, and she has a much better understanding of marketing as well.

If I think about whether I will do it or not, well, I'm not quite as sure about it as I was a couple of years ago, as the world economy is having a few problems, but I'm sure in a few years you will see my school opening up in Malta.

🎧 20 Unit 8, Listening, Skills focus, Exercise 1 (p. 112)

Hello, and welcome to today's talk on the state of contemporary cities. I'm going to be talking about four aspects of modern city life – costs, and the impact of rising costs on city dwellers, transport, leisure opportunities and multi-culturalism. I'll be making primary reference to London, but I'll be talking about city issues in general.

🎧 21 Unit 8, Listening, Skills focus, Exercise 3 (p. 113)

Firstly, let's look at the rising cost of living in cities, and the impact of that on people earning an average salary. Going back a generation, in a city like London, it was a reasonable aspiration for a family or even a single person with a normal job, like a nurse or a teacher, to be able to cover the rent and bills, have a reasonable lifestyle and still live close to the city centre. Areas like Hackney, for example, in East London, where I grew up, had cheap rents and mortgages, and therefore were extremely mixed in terms of the type of people living there. However, the cost of living in areas like Hackney in big cities like London has spiralled in recent years, and many people have now had to move out. This process, by which poorer areas suddenly get rich, is known as gentrification, and it happens in cities all over the world, but is a particular problem in London. No solution has yet been found to this problem, but one possible avenue for the future is for the government to set a maximum amount per month or per year that a landlord can charge to rent out a house. This works successfully in some European cities, and perhaps this might help to reduce the cost of housing in London.

🎧 22 Unit 8, Listening, Skills application, Exercise 1 (p. 113)

Another issue in London is transport. Visitors to London are often surprised by the variations in the provision of transport in London. Some Tube trains are very modern, but on the lines outside of tourist areas, the trains often seem very old and dirty. Although a lot of effort has been made to reduce traffic in central London, mainly due to the introduction of the congestion charge in the 1990s, roads are still full of traffic at rush hour, and getting from A to B can be difficult. A final issue in relation to traffic is the price. The cost of a monthly travelcard is more than twice that of Paris, for example, adding to the general high cost of living in London.

My third area today is leisure. London is well-known for its sheer variety of entertainment, leisure and cultural opportunities. One area I'd like to highlight is the range of museums in London. As a result of the decision of the Labour government in the 1990s to remove fees for the main museums, visitors to London can enjoy a trip to the National Gallery or the Tate Modern, for example, free of charge. This has definitely led to an increase in the number of visitors and has proved a successful model, copied by many other major world cities.

A first-time visitor to London will also be struck by the number of large parks in central London. Largely built in the Victorian era, London has a high number of large green spaces, ranging from the iconic Hyde Park to smaller neighbourhood parks and kids' playgrounds. This cannot be underestimated in terms of quality of life – just having space to get away from the traffic and the hustle and bustle of city life is a boon for city dwellers.

Finally, I'd like to touch briefly on multi-culturalism. London today is truly a melting-pot for people all over the world – in the last census in 2011, there were over 200 different nationalities living in London, and at least a quarter of the population of London were born overseas. I see this as a great strength of London – a vibrant, diverse city, where people of all nationalities live side-by-side, working and living together. Going back 30 years, for example, it was difficult to find the same range of restaurants and shops – now you can find food from pretty much anywhere in the world. There can be problems when so many people from different countries live together, but this is where the benefit of English being a common language comes in – when there are problems, people can at least communicate with each other about them.

So, there you have it. London is not without its problems, and I've touched on some of them, like the cost of living or issues surrounding transport. However, it's a great city, and I for one would not like to live anywhere else.

🎧 23 Unit 8, Speaking, Exercises 2 and 3 (p. 116)

I'm going to tell you about a city I enjoyed visiting, which was Barcelona. I went there last year on holiday for a week, in June. I'd been working for about six months without a break, and I was really tired, so I decided it was time to get away from it all. The reason I chose to go to Barcelona was because my friend Matt, who was working there as a teacher, had invited me to visit him, and said that he could put me up and that he could show me around the city, and take me to the best places. It was the first time I'd ever been to Spain, so I was really excited before I went and it was as fantastic as I thought it would be.

One thing I really liked about Barcelona was the weather. It was baking hot all the time, and I really enjoyed strolling around the city in the sun, feeling the heat on my face, and getting a tan. Another great thing about Barcelona was the food. On my first day, Matt took me to an amazing family-run restaurant, where the home-cooked food was amazing and the service was really friendly. It was really

good value for money as well. We left them a really big tip to say thank you for such a great meal.

One of the highlights of my trip to Barcelona was seeing all the famous tourist attractions, like the Sagrada Família and the Gaudí buildings. On the third day of my trip, Matt was working all day, so I decided to take a bus tour around Barcelona, to see all the sights. I took loads of photos and I even picked up a few souvenirs to take home for my friends and family.

As well as seeing the sights, I also spent a couple of days chilling out on the beach. It was great to sunbathe on the sand and then go for a dip in the sea every now and then. The sea was really warm and it was a great way to switch off from my job and everything I had to do in my everyday life.

If I had to choose one thing that I enjoyed most about the holiday, it would be hanging out with my friend Matt. We hadn't seen each other for ages, and it was great to spend some time together and to catch up. So, that was a great holiday I really enjoyed.

🎧 24 Unit 9, Listening, Skills application, Exercise 1 (p. 128)

Hello, and thank you for coming. I'm Councillor James Madison, from the city council, and I'm here to talk to you about some proposed changes to the city centre. First of all, I'm going to outline the main changes which we propose for the city, and then there will be time at the end if anyone has any questions.

So, we've thought long and hard about the changes that we'd like to make to the city centre. One big change that we'd like to bring in is regarding the sports centre, as it's really not fit for purpose any more. It's old and run-down – and no wonder, as it's over 50 years old! We did consider renovating and expanding it on the present site, but in the end it proved too costly, so we're proposing that we build a brand-new sports complex on land just outside the city centre. It gives us the opportunity to create a state-of-the-art facility, with totally modern equipment and premises.

Now, on to the city museum. It has been clear for several years that visitor numbers have been falling, and as a result, we did consider shutting it down, but we don't feel the city should be without a museum, as it's a key part of the local community. So what we've decided to do is to slash the ticket prices by 50 percent for adults, and make it free for under 18s, students and pensioners, in the hope that more people will visit. We really want everyone to be able to enjoy the great exhibits the museum has to offer.

Another change is the car park under the town centre. We know that it's essential to keep the car park, but we're worried about the amount of traffic at weekends in the city centre, particularly among shoppers who need a place to leave the car. We have two proposals here. One is to build a tram line from the outskirts to the city centre, so that more of you can come into town using a park-and-ride system. The other thing is to up the price of leaving your car in the car park, in the hope that more of you will then consider taking a bus, or a tram once the line's built.

On a brighter note, you'll all know that the city offices building near the town hall has been empty for several years. We've been thinking long and hard about what to do with it, and although several private companies wanted to buy it, we're going to keep it council-owned. We propose turning the offices into flats, which will be sold at reasonable rates, so that local people can afford them. We know there's a shortage of housing in the city, so we think this will be welcomed by local people.

Finally, the swimming pool. As you know, the city would like to host more sporting events, and last year we held our very first half marathon, which was a great success. Our much-loved swimming pool needs to be refurbished, and in fact what we want to do is turn the current 25-metre pool into an Olympic-size 50-metre pool, so that we can host swimming competitions in the future, as well as giving the opportunity for more local people to use the facilities.

So, that's about it for our proposals. If anyone has any questions, please ask.

25 Unit 9, Listening, Skills application, Exercise 2 (p. 128)

Thank you for all your questions. Now I'd like to answer some of them and talk a bit more about what happens next. So, the first thing is the timescale. We hope to have completed all the building work and the changes within two years, but we know that these projects often take longer than expected, so our absolute latest deadline is three years from now. In terms of finance, which many of you asked about, rest assured that we absolutely pledge that we will not raise taxes to fund the changes. We have a budget already in place, and we've made savings elsewhere, so we will not need to ask the public for more money.

Now, in terms of the consultation, we hope you will agree that these are positive changes for the city, but of course you may disagree. If you're not in agreement, please do email your local councillor with your thoughts, any time up to May. In May, we will take the final decision, so you have until then to let us know of any objections. Someone asked me about the impact of the changes on tourism. Well, when you factor in the new sports facilities and the museum, we hope to attract anywhere between 50,000 and 100,000 new visitors a year. This will bring in more income to the city, and if we can host more sporting events, it will also put us on the map. We also estimate that with the new facilities and the influx of tourists, there should be around 5,000 new jobs for local people.

So, once again, many thanks for listening, and here's to a great future to our wonderful city.

26 Unit 9, Speaking Part 3, Exercises 2 and 3 (p. 130)

1

Student 1: Do you think English will continue to be the international language in the future?

Student 2: I think it's highly likely that English will continue as the international language, because I think that now so many people speak English that it would be difficult for another language to compete. I also think that English isn't as difficult as some other widely spoken languages, like Chinese, so for me, there's a really good chance that English will stay as number one.

2

Student 2: Do you think more people will work from home in the future?

Student 1: Yes, I think more people will definitely work from home in the future, because technology makes it easier to do that, for more jobs. The other thing is that it's really popular with people who have children, or for people who don't want to commute long distances to work every day, so yes, I can definitely see more people working from home in the future.

3

Student 1: Do you think the population of cities will continue to grow?

Student 2: I think there's no doubt that cities will continue to grow in the future, because they are the places with the most opportunities in terms of jobs, and also entertainment and things to do in your free time. I predict that cities will keep growing at a faster and faster rate every year, and it's going to be difficult for governments to deal with the problems that will cause.

4

Student 2: Do you think smoking will be made illegal?

Student 1: I think there's not much chance that smoking will become illegal, because I think it's people's right to smoke if they want to, especially in their own home. I definitely think that more countries will ban smoking in public places, but I think it's very unlikely that smoking will become illegal.

27 Unit 9, Speaking Part 1, Exercises 2 and 3 (p. 131)

1 So, I've just finished university, and I'm taking a gap year at the moment. I'm waiting for my final exam results, but hopefully I'll get a good grade overall. In the short term, I'm going to take a break and have a month off, and then I have a work placement in a fashion company lined up in September, so I'm really looking forward to that.

2 So, if all goes to plan, I'll start a Master's degree in fashion design next year, and my dream is to set up my own fashion company in the long term. First of all, I need to learn how the fashion business works by working for someone else, but hopefully by the time I'm 30, I'll have started my own company.

3 It's hard to predict the future, but in ten years' time, I'd like to be running my own company, as I said, and hopefully I'll have met the right person and settled down. I'd love to start a family one day, as well, but it's too far in the future to make concrete plans.

28 Unit 10, Speaking, Grammar: Linking phrases, Exercise 1 (p. 140)

I'm going to talk about a friend I admire, which is my friend Paul. Paul is a friend from school, and in terms of how long I've known him, it must be about 20 years now, because we met when we were 11, and now we've just turned 30.

As I said, regarding where we met, it was at primary school, in the last year, and the teacher made us sit next to each other that year. We hadn't really spoken before that, but we hit it off and became really good mates.

If I think about how often we meet, well, unfortunately we don't meet so often these days, because we live in different countries, but we try to meet up at least once a year, for an evening or a weekend, and catch up on what we've been doing.

Talking about Paul's job, so he's a teacher of kids with special needs, he works in a school in Scotland, and his job is to help those kids to learn, to socialise and to get as much out of school as possible.

What I really admire about Paul is that he is so patient and kind with the kids. I know that for me I would find this kind of job really stressful, and I don't think I'd be very good at it, but Paul never loses his temper and he's always positive and friendly with them. Another thing that I admire about him is that he always goes the extra mile with the kids – if they need extra help after school, he's always willing to stay late, and with a smile on his face, so that's amazing.

29 Unit 10, Speaking, Grammar: Modal verbs to talk about the past, Exercise 2 (p. 141)

1 So, I'm going to talk about a time when I got lost. I can't remember exactly how old I was, but I think I must have been around 11 or 12. Anyway, I was staying in the countryside with my grandparents, and what happened was I went in the woods …

2 I'm going to tell you about a great meal I had, which was for a friend's birthday at university, so I would have been 19 or 20, something like that. So, we all went to an Italian restaurant, and when we got there …

3 I'm going to talk about I time I was late. It was in my final year at university, so it must have been about 2011 or 2012, around then. One day, I woke up at 9 a.m. and I suddenly realised I had overslept and missed my bus …

4 So, I'm going to tell you about a great holiday I had. I was 11 or 12, I think, so it would have been about 2008 or 2009, that kind of time. Anyway, my parents decided to take us on a round-the-world trip for a month and when I got started …

30 Unit 10, Listening, Skills focus, Exercise 2 (p. 142)

Presenter: Hello, and welcome to the programme. I'm joined today by Maria Jenkins, a restaurant reviewer for the local newspaper. She's going to talk about some restaurants that she's dined in recently, and give you her verdict about the food and the experience in general. Maria, over to you.

Maria: Thank you very much for inviting me onto the programme. So, yes, I'm going to talk about four restaurants that I've been to undercover recently, most of which have seen some big changes, which I'll tell you about as I'm going along. So, first of all, I recently ate at A Taste of Italy, which is a charming family-run Italian restaurant on the high street. I'm sure many of you know it well, as it's been there for over 20 years, and the owners have remained the same ever since it opened, but one thing that you do need to know is that the food on offer at A Taste of Italy has been updated and modernised. Gone are many of the old pasta dishes and now there's a streamlined menu, with a choice of six pizzas, six pasta dishes, a steak and two fresh fish courses. I think you'll find these choices appealing – I know I did. A great romantic night out, in a lovely atmosphere.

Now, onto the Taj Mahal. Again, this is an old favourite for many of you, despite the fact that it's always been hard to get a table, as the restaurant is tiny, and there's only room for about ten tables. The owners have been looking to move somewhere bigger for ages, but as yet there's no news on that. What I can say, though, is that the Taj's traditional menu definitely hits the spot. Book at least two weeks in advance, though, if you're thinking of having a curry at the Taj.

Onto The Tokyo House … this Japanese restaurant is having a bit of a makeover at the moment. The business is under new management, and they've decided to go for a change of atmosphere and clientele. The Tokyo House used to be quite formal – the place for a business meeting or a work event – but the new proprietors have decided to aim for a more casual dining experience. You can now order a couple of sushi dishes at the bar while you have a drink, and the new music and décor is definitely designed for a younger crowd.

Finally, The Parisian Bistro. I'm glad to say that the big news about the Parisian has nothing to do with their excellent menu, but that they have just moved into a new, much bigger location on the outskirts of town. It's a bit of a trek to get there, but I'm sure you'll find it worth the trip. Light, airy and with great modern French décor, this really is an appealing new place to visit. There's even a stage for live gigs and entertainment. Evening tables are all booked up for the next month or so, so get your reservation in well in advance is my advice.

Presenter: Well, that's great, Maria, and thank you so much for coming in and sharing your experiences. All that talk of food is making me hungry and I think …

🎧31 Unit 10, Listening, Skills focus, Exercise 5 (p. 142)

Presenter: So, Maria, you're going to tell us a little bit more about the new Parisian Bistro, is that right?

Maria: Yes, that's right. Well, firstly, as they've moved to new premises, they've brought in some special offers to attract new business. In fact, if you go for lunch, and you take someone with you, they offer a 50% discount between midday and 2 p.m.

Presenter: That sounds great.

Maria: Yes, and I'd also recommend the Parisian if you just fancy a drink after work. As well as some great wines, as you'd expect from a French-owned establishment, they also have some excellent craft beers. The food is pretty good, too. The Parisian is well known for its cheese and mushroom omelette – it might sound a simple dish, but they do it perfectly. One of the secrets of the food, I think, is that everything is cooked on the spot and all the ingredients are locally sourced.

Presenter: What about desserts? I love French desserts and pastry.

Maria: Well, the Parisian's signature dessert is their Tarte Tatin. If you've never heard of it, it's an amazingly sweet tart, made from apples and crispy pastry. Finally, as I was saying earlier, the Parisian now offers live music – if you go on the first Saturday of the month, there's an excellent jazz band, all of whom are local musicians.

Presenter: Well, I'm sold! Many thanks again, Maria.

🎧32 Unit 10, Listening, Skills application, Exercise 2 (p. 143)

Presenter: Hi, Maria, welcome back. Today you're going to talk about four more local restaurants.

Maria: That's right, thanks for inviting me back. So, first of all, I'd like to talk about The Pancake Palace. This is an American-style diner, serving burgers, ice-cream and, of course, pancakes. You might imagine this to be quite a low-priced place, but actually the prices are fairly high, so beware. One thing that *is* good here is the dedicated menu for kids – it has smaller portions and the whole restaurant is very child-friendly.

Next up is Tang's Chinese. Older listeners may remember a similarly named restaurant in the town years ago, but this place is fairly new. In fact, they're celebrating the first anniversary of their opening night next week. The food is great, very authentic, with Chinese chefs and traditional recipes. Definitely highly recommended.

Another restaurant aiming to bring a real taste of the home country to the table is The Argentine Steakhouse. This restaurant is not for those on a budget, as their prime-quality steaks are flown in directly from Buenos Aires, but it's well worth splashing out on payday or a special occasion. This is simply top-quality beef, cooked to perfection, in a great atmosphere. Maybe slightly surprisingly, the restaurant claims to be open every single day of the year, so if you ever fancy a steak on Christmas Day, this is the place! Seriously, though, this a great place for meat-lovers.

Finally, we have The Thai Temple. This is definitely a cheap and cheerful option – there are no frills to the décor and the menu is fairly limited, but if you're after a nice, low-cost meal, this is the place. It has great food, home-cooked with love by proper Thai chefs. One curious thing about this place is that there are only soft drinks on the menu, but the owners say you're welcome to bring your own wine and beer if you want to, for no extra charge.

Presenter: Well, plenty of food for thought, so to speak! Maria will be back in a moment to talk a bit more about The Thai Temple …

🎧33 Unit 10, Listening, Skills application, Exercise 5 (p. 143)

Maria: Now, I'm just going to talk briefly about The Thai Temple, as it's such an unusual place. The restaurant is owned by a young couple, Aiden and Abi, who went backpacking in Thailand after they finished university, and fell in love with the country and the food. When they came back at the end of their year off, they decided to open a Thai café here in the UK. The main thing they wanted was to try to recreate the food and atmosphere of the restaurants they had visited in Thailand, so the first thing they did was to employ a chef from Thailand, so that the food was as authentic as they could make it.

The USP of The Thai Temple is that it's home-cooked food for not a lot of money. The dishes are all pretty straightforward, the kind of thing you'd get in a Thai home, and the prices are low. The food is pretty nutritious as well. You can eat really well for a few pounds here.

In terms of the clientele, the owners say everyone is welcome, and they have people of all ages eating at the restaurant, but the majority of their customers are young people, students or tourists who've seen the restaurant in a good-food guide.

One thing I should mention is that every May, the restaurant puts on a special chilli-eating competition. Whoever can eat the spiciest chilli wins a cash prize, plus a free meal for up to 12 guests. If you think you can handle hot Thai chillis, then why not enter? Or just go along and watch others for fun.

Finally, just a word on the food. They do great soups and a really good Pad Thai, but the number-one dish is actually the vegetarian red curry. I tried it last time I was there, and I'd agree – it's superb.

Presenter: Thank you very much, Maria.

Answer key

Writing Task 2: Advantage/ disadvantage essays
Model essay
Exercise 4
2 Four paragraphs.
3 Two advantages and two disadvantages
4 In the conclusion

Topic sentences for advantage/ disadvantage essays
Exercise 1
Another benefit of living abroad is that you can learn about new cultures.
One drawback of living abroad is that people may feel homesick.
Another important drawback of living abroad is that it can be difficult at first to adapt to the new country.

Exercise 2
1 advantage; living
2 Another benefit; you
3 drawback; is that; may
4 important; it can

Exercise 3
1 One advantage of **studying** English is that you can get a better job.
2 Another benefit **of** studying English is that you can communicate with people all round the world.
3 One advantage of living in the countryside is that **it is** peaceful.
4 Another benefit of living in the countryside **is that** it is friendly.
5 One disadvantage **of living** in the countryside is that it can take a long time to get to work.
6 Another downside of living in the countryside **is** that there is not much to do in the evening.

Exercise 5
1 One advantage of going abroad on holiday is that you come into contact with a new culture.
2 Another advantage of going abroad on holiday is that the weather can be better than at home.
3 One drawback of going on holiday abroad is that there may be a language barrier.
4 Another drawback of going on holiday abroad is that it can take a long time to get there

Supporting the topic sentence
Exercise 1
1 a 2 b 3 a 4 b 5 b 6 c

Exercise 2
Suggested answers
1 Having a mobile phone means that you can text or call your friends and family whenever you like.

2 By having a mobile phone, you can look up information on the internet with just a few taps on the screen.
3 If you have a mobile phone, you may have to pay quite a lot of money each month to make calls, send texts and use online apps.
4 In other words, some people find that they use their phone all the time and cannot stop messaging their friend or checking their social-media accounts.

Exercise 3
1 result 2 result 3 result 4 reason
5 reason

Exercise 4
1 This is because / The reason is that
2 The consequence is that / As a result, / This means that / As a consequence,
3 This is because / The reason is that
4 The consequence is that / As a result, / This means that / As a consequence,

Exercise 5
Suggested answers
1 … most large companies want their employees to speak good English.
2 … you can communicate with people from lots of different countries.
3 … it can be difficult to do your university work properly.
4 … it can be more risky to run your own business than to work for a company.

Exercise 6
Suggested answers
1 This is because you do not have to pay for things such as rent and electricity.
2 As a result, their life will be easier and they will be more relaxed.
3 As a consequence, you may not be able to do all the things you would like to.
4 This means that you do not always get to make your own decisions.

Giving examples
Exercise 1
a Not suitable: too informal and personal
b Not suitable: you should not make up statistics
c Suitable

Exercise 2
1 example 2 instance 3 Take 4 good
5 case

Exercise 3
Suggested answers
1 Take living in London, for example. Many commuters spend over two hours a day getting to and from work.
2 For instance, if you do the washing-up after they have cooked a meal, they can sit down and relax when they are tired.
3 A case in point is social media – many people cannot bear to go for long without checking their Facebook page or Instagram account.
4 A good example is Paris, where a simple coffee can cost up to €5.

Introductions for advantage/ disadvantage essays
Exercise 1
1 You need to rephrase the question and introduce the topic. You should then describe the two different opinions about the topic, and finally say what the essay will do.
2 You need to write three or four sentences.
3 No, you should rephrase it. If you repeat it word for word, you will be penalised by the examiner.

Exercise 3
1 c 2 b 3 a

Exercise 4
1 has become 2 want 3 has increased
4 choose / are choosing 5 is increasing
6 has been rising / has risen

Exercise 5

Rules	Tense
1 Facts about now	Present simple
2 Recent changes	Present perfect
3 Things changing now	Present continuous

Exercise 6
1 Many 2 believe 3 benefits 4 while/ whereas 5 admit/argue 6 connected to
7 essay 8 look 9 points 10 view
11 give

Exercise 7
1 who 2 rising 3 believe 4 significant
5 doing 6 while 7 disadvantages 8 This
9 will 10 points of view 11 will

Exercise 8
Suggested answer
The number of people who own a mobile phone is increasing daily, with some people upgrading their phone several times a year. While there are obvious benefits to having a mobile, there are also some important drawbacks. I will be looking at both points of view in this essay.

Conclusions for advantage/ disadvantage essays
Exercise 2
1 You should say that you have examined both sides of the argument, then give your opinion. Then give more detail about your opinion.
2 Three sentences

Exercise 3
1 c 2 a 3 b

Exercise 4
1 advantages 2 disadvantages

Exercise 5
1 sum 2 having 3 detail 4 clear
5 advantages* 6 disadvantages*
7 opinion 8 outweigh 9 Although
10 balance 11 experiences
* Although it is grammatically possible to say *disadvantages and advantages*, it is usually treated as a phrase, with *advantages* coming first.

Exercise 6
Suggested answers
1 To sum up, having looked at this topic in detail, in my opinion, it is clear that there are both advantages and disadvantages of working from home. In my view, the drawbacks outweigh the benefits. Although it is true some people would enjoy working home, on balance, I think that for me it would be isolating, and I would miss the interaction with colleagues.
2 To sum up, having looked at this topic in detail, in my opinion, it is clear that there are both advantages and disadvantages of living in the country. In my view, the drawbacks outweigh the benefits. Although it is true that it is less stressful to live in the country, on balance, I think that there are greater job and entertainment opportunities in a city, and I would prefer to live in this kind of environment.

Listening Part 2: Multiple-choice questions
Skills focus
Exercise 1
a 1 moved, new building; 1992, 1978, 2001
  2 send people abroad; less than a month, maximum of a year, more than a year
b *Suggested answers*
  1 changed to a new office, relocated
  2 organise for people to go overseas; under a month; up to a year; over a year

Exercise 2
1 C   2 B

Exercise 3
1 … especially after we got new premises in 2001
(The key phrase *moved into a new building* matches with *we got new premises in 2001*. Option A (1978) is when Overseas Opportunities started, and B (1992) is when James Stevens started working for the organisation.)
2 We normally post around 500 people abroad to work or study for up to a year.
(*A maximum of a year* matches with *up to a year*. Option A is incorrect because the speaker says that the placement can be *as short as a month*, so one month is the minimum time possible. Option B is incorrect because the placements are *up to a year*, so not more than a year.)

Exercise 4
Suggested underlining
3 charity placement do not have to pay; shopping, house, bus, train, other parts of the country
4 voluntary placement should; similar placement, happy, simple way, local language
5 sends more volunteers; South-East Asia, India, Sub-Saharan Africa
6 Most internships, salary; do not pay, good salary, limited salary

7 work placement, pay; pay, once, not pay, pay, company
8 number-one thing, work placement; saving, better work record, new things

Skills application
Exercise 1
3 B   4 B   5 C   6 C   7 A   8 C

Speaking Part 1
Talking about what you do
Exercise 4
Speaker 1: 1 'm/am studying   2 'm/am living   3 've/have been studying   4 've/have met   5 came; worked; decided; wanted; quit; came   6 'm/am planning   7 'll/will start
Speaker 2: 1 work; specialise   2 've/have been working; worked; 've/have been working   3 like   4 finished; took; travelled   5 'm/am going to apply   6 'll/will have

Exercise 5
Other possibilities
Speaker 1: 1 –   2 live   3 –   4 meet   5 –   6 plan   7 –
Speaker 2: 1 –   2 've/have worked; worked; 've/have worked   3 –   4 –   5 'm/am applying   6 –

Grammar: Tenses
Exercise 1
Sentence 1 is the present continuous tense, which is used for temporary or short-term situations. Sentence 2 is the present simple, which is used for permanent or long-term situations.

Exercise 2
The verbs are all in the past simple, which is used for completed actions in the past.

Exercise 3
1 F (past simple)
2 U (present perfect continous)
3 F (past simple)
4 U (present perfect continous)

Exercise 4
Sentences 1 and 3 describe definite future plans; sentences 2 and 4 describe things the speakers hope to do if certain conditions are fulfilled (i.e. if she gets the promotion; if he gets a good result in IELTS).

Exercise 5
1 finished; took; worked   2 'm/am doing   3 'll/will start / 'm/am going to start   4 plan / 'm/am planning   5 've/have been working   6 'm/am living; 'm/am going to look   7 work; 've/have been working   8 came; spent; didn't / did not like; gave   9 applied; start / 'm/am going to start / 'm/am starting   10 graduated; got; 've/have been working

Reading: Matching information
Skills focus
Exercise 3
The phrase *spent their childhood* refers to *I was brought up in a small village*; the phrase *doesn't live there any more* relates to the section where Arthur describes how he moved to London.

Exercise 4
1 Arthur   2 James   3 Rose   4 Rose   5 Maria   6 Arthur   7 Arthur   8 James   9 Maria   10 Maria   11 Rose   12 Arthur

Exercise 5
2 commute   3 property   4 There's fresh air   5 enjoying the peace and quiet   6 nightlife   7 gossip   8 The cost of living is much higher   9 cosmopolitan   10 job opportunities   11 I've been able to build a really good career.   12 museums and galleries   13 the fast pace of life   14 switch off from the stress of the city   15 bring up children   16 part of a community   17 isolated

Exercise 6
1 pace; life   2 commute   3 museums; galleries   4 isolated   5 gossip   6 nightlife   7 fresh   8 bring up   9 opportunities   10 cost; living

Pulling it all together
Review
Exercises 1 and 2
See pages 8 and 9.

Exercise 3
For example; Take … , for example; A good example is …; A case in point is …

Exercise 4
1 Three sentences
2 The first sentence should rephrase the question and introduce the topic. The second sentence should describe the two different opinions about the topic. The third sentence should explain what the essay will do.

Exercise 5
1 has become   2 choose   3 is rising

Exercise 6
1 Three sentences
2 The first sentence should say that you have examined both sides of the argument. The second sentence should state your opinion. The third sentence should say that the other side of the argument has some good points, then give more detail about your opinion.

Exercise 7
1 sum   2 Having; detail   3 clear; both   4 Although   5 balance; outweigh; disadvantages/drawbacks

Final practice essay
Exercise 2
Sample answer
In recent years, a significant number of people have decided to move out of big cities and live in the countryside. Many believe that there are significant benefits of doing this, while others think that there are also drawbacks connected to living in the country. This essay will look at both points of view, and then I will give my opinion.
First of all, one advantage of living in the country is that the pace of life is slower. If you live in the country, life is not so busy, and

there are fewer cars and roads. As a result, people who live in the country tend to feel more relaxed and less stressed. Another benefit of living in the country is that there tends to be less pollution. In other words, there are more green areas and the air is fresher away from the towns and cities. As a consequence, many parents choose to bring up their children in the countryside.

On the other hand, there are some disadvantages. One drawback of living in the countryside for young people is that there is not much to do. There is often not much entertainment or nightlife, and this means that it can be boring for teenagers and young adults. Another important drawback is that there are fewer job opportunities. Living in the country means that it is generally difficult to find a good job, particularly if you want to work for a big company.

To sum up, having looked at this topic in detail, it is clear that there are both advantages and disadvantages of living in the country. In my opinion, the drawbacks outweigh the benefits, particularly for young people. Although it is true that cities are busy and stressful, on balance I think they are more interesting and there are more opportunities for people than in the country. (310 words)

Unit 2

Writing Task 2: Opinion essays
Model essay
Exercise 3
1 Yes
2 Two
3 It talks about the other side of the argument.
4 An opinion essay has three paragraphs in the main body, two of which support the writer's opinion, and one which looks at the other side. An advantage/disadvantage essay has two paragraphs in the main body. Each paragraph has two points in – two advantages and two disadvantages.

Introductions for opinion essays
Exercise 1
The main difference between this opinion essay introduction and the introduction to the advantage/disadvantage essay on page 7 is that in an opinion essay you need to state your opinion in the introduction, but in an advantage/disadvantage essay, you shouldn't give your opinion until the conclusion.

Exercise 2
1 b   2 d   3 a   4 c

Exercise 3
1 Some people argue that … , but my opinion is …
2 Many people believe that … . However, I think that …
3 Some people put forward the argument that … . I disagree with this and I belive that …

4 It is thought by some people that … . However, I hold the view that …

Exercise 4
Suggested answers
2 Many people believe that all criminals should be sent to prison. However, I believe that it depends on the crime and the age of the criminal.
3 Some people put forward the argument that children should go to single-sex schools. I disagree with this and I believe that children are more successful in mixed-sex schools.
4 It is thought by some peole that all adult men should have to join the army for a period of time. However, I hold the view that it should be people's choice if they want to sign up for the military.

Exercise 5
1 longer   2 result   3 argued   4 should
5 However   6 view   7 by   8 essay
9 explain   10 detail

Exercise 6
Suggested answers
1 It is common these days for the majority of students to go to schools where boys and girls study together. Some people argue that it is better to send children to single-sex schools, but I hold the view that mixed schools provide children with a better education. This essay will explain my opinion in more detail.
2 In the modern world, crime rates are rising, and people feel increasingly under threat from crime. It is argued by some people that the answer is to send all criminals to prison. However, I think that only people who commit serious crimes should be sent to jail. This essay will explain my opinion in more detail.

Exercise 7
Suggested answers
1 These days, there are more and more threats to security in many countries, and the world is becoming more dangerous. Some people put forward the opinion that all men should have to join the army for a period of time. However, my view is that it should be optional for people to join the army. This essay will explain my opinion in more detail.
2 These days, shops tend to be open longer and longer, and many retail workers have to work on Sundays. It is thought by some people that shops should not be allowed to open on Sundays so that workers can take a break. However, I hold the view that shops should be open on Sundays. This essay will explain my opinion in more detail.

Topic sentences for opinion essays
Exercise 1
The topic sentences in the model essay in Unit 1 introduce the advantages and disadvantages of living abroad. The topic sentences use phrases like *One advantage*

of … or *One drawback of …* . In the opinion essay on page 21, the writer is explaining their opinion, so the topic sentences use different language, e.g. *One reason I believe … is …*

Exercise 2
1 reason; believe
2 argument; favour
3 main; think
4 another; support
5 favour of
6 second

Exercise 3
1 Not only should the government invest in public transport, but it should also build more cycle lanes.
2 Not only are mobile phones addictive for children, but they also stop children from communicating face to face.
3 Not only do you save money on travel costs if you work from home, but you also do not have to spend time commuting.
4 Not only would banning cars from city centres on Sundays reduce pollution, but it would also make it safer to cycle.

Exercise 4
1 Not only should healthcare be free, but it should also be available to everyone.
2 Not only should the government increase tax on junk food, but it should also ban junk-food advertising.
3 Not only is military service expensive, but it also does not benefit young people.
4 Not only does sending criminals to prison protect society, it also deters potential criminals from breaking the law.

Exercise 5
Suggested answers
One argument in favour of military service is that it teaches young people respect.
Not only does military service teach young people respect, but it also means there will be more trained people to defend the country if there is a conflict.

Giving opinions
Exercise 1
1 concerned   2 view/opinion   3 opinion/view   4 would   5 point   6 am

Exercise 2
1 starting   2 should   3 ought/need
4 support   5 advise   6 need/ought

Conclusions for opinion essays
Exercise 1
1 Governments should pay for higher education.
2 Education should be available to everyone, not just to people who have enough money to pay for it.
3 Graduates generally earn more money than people who do not go to university.

Exercise 2
1 Although it is true that working from home can save you money, on balance I believe that it is better to work in an office.

2 Although it is true that living in the countryside is relaxing, on balance my view is that it is better to live in a big city.

3 Although it is true that university education is expensive for the government, on balance I am of the opinion that it should be free.

4 Although it is true that mobile phones can be addictive, on balance I would argue that they are really useful for communication and getting information.

Exercise 3

1 conclusion   2 having   3 detail
4 although   5 am   6 opinion   7 should
8 main   9 reason   10 regardless

Identifying opinion and advantage/ disadvantage questions
Exercise 1
1 advantage/disadvantage
2 opinion
3 advantage/disadvantage
4 opinion

Reading: True/False/Not Given questions
Skills focus
Exercise 3
2 True   3 False   4 True   5 Not Given
6 Not Given

Exercise 4
2 True   3 False   4 True   5 False
6 Not Given

Skills application
Exercise 1
1 False (In paragraph 1, the text says *there are rumours that exams for five-year-olds are on the way, with a decision expected next year*, so the decision has not been made yet.)

2 True (In paragraph 2, the text says *school-leaving exam results are higher now than at any time in the past*.)

3 True (At the end of paragraph 2, the text says *parents and school managers can see the results of age-seven tests in black and white*.)

4 True (In paragraph 3, the text says *In the modern world, the skills that people will need when they enter the workplace are soft ones … Knowing your times tables or memorising dates and facts are not enough to equip young people for the future world of work*.)

5 Not Given (There is no mention of *other countries* in the text.)

6 False (In the last paragraph, the text says *According to a recent survey of parents, around three-quarters would like there to be fewer tests in schools*.)

Listening Part 1: Distractors
Skills focus
Exercise 1
1 Full   2 Standard   3 Basic   4 standard
5 £215   6 £5

Exercise 2
The answer for Question 4 is *standard*. It is correct because the man says *I think standard membership is the one I'll go for*. Distractor 1 is *full*. It is wrong because he says *I'll probably only go to one or two classes a month, so I won't need the full membership*. Distractor 2 is *basic*, because he says *If I sign up for the basic, I'll end up paying for the classes anyway*.

Exercise 3
1 boxfit   2 induction   3 Stephenson
4 17/6/74   5 4453 3608 0987 1421   6 588
7 Thursday   8 4.15

Exercise 4
1 Distractor: £200 (not correct because that was last year's price)

2 Distractor: £15 (not correct because that was the amount that prices went up by)

3 Distractor: yoga (not correct because there are currently no yoga classes running)

4 Distractor: pilates (not correct because that was last year's most popular class)

5 Distractor: 585 (not correct because the man corrects himself by saying No, hang on)

6 Distractor: Wednesday (not correct because the man says he's working on Wednesday, so he can't come then)

7 Distractor: four o'clock (not correct because the receptionist asks if he can come at 4.15 pm instead)

Exercise 5
1 e   2 e   3 b   4 c   5 a   6 d   7 d

Skills application
Exercise 1
1 General English   2 Part-time / Evening
3 Evening / Part-time   4 part-time   5 9.30
(a.m.)   6 12.30 (p.m.)   7 £150   8 10%
9 registration fee   10 11 a.m.   11 £15
12 Kasatkina   13 Swiss   14 21/4/82
15 KM1453446791   16 07745 671239

Speaking: Part 3
Giving opinions
Exercise 3
1 point   2 see   3 strengths   4 weaknesses
5 Not only   6 view   7 strike a balance
8 case   9 example   10 stressed
11 pressure   12 aware   13 heart
14 memorising   15 for one   16 would
17 good   18 said before   19 coursework
20 for another   21 see   22 scrap
23 tuition

Exercise 5
2 strike a balance between   3 As far as I'm
aware   4 learning by heart / memorising
5 coursework   6 tuition fees.

Pulling it all together
Review
Exercise 1
Four sentences: you should rephrase the question, explain what other people think, give your opinion, and say what your essay will do.

Exercise 2
Suggested answers
Some people argue that … but my opinion is …
Many people believe that … However, I think that …
Some people put forward the argument that … . I disagree with this and I believe that …
It is thought by some people that …
However, I hold the view that …

Exercise 3
One argument in favour of … is …
The main reason that I think … is …
Another reason to support … is that …
Another argument in favour of … is …
A second argument to support … is that …

Exercise 4
1 Not only do exams help students see their strong and weak points, but they also motivate students to work harder.

2 Not only are exams really stressful for children, but children can also have a bad day, and therefore the result is not fair.

Exercise 5
1 conclusion   2 Having looked   3 detail
4 Although; true   5 balance; opinion
6 main reason

Exercise 6
1 should   2 recommend   3 advise; to
4 ought to   5 suggest

Exercise 7
See Exercise 5 on page 31.

Exercise 8
See pages 27–28.

Final practice essay
Exercise 2
Sample answer
These days, the trend in education is for students to have more and more tests. Some people argue that this is necessary to improve exam results. However, my opinion is that schools have too many exams. This essay will explain my opinion in more detail.

One reason that I believe students do too many tests is that it often leads to stress and illness among children. In many countries, children now are tested from the age of seven, or even younger, and as a result, more and more young children are suffering from stress or depression. If there were fewer tests, children would enjoy school more, and probably learn better as well.

Another argument in favour of reducing the number of tests is that children need to learn a range of skills at school, not just how to pass exams. For instance, it is important for them to learn to co-operate, to share and to work in a team. These skills are essential for life, but also for their future job prospects. If schools had fewer tests, teachers could focus more on these types of skills and lessons.

Having said that, there are those who argue that exams are important because they raise standards in schools. They believe that if

children take tests at seven, for example, teachers will have to improve the quality of their lessons, and children will study harder as well. As a consequence, educational standards will improve, and children will get better results in the long-term as well.
In conclusion, having looked at this topic in detail, although it is true that testing is important, on balance my view is that schools should test children less than now, and should spend more time on other types of lessons and skills. Children should have a balance between testing, learning and play. (304 words)

Unit 3

Writing Task 2: Problem/solution essays
Model essay
Exercise 2
1 Obesity is mentioned in paragraph 2. The reason given is the high level of processed meals, junk food and take-aways that people eat. The proposed solution is for governments to increase tax on unhealthy food.
2 Lack of exercise is mentioned in paragraph 3. The reasons given are the high cost of gym membership and lack of sports facilities. Two solutions are proposed: government subsidies for gym membership and the construction of more sports facilities.
3 Paragraph 4 mentions the high rates of smoking and alcohol consumption. The result is an increase in the number of serious related illnesses. The writer suggests that governments should increase spending on publicity campaigns to tell people about the health risks involved.
4 The writer says that sales of unhealthy foods are increasing year on year in the UK.
5 The writer concludes that although individuals must take some responsbility for their health, the main responsibility lies with the government.

Topic sentences for problem/solution essays
Exercise 1
1 major, connected   2 issue, that   3 final, is

Exercise 2
1 cause   2 for   3 additional   4 explanation
5 explain   6 factor   7 contributing
8 related

Exercise 3
Suggested answers
1 One reason for the shortage of nurses is that they earn a low salary.
2 One cause of air pollution in cities is that there are not many green areas and parks.
3 Another way to explain obesity is that many people have a poor diet.
4 One contributing factor to traffic congestion is the high cost of public transport.

5 One issue related to high rates of alcohol consumption is the low cost of alcohol in supermarkets.
6 A final cause of homelessness is the lack of jobs for unskilled workers.

Exercise 4
Suggested answers
1 One reason for teacher shortages is that they have to do a lot of marking in their free time.
2 One cause of obesity is people's lack of ability to cook healthy food.
3 One way to explain people's lack of fitness is that many people drive to work instead of walking or cycling.
4 A contributing factor to crime is the lack of CCTV cameras on the streets.

Language for writing about solutions
Exercise 1
1 solve, should   2 answer, for, to   3 way, issue

Exercise 2
1 deal, could   2 forward, be   3 solution, for
4 order, tackle

Exercise 3
Suggested answers
2 To try to solve this problem, governments should introduce stricter pollution limits on factories.
3 In order to tackle this issue, governments should employ more police officers.
4 To deal with the problem, local councils could create more cycle lanes.

Exercise 4
Suggested answers
2 The solution is for the government to invest in more trains and buses.
3 The answer could be for local councils to make it compulsory to recycle.
4 To try to deal with this problem, teachers could make children switch off their mobiles at the beginning of the school day.

Vocabulary for writing about solutions
Exercise 2
2 a   3 c   4 d   5 h   6 f   7 b   8 i   9 e   10 g

Exercise 3
B 4   C 9   D 1   E 7   F 5   G 2   H 6   I 3   J 10
K 8

Exercise 4
1 class sizes   2 allocate more money to something   3 bring in a law   4 There are long delays for hospital treatment.   5 fine people   6 sleeping rough   7 shelters
8 impose higher taxes (on)   9 ban something
10 first-time buyers

Conclusions for problem/solution essays
Exercise 1
1 b   2 c   3 a

Exercise 2
2 This is an **increasingly** serious problem.
3 The main responsibility **lies** with the government.

4 To sum up, there is no doubt that these problems need to be **addressed** quickly.
5 I think that everyone has a **duty** to recycle and care about our environment.
6 There are a **range** of problems facing people who live in the countryside.
7 There is no **simple** solution to the problem of teacher shortages.
8 Governments need to **act** now before the problem gets even worse.

Exercise 3
1 You have to write *otherwise* at the beginning of the second clause of the sentence. It is followed by *will/won't* + infinitive.
2 *Unless* is followed by the present simple. In the second clause of the sentence, you need to use *will/won't* + infinitive.
3 The present simple
4 Yes, with *unless* you can change the order of the clauses if you want. If you do this, you do not need a comma: *These problems will become even greater in the future unless the government invests more money in health education soon.*

Exercise 4
1 Unless we raise teachers' pay, fewer and fewer people will choose to go into teaching. / Fewer and fewer people will choose to go into teaching unless we raise teachers' pay.
2 Governments should ban the use of mobiles while driving, otherwise there will continue to be a large number of accidents.
3 Unless governments make recycling compulsory, many people will continue to throw recyclable material away. / Many people will continue to throw recyclable material away unless governments make recycling compulsory.
4 Supermarkets should use much less packaging, otherwise the seas will continue to be full of plastic.

Exercise 5
Suggested answers
1 We need to charge people to drive into city centres, otherwise cities will be full of traffic.
2 Unless we increase the price of plastic bags in supermarkets, people will continue to throw them away and not use them again.
3 Unless we cut waiting times, people will continue to suffer for long periods before being treated.
4 Governments should make public transport cheaper, otherwise many people will keep using their cars.

Writing about the result of the solution
Exercise 1
2 **This would mean that** people would eat more healthy food.
3 **If this was done**, people would be more aware of the dangers of a lack of exercise.
4 **The result of this would be that** more people would give up smoking.

5 **If the government did this**, people would probably cook more often from scratch.

Exercise 2
Suggested answers

1 If they did this, fewer people would have to sleep rough.
2 If this was done, it would reduce the stress on teachers.
3 This would mean that everyone would have more time to rest and exercise.

Exercise 3
Suggested answers

1 If they did this, children would be less likely to ask their parents for this kind of unhealthy food.
2 This would mean that people would be able to fit exercise into their daily routine more easily.

Introductions for problem/solution essays
Exercise 1

1 has risen   2 has become   3 has been

Exercise 2

1 Over   2 reached   3 face   4 related
5 major   6 addressed   7 examine
8 detail   9 propose   10 tackle

Reading: Identifying information
Skills focus
Exercise 1

1 Key words: long tradition, vegan and vegetarian diet
Possible synonyms: going back centuries; non-meat diet
2 Key words: explanation, recently, grown in popularity
Possible synonyms: reason, why; in the last few years, become more popular
3 Key words: positive change, attitude
Possible synonyms: improvement; the way veganism is seen
4 Key words: environmental reason
Possible synonym: in order to help the planet
5 Key words: possible dangers
Possible synonym: potential risks

Exercise 2

2 B (Surveys suggest that the primary motivation for this mass conversion to veganism is health-related.)
3 A (Now, though, veganism is seen as a positive lifestyle choice.)
4 B (A minority of those asked in a recent survey also said that they became vegan in order to protect the planet, the reason being that so much land, water and resources are taken up with feeding livestock for meat and dairy production.)
5 D (… if you do not eat vegan foods in the right combinations, for example rice and beans together, there is a risk of your diet lacking essential nutrients and proteins.)

Skills application
Exercise 1

1 C ('*I have a very poor work–life balance – I hardly ever see my husband, and when I do get home, I'm normally exhausted and I'm in bed by 9.30. It's really bad for our relationship.*')
2 B (*By law, workers are not allowed to work more than 48 hours a week in the UK, but 42% of people reported that they worked more than 48 hours a week on a regular basis.*)
3 F (*In previous generations, many people got their first job and then had a job for life, with no need to worry about losing it. However, in today's job market, many workers are employed on temporary and short-term contracts.*)
4 D (*… in the past when people left work, it was impossible for their boss to contact them; now many people are checking work emails in evenings and weekends, and never really get a chance to stop working.*)
5 E (*Half of those surveyed said that spending several hours a day commuting to work and back was their number-one source of stress.*)
6 D (*Another issue which affects many people is the inability to switch off from work. This is caused by internet technology.*)
7 C ('*… there's also a culture of staying late in the office, which I feel pressure to fit into. Everyone else stays late, so if I went home at 5.30 p.m., I feel like my boss would think I was lazy.*')
8 F (*The result of all of this is to place workers under great amounts of stress and pressure, and often leads to people working too much.*)

Exercise 2

2 a lack of time   3 long working hours
4 a key source of stress   5 I feel pressure to fit into.   6 I have a very poor work–life balance.   7 the inability to switch off from work   8 commuting   9 permanent contracts   10 short-term contracts
11 zero-hours contracts

Exercise 3

1 work–life   2 zero-hours   3 switch off
4 working hours   5 commuting

Listening Part 1: Predicting answers
Skills focus
Exercise 1

1 The names of two sports, e.g. tennis and rugby.
2 The key word is *maximum*. A possible synonym could be *the highest/greatest number of tickets*.
3 2: it's unlikely that someone would buy 20 or 200 tickets.
4 A possible synonym could be *still on sale*. The speaker might say *We've run out of tickets*, *There are none left* or *They're sold out* as a synonym of *not available*.
5 £35, as it's the cheapest ticket.

6 Smith, because family names always start with a capital letter.
7 It is likely that you will have to write eight digits, as a typical credit-card number has 16 digits.
8 Possible synonyms could be *They will be delivered, You will receive them*. You can expect to hear a day of the week, a date or maybe *tomorrow*.
9 A word meaning 'get your money back'.

Exercise 2

1/2 swimming/baseball   3 six/6   4 three/3
5 June 14th/14th June   6 £30   7 Wilkinson
8 Commercial   9 2341 8875   10 Thursday
11 refunds

Exercise 4

1/2: tennis, golf   3 15, 20   4 one, two
5 June 28th   6 £40, £50, £150
7 *No distractors*   8 *No distractors*   9 8879
10 tomorrow, Tuesday   11 *No distractors*

Speaking Parts 1 and 2
Common questions related to health and fitness
Exercise 1

1 in shape   2 member   3 trainer   4 team/individual, individual/team   5 taken part
6 encouraged   7 been   8 cut down
9 moderation   10 cook   11 enough
12 food

Speaking Part 3
Giving examples from your experience
Exercise 1

Speaker's personal experience: In my case, for example, my parents took me to football training every Saturday morning (A), For me personally, I gave up meat two years ago and it was definitely for health reasons (B).
Experience of someone the speaker knows: My brother, for instance, gave up meat when he was 14 for this reason (B), If I think about my father, for example, … after work (C).
Examples from the speaker's country: Children in my country only have sport once or twice a week (A), Where I'm from, you have to pay quite a lot of money to join a gym (C)

Exercise 2

1 case   2 personally   3 think   4 Where
5 know   6 country   7 instance
8 experience   9 average   10 Take

Pulling it all together
Review
Exercise 1
Suggested answers

1 One cause of stress in the modern world is that the pace of life is so fast.
2 Another reason for stress is long working hours.
3 One contributing factor to teacher shortages is rising class sizes.
4 One issue related to obesity is that many people do not do much exercise.

Exercise 2
1 Introduce   2 Bring   3 Employ   4 Impose
5 Fine   6 aside   7 rough   8 first-time
9 Allocate   10 Subsidise

Exercise 3
1 Unless action is taken immediately, the healthcare system will face a crisis.
2 The government should invest substantial resources in healthcare, otherwise people will continue to face a long wait for hospital treatment.

Exercise 4
Suggested answers
If this was done, … would …
If they did this, …would …
This would mean that … would …
The result of this would be …

Exercise 5
See box on page 42.

Final practice essay
Exercise 2
Sample answer
There has been a sharp increase in recent times in the number of people who are suffering with illnesses connected to stress. There are several reasons why stress is increasing in modern life, including job insecurity, technology and long working hours. This essay will examine these issues in more detail and propose some ways to tackle them.

One factor behind stress in modern life is job insecurity. These days, many people are employed on zero-hour contracts, and as a result they tend to worry about how much work they will get each week, and how much they will be paid. To deal with this problem, governments could bring in a law to ban this type of contract. If they did this, people would have more job security and they would feel less stressed.

Another cause of stress is technology. Although technology brings many benefits to people, it also can have a negative effect on working patterns. For example, many employees have to answer work emails in their free time, and this can make it difficult to have a good work–life balance. The way forward might be for companies to make it clear to their staff that they should not continue working outside their normal hours. A further contributing factor to stress is long working hours. In many cases, people are working longer and longer, and many people feel they should stay in the workplace late in the evening in order to prove that they are good employees. The answer could be for governments to enforce the laws on maximum working time more strictly. This would make sure that people do not work too much.

In conclusion, it is clear that stress in modern life has a range of causes, often connected to work and technology. Unless these issues are addressed, rates of stress-related illness will continue to increase. I believe that both

governments and employers have a duty to take better care of people's physical and mental well-being.
(329 words)

Unit 4
Writing Task 2: Two-part essay questions
Model essay 1
Exercise 5
1 There are three sentences. The first sentence rephrases the question, the second sentence gives opinions about both parts of the question, and the third sentence says what the essay will do.
2 Both questions
3 The main idea is that it is easier to gain information and knowledge via the internet.
4 There are two examples to support the main point – one about access to education and one about consumer information.
5 The main ideas are that children can come across more adult content because of the internet, and that parents should control what children can access.
6 Both questions
7 The conclusion is that adults should have free access to information, but parents should control what children have access to.
8 The main differences are answering two questions in the introduction and conclusion, and then breaking up the main body into two separate parts, each dealing with one of the questions.

Exercise 6
2 find something at the touch of a button
3 To take one example, …
4 a face-to-face course
5 the biggest downside
6 come across violent or sexual images
7 This can have a negative effect on their well-being.
8 a filter
9 prevent adults from getting information

Grammar: Noun phrases
Exercise 1
1 the expansion of the internet
2 the introduction of free online courses.
3 the globalisation of business
4 the invention of catch-up television

Exercise 2
2 a   3 b   4 e   5 g   6 f   7 h   8 d

Exercise 3
1 In the last few years, there has been an increase in the number of people who go abroad to study English.
2 The last few years have seen a rise in the number of people who change jobs several times in their career.
3 In the last few years, there has been a fall in the number of women who stay at home to look after children.

4 The last few years have seen a decrease in the number of people who can afford to buy a house in London.
5 In the last few years there has been a rise in the number of people who study free online courses.
6 The last few years have seen an increase in the number of people who want to move out of big cities and live in the countryside.

Exercise 4
1 the invention of the internet
2 the need to speak / the necessity of speaking English to get a good job
3 rising house prices / the rising cost of a house
4 an increase / increases in global temperatures

Model essay 2
Exercise 2
1 It asks you to give suggestions/solutions instead of just an opinion.
2 Four sentences: The first rephrases the question, the second and third sentences give the writer's opinion, and the fourth says what the essay will do.
3 The writer agrees with banning mobiles in schools.
4 The writer says parents should limit children's mobile phone use.
5 Paragraph 2 deals with the first of the two questions.
6 Paragraph 3 deals with the second of the two questions.
7 Two opinions, answering both questions

Exercise 3
1 set clear rules and limits (on how long children can use mobile phones)
2 check their phone frequently
3 interpersonal skills
4 concentrate on their lessons
5 In terms of
6 By doing this, …
7 strike a balance between
8 social media
9 mainly because
10 Parents set clear boundaries.

Language for avoiding generalisations
Exercise 1
Sentence b is better because by adding *tend to*, you show that you understand that not every person who studies abroad gets homesick, but that it happens quite often.

Exercise 2
Suggested answers
generally (speaking), often, by and large, sometimes, more often than not, be likely, in most cases

Exercise 3
1 People who cycle to work are generally fitter than those who drive. / Generally, people who cycle to work are fitter than those who drive.
2 People who live in the capital city often spend a long time getting to work each day. / Often, people who live in the capital

city spend a long time getting to work each day.
3 Children who use mobile phones too much can become less sociable.
4 Generally speaking, people who live abroad for a year or two become more open-minded and tolerant. / People who live abroad for a year or two become, generally speaking, more open-minded and tolerant.
5 People who do a lot of exercise and eat healthily tend not to become overweight or obese.
6 More often than not, people who get good degrees from a top university get good jobs. / People who get good degrees from a top university more often than not get good jobs.
7 If children have their mobile phones during school, it is likely that they will check the phone frequently and send messages to people.
8 In most cases, children whose parents read a lot at home will enjoy reading too. / Children whose parents read a lot at home will, in most cases, enjoy reading too.

Exercise 4
Suggested answers
1 People who work from home tend to get easily distracted.
2 People who run their own businesses generally make more money.
3 By and large, those who work in jobs like teaching or medicine enjoy their jobs more than people who work in business.
4 People who do not do sport often suffer from illnesses later in life.
5 Generally speaking, people who live in the countryside have more peace and quiet than those who live in cities.
6 In most cases, access to unlimited information on the internet is a good thing.
7 Students who take a gap year after they finish high school tend to be more mature and more successful when they go to university.
8 If smoking is banned in public places, it is likely that more people will give up smoking.

Exercise 6
… it is likely that they will check their phone …
As a result, they tend not to …

Reading: Matching headings
Skills focus
Exercise 1
1 second sentence   2 last sentence
3 first sentence   4 no topic sentence

Exercise 2
2 The main idea of paragraph 4 is the benefits of pet ownership.

Exercise 3
1 b   2 c   3 a   4 c

Exercise 5
benefits: a positive effect, the advantage of

young people: children, young children, teenagers
researchers: experts, educational academics

Exercise 6
Key words	*Suggested synonyms*
drawbacks	disadvantages, downsides
running a business	owning a company
in your 20s	between the age of 20 and 29

Exercise 7
drawbacks: potential problem, downside, it can be tough
running a business: set up a company, found your company, open a business
in your 20s: before your 30th birthday, young people fresh out of college

Skills application
Exercise 1
B vi   C ii   D viii   E x   F ix   G i   H vii   I iv
J v

Listening Part 2: Predicting answers
Skills focus
Exercise 1
1 A phrase that indicates an amount
2 A comparative adjective
3 Something that you can see from a high point
4 An adjective

Exercise 2
1 twice   2 brighter   3 river   4 interactive
5 mock   6 staff

Skills application
Exercise 1
1 relaxed   2 snacks   3 drinks   4 design
5 pricy   6 Thursday (the) 17th 7 50, 60
8 New Year's Day   9 valid   10 70s

Speaking Parts 2 and 3
The news
Exercise 3
1 up-to-date   2 informed   3 browse
4 catch   5 lose touch   6 headlines
7 community   8 fake news   9 trust
10 bias

Communication
Exercise 3
1 debates   2 argument   3 apologised
4 presenting, relationships   5 therapist
6 interrupt   7 misunderstand   8 get on with

Pulling it all together
Review
Exercise 1
1 button   2 filter   3 limits   4 balance
5 concentrate

Exercise 2
Suggested answers
1 Generally speaking, people who live in big cities have to spend longer getting to work than people who live in the countryside.

2 People who work for themselves tend to find it harder to switch off from work at the end of the day.
3 People who work for private companies often now have less job security than in the past.
4 By and large, children who spend too long in front of the television become badly behaved and overweight.

Exercise 3
1 Identifying topic sentences in paragraphs
2 Identifying key words in headings, and matching with synonyms

Exercise 4
1 last, seen   2 development, transformation
3 due to   4 consequence, rise

Final practice essays
Exercise 2
Sample answers
1 In recent years, some governments have abolished the entry fees for some of their most important museums. Some people believe that doing this is too expensive, and that governments should spend money on more important things. However, my view is that it is a good use of government resources to make museums free. This essay will explain my opinion in more detail.
One argument in favour of making museums free to the public is that it attracts tourists. Every year, millions of tourists visit major capital cities on holiday, and one of the factors which influences their choice of city is the possibility to visit museums and galleries free of charge. In addition, there are benefits for local people, because free entrance to museums widens access to culture and learning for people who live in or visit the city. This is particularly the case for people on low incomes, who might otherwise choose not to visit museums.
On the other hand, there are those who argue that governments should have other priorities when it comes to spending money. They believe that governments should prioritise areas of expenditure like health and education, because these are more fundamental to people's lives. In a time of austerity, the argument is that spending money on museums is not really affordable or desirable. In addition, it can be argued that people are generally willing to pay to enter museums, and that in most cases the entrance fees are not very high.
In conclusion, although I think it is true that allocating government resources to areas like health and education is important, on balance I agree with making museums free, mainly because it allows everyone to enjoy a country's cultural riches. If museums charge people to enter, only those who can afford to pay will go to museums, and this will significantly disadvantage people on the lowest incomes.
(312 words)

2 These days, a common stage of life for young people is to take a break between school and university, or after finishing university. In my view, the main reasons that young people do this are to have time to think about what they want to do in life, and to acquire new skills. I think the best way to spend a gap year is to do a combination of different things. This essay will explain my ideas in more detail.
First of all, one reason that people like to take a year's break is that it gives them time and space to reflect. Some young people decide early on in life what they would like to do as a career, but many others need time to consider what their skills and interests are before they start a university course or a job. In addition, taking a year out from studies or work offers the possibility to learn new skills and have new experiences. For instance, many people go abroad for a period of time to learn a foreign language or to undertake some voluntary work.
In my view, the best way to spend a gap year is to have a balance of different activities during the year. I think it is important to travel during a gap year, in order to see different places, and to try to understand people from different cultural backgrounds. In addition, learning a new skill is very good for people's confidence and for their future job prospects. Finally, it is also essential to have a break from study and the pressure of exams, and have time to relax.
To sum up, my view is that having a gap year is an important part of each person's life, and that if possible, everyone should have the opportunity to take an extended break. I believe that spending a year combining learning, travelling and reflecting is the best way to develop as an individual in that year, and is very important for a person's future.
(337 words)

Unit 5
Writing Task 2: Discussion essays
Model essay
Exercise 2
1 No
2 There are four sentences. The first sentence gives examples of environmental problems. Sentences 2 and 3 rephrase the two opinions in the question. Sentence 4 explains what the essay will do.
3 Two: one is that governments have the power and money to make changes, and the second is that we need governments to work together to make real changes.
4 Two: one is that each person should make small changes in their own lives. The second is that people can do things in their local community, and work together to persuade local councils to be greener.

5 The writer's opinion is that both the individual and the government have a responsibility for the environment.

Exercise 3
1 climate change   2 marine pollution
3 fossil fuels   4 renewable energy
5 resources   6 international co-operation
7 reducing carbon emissions   8 local produce   9 litter   10 lobby

Language for introducing ideas
Exercise 1
2 It is believed that recycling should be made compulsory.
3 It is often claimed that renewable energy is cheaper than energy from fossil fuels.
4 The argument is often put forward that only governments can make major environmental changes.
5 It is generally thought that supermarkets use too much plastic in their packaging.
6 It is often said that people should think globally but act locally when it comes to the environment.
7 It is commonly argued that environmental problems cannot be solved by one government acting alone.

Exercise 2
1 There is an argument that …
2 One reason people that people believe that …
3 There are many people who think that …
4 There are those who say that …
5 One line of argument is that …
6 There is a point of view that …

Exercise 3
Suggested answers
1 There are many people who believe that governments should double their investment in solar and wind power.
2 One reason that people believe that governments should close down nuclear power plants is because they are too dangerous.
3 There is a point of view that governments should help people save energy by providing money to insulate homes from the cold.
4 There is an argument that water companies should charge people for the amount of water they use.
5 There are those who say that local councils should set up park-and-ride schemes in order to reduce car use in city centres.
6 There are many people who believe that people should take showers instead of baths in order to reduce their water consumption.

Grammar: Relative clauses
Exercise 1
1 d   2 b   3 a   4 c

Exercise 2
1 which means that   2 which enables them to   3 which would make it easier   4 which would lead to   5 which is a negative development   6 which would help them

realise   7 which would encourage more people to   8 which is a positive development

Exercise 3
Suggested answers
1 Tuition fees for university now cost over £9,000 a year in the UK, which means that people from poorer families find it difficult to access higher education.
2 There is much more choice of organic food and vegetables in supermarkets than there used to be, which enables people to eat organic produce whenever they like.
3 Governments could offer cheap business loans to people who want to start green businesses, which would encourage more people to set up environmentally friendly companies.
4 Supermarkets now charge people if they want a plastic bag for their shopping, which is a positive development, because it means that people use fewer plastic bags.

Language for key topics: Crime
Exercise 3
1 C   2 B   3 D   4 B   5 A   6 C   7 A   8 C

Exercise 4
1 It is a deterrent to potential criminals.
2 prison sentences   3 behind bars
4 heinous crimes   5 lock criminals up   6 the root cause   7 My objection to prison […]
is …   8 first offender   9 community service
10 give something back to society
11 Prisons don't do a very good job of rehabilitating criminals.   12 counselling

Exercise 6
Sample answer
There is no doubt that tackling crime is one of the most significant issues facing governments all across the world. It is often argued that sending criminals to jail is the best way to punish them and to reduce crime. However, there are also those who argue that community-based punishments are more effective. This essay will examine both points of view.
One reason that people believe that criminals should be send to prison is to protect society. If criminals are behind bars, they will not be able to re-offend, and therefore society will be safer. This is particularly the case in terms of violent crime, such as murder or serious assault. Another argument that can be put forward is that prison works as a deterrent to potential criminals. In other words, if people know that by committing crime they will go to jail, it is likely that they will think twice before offending.
On the other hand, there are many people who believe that community punishments are a better way of dealing with criminals. They say that sending criminals to jail does not help offenders to learn from their mistakes or to be rehabilitated, because prisons often do not offer much education or counselling to offenders, and they often return to society and re-offend. In addition, it is argued that punishments such as community service give

offenders a chance to give something back to society, and even to learn new skills at the same time.

In conclusion, having looked at both opinions, my view is that societies need a mix of punishments, depending on the type of crime. For serious, violent crimes, criminals should be sent to prison, to protect society; but for minor crime, I believe it is much better to keep offenders out of jail and to punish them in society.

(303 words)

Language for key topics: The 'good society'
Exercise 2
Texts A and D agree more with the first statement. Texts B and C agree more with the second statement.

Exercise 3
1 A   2 D   3 C   4 A   5 B   6 C

Exercise 4
1 eradicate poverty   2 a roof over your head
3 living on the breadline   4 on benefits
5 access to education   6 lifelong education
7 The wealth should be shared out.   8 There is still a lot of discrimination against women.
9 government resources

Exercise 6
Sample answer
In the modern world, most governments put economic growth at the heart of what they do. They believe that the main goal for society should be expanding the economy and making people richer. However, there is also an argument that governments should also be aiming to create a fairer and more equal society. This essay will examine both points of view.

One reason that many people think that economic development is the primary goal of society is to eradicate poverty. Many countries of the world have a large number of people who are living below the poverty line, and governments believe they should first and foremost try to create wealth so that poverty rates are reduced. In addition, there is a line of argument that in order to pay for services such as education, health and transport, governments need to be economically successful. If they create wealth and grow the economy, they can use this money to fund services and welfare.

On the other hand, there are many people who think that it is not just economic growth that should be the aim of society or the government. They say that social justice and equality are at least as important. For instance, there are some countries in the world which are extremely wealthy overall, but still have millions of people living in poverty. Therefore, it is not just how much money a country has, but how equally that money is shared. Moreover, the argument can be put forward that life is about more than just money. Governments should aim to eliminate poverty,

but they should also create access to education, travel and culture for their people. In conclusion, having looked at both opinions, my view is that economic growth should not be the only goal of society. Although I think it is essential to grow the economy and to reduce poverty, it is as important to make sure that wealth is shared, and that people are able to have the opportunities to lead interesting and fulfilling lives.

(337 words)

Reading: Note completion
Skills focus
Exercise 2
1 trapped   2 thrown away

Skills application
Exercise 1
3 toxic   4 Styrofoam boxes   5 landfill sites
6 disposed of   7 plastic bags   8 200 years
9 garbage patches   10 single-use
11 bamboo   12 roll-out   13 awareness
14 Discounts

Listening Part 3: Multiple choice and sentence completion
Skills focus
Exercise 3
1 A   2 B   3 C   4 deadline   5 electronic
6 trading centre   7 shipbuilding techniques
8 poor housing   9 *The Working Poor*
10 factory pollution

Skills application
Exercise 1
1 C   2 B   3 C   4 C   5 A   6 green energy
7 wind turbines   8 start-up costs
9 tidal power   10 hot countries

Speaking Parts 2 and 3
The environment
Exercise 1
1 d   2 c   3 a   4 b   5 f   6 e

Exercise 3
1 c   2 a   3 e   4 f   5 b   6 d

Pulling it all together
Review
Exercise 1
1 It is often said that governments should tax older cars which pollute the environment more than newer, cleaner ones.
2 The argument is often put forward that any environmental change has to start locally.
3 It is generally thought that there is too much packaging on the goods we buy.

Exercise 2
1 argument   2 reason, believe   3 many, who   4 those   5 line   6 point, view

Exercise 3
1 See Exercise 2 on page 73.
2 See the box on page 71.

Exercise 4
1 solar, tidal   2 renewable   3 fossil fuels
4 pick, litter   5 lobby   6 compulsory

7 park, ride   8 single-use   9 staycation
10 pressure group   11 local produce
12 raise awareness

Final practice essay
Exercise 2
Sample answer
It is clear that the world is facing a large number of serious environmental problems. It is argued by some people that the best way to deal with these issues is for the government to bring in strict laws to protect the environment. However, there are also those who say that the government's role should be to try to persuade people to become more green, instead of legislating. This essay will examine both points of view.

One reason that people believe that governments should legislate for environmental change is that it ensures that environmental rules and standards are followed. If environmental rules are voluntary, some people and companies will follow them, but others may not. Therefore, laws are needed to make sure everyone complies with environmental standards. Another argument that can be put forward is that by introducing laws, governments can change behaviour more effectively. For instance, if governments bring in a law to charge people for plastic bags in supermarkets, people will use far less of them, and this will happen very quickly.

On the other hand, there are many people who believe that it is better to educate and persuade the public to make environmental changes. They say that if you can convince people that they need to recycle, for instance, it is more effective that forcing people to do it, because people will recycle willingly, and they will also persuade others to do the same. In addition, it can be argued that governments should treat citizens like adults, and should provide them with information and facts about the environment, and then let them make up their own minds about what to do.

In conclusion, having looked at both opinions, my view is that governments should do both things. They should make strict laws in areas such as setting limits on the amount of pollution that cars can emit, for instance, but they should also undertake more public education and persuasion, so that people will act in green ways out of choice, not just because they are forced to.

(341 words)

Unit 6
Writing Task 1: Graphs with a trend
Model essay
Exercise 1
1 Ten years
2 How many people visited the cities over the period
3 New York
4 London
5 An upward trend for London and a downward trend for New York, overall
6 The number of visitors to London overtook that of New York.

Exercise 2
1 Four paragraphs
2 In general
3 Two ideas (the general trend of the graph + the relative popularity of the cities)
4 Past simple
5 *started at / began at*
6 *around, approximately, just under, about, just over*
7 *soared*
8 *remained stable*
9 *In detail, …*
10 Because paragraph 3 describes an upward trend (London), but paragraph 4 describes a downward trend (New York).

Verbs and adverbs to describe changes
Exercise 1

Increases	Big increases	Decreases	Big decreases
go up, grow, increase, rise	jump, rocket, shoot up, soar, surge	decrease, decline, drop, fall, go down	plunge

Exercise 2
1 a present perfect   b past simple   c present simple
2 Sentence b is correct because we are describing a finished period in the past.

Exercise 3

Verb	Past simple
decrease	decreased
drop	dropped
fall	fell
go down	went down
go up	went up
grow	grew
increase	increased
jump	jumped
plummet	plummeted
plunge	plunged
rise	rose
rocket	rocketed
shoot up	shot up
soar	soared
surge	surged

Exercise 4
2 considerably, significantly   3 dramatically
4 rapidly, sharply   5 gradually   6 steadily

Exercise 5
1 considerably/significantly   2 sharply/rapidly/dramatically   3 considerably/significantly   4 slightly   5 steadily/gradually

Exercise 6
Suggested answers
2 The number of visitors to New York went up slightly to just over 3m in 2013.
3 The number of visitors to London rose considerably to 2.2m in 2011.
4 The number of visitors to London increased sharply to around 3.8m in 2015.
5 The number of visitors to London grew steadily to 4.2m in 2018.

Adjectives and nouns to describe changes
Exercise 1

Verb	Noun
decrease	a decrease
drop	a drop
fall	a fall
fluctuate	a fluctuation
improve	an improvement
increase	an increase
jump	a jump
level off	a levelling off
plunge	a plunge
rise	a rise
surge	a surge

Exercise 2

Adverb	Adjective
dramatically	dramatic
gradually	gradual
rapidly	rapid
sharply	sharp
significantly	signficant
slightly	slight
steadily	steady

Exercise 3
2 There was a dramatic fall in the number of visitors to Cairo.
3 There was a steady rise in the number of travellers in South America.
4 There was a gradual drop in the number of tourists in Italy.
5 There was a considerable decrease in the number of visitors to Milan.
6 There was a significant decline in the number of people visiting Dubai.

Introductions for Task 1 essays
Exercise 1

Countable	Uncountable
cars, DVDs, employees, people, smokers, tourists, visitors	chocolate, coffee, electricity, gas, money, oil, profit, spending, water

Exercise 2
1 how many, visited   2 number, who visited

Exercise 3
1 much, was   2 amount, which

Exercise 4
1 the amount of coffee which was produced
2 how much gas was used
3 the number of cars which were sold
4 how many people worked

Exercise 5
Suggested answers
1 The graph shows information about how much electricity was used in the UK.
   The graph shows information about the amount of electricity which was used in the UK.
2 The graph shows information about how many people viewed/watched the World Cup final in the UK.
   The graph shows information about the number of people who viewed/watched the World Cup final in the UK.

Exercise 6
1 information   2 many   3 over   4 between
5 and

Exercise 7
Suggested answers
1 The graph shows information about how many cars were sold in the UK and the USA, over a 15-year period between 2000 and 2015.
2 The graph shows information about the amount of coffee which was produced in Brazil, over an eight-year period between 2010 and 2018.

Overviews for Task 1 essays
Exercise 1
1 Overall
2 There was an upward trend in the number of visitors; The number of visitors … saw a significant decrease over the period.
3 Another interesting point is that …
4 Comparative (*more visitors than, much more popular than*)

Exercise 2
1 an upward trend in
2 a downward trend in
3 saw a significant rise over
4 saw a considerable fall over
5 had more visitors than/was more popular than
6 was more popular than

Exercise 3
Overall, **what** stands **out** from the graph is that there was an upward **trend** in the number of visitors to Paris, **while** the number of people who visited Barcelona **saw** a slight fall over the **period**. Another **interesting** point is that in 2005, Barcelona **had** more visitors than Paris, but in 2015, Paris was more popular **than** Barcelona.
(Note that the first sentence could also be: *Overall, **what** stands **out** from the graph is that **while** there was an upward **trend** in the number of visitors to Paris, the number of people who visited Barcelona **saw** a slight fall over the **period**.*)

Writing a main body paragraph
Exercise 1
and then, At this point, Subsequently, and following this

Exercise 2
1 To begin with,   2 To start with,
3 … and then,   4 At this point,
5 Subsequently,   6 and following this,
7 Then,   8 After that,   9 Next,
10 Afterwards,   11 Finally
12 and finished at   13 with the figure finishing at

Exercise 3
approximately, just over, around
Other possiblities: roughly, about, nearly

Exercise 4
1 at   2 to   3 to   4 at   5 at   6 at

Exercise 5
1 to   2 at   3 at

Exercise 6
1 at   2 to   3 at   4 to   5 to   6 at

Grammar: Describing changes
Exercise 1
1 falling   2 fallen

Exercise 2
1 fallen   2 grown   3 risen   4 gone up

Exercise 3
1 After increasing slightly to 2.2m in 2005, the number of visitors to Paris then rose sharply to 4.5m in 2007.
2 Having fallen slightly to 2.4m in 2008, the number of visitors to Barcelona then went up gradually to 2.8m in 2012.
3 After remaining stable at 4.7m between 2008 and 2011, the number of visitors to Paris then rose steadily to 5.5m in 2015.
4 Having grown considerably between 2005 and 2010, from 2.1m to 4.2m, the number of visitors to Barcelona then levelled off until 2012.

Exercise 4
1 There was a steady rise in the number of cars sold in the UK to 4.2m in 2015, after which/at which point the figure went up gradually to 4.6m in 2018.
2 The number of cars sold in the USA fell significantly to 21.5m in 2008, after which/at which point there was a steady rise to 28.1m in 2012.
3 There was a sharp increase in the unemployment rate in the EU to 6.2% in 2011, after which/at which point the figure recovered to 4.1% in 2015.
4 The employment rate in the public sector in the UK decreased considerably to 8.3m people in 2015, after which/at which point the figure went up gradually to 8.7m in 2017.

Exercise 5
Suggested answers
1 After going up slightly to 3.1m in 2013, the number of visitors to New York then fell steadily to 2.2m in 2017.

2 Having risen considerably to 2.2m in 2011, the figure than levelled off until 2012.
3 The number went down considerably to 1.6m in 2014, after which it soared to 3.7m in 2015.
4 The figure rose sharply to 3.7m in 2015, at which point it went up steadily to 4.2m in 2018.

Reading: Matching
Skills focus
Exercise 2
1 Key words: *accommodation, wasn't finished*
   Possible synonyms: *hotel, bed and breakfast, apartment; half built, under construction*
2 Key words: *didn't get to, destination*
   Possible synonyms: *didn't arrive; holiday location*
3 Key words: *a meal, wasn't what they expected*
   Possible synonyms: *dinner, restaurant; different from what they thought*
4 Key words: *at the same time, big local event*
   Possible synonyms: *during; a festival, a carnival, a parade*

Exercise 3
1 B   2 A   3 A   4 B

Skills application
Exercise 1
1 A   2 C   3 B   4 D   5 C   6 D   7 A
8 B   9 C   10 B

Listening Part 4: Sentence completion
Skills focus 1
Exercise 3
1 cultural understanding   2 sharing knowledge   3 spring up   4 well-known; trusted   5 mature   6 disadvantage

Skills focus 2
Exercise 1
7 Key words: *best-known person, is believed to be*
   Possible synonyms: *famous person, celebrity; is said to be*
8 Key words: *mainly because of*
   Possible synonym: *the major reason is*
9 Key words: *particularly, backgrounds*
   Possible synonyms: *especially; families*
10 Key words: *referred to as*
   Possible synonym: *is called*
11 Key words: *return to work, enthusiastic*
   Possible synonyms: *go back to their jobs; with a positive attitude*
12 Key words: *extended travel, easily*
   Possible synonyms: *a long break; not a problem to*
13 Key word: *predict*
   Possible synonyms: *expect, estimate*

Exercise 2
7 Prince William   8 university fees
9 poorer   10 late gapping   11 refreshed
12 affordable   13 shorter

Exercise 3
7 famous gap-year participant, is thought to be
8 essentially due to
9 particularly the case among poorer students
10 generally known as
11 come back from a break enthused
12 a gap year is absolutely
13 anticipate

Speaking: Part 3
Tourism
Exercise 3
1 key benefits   2 brings   3 creates
4 particular   5 opportunities   6 only
7 upside   8 effect   9 mixing   10 open-minded   11 main drawbacks   12 impact
13 good example   14 afford   15 well
16 that   17 result

Exercise 4
2 creates more jobs   3 sectors like hospitality
4 not only that   5 another upside   6 It often has a positive effect on the local culture.   7 mixing with
8 one of the main drawbacks   9 It can have a negative impact on local people.   10 a good example is   11 Many local people can't afford to buy or rent a house.   12 as well as that   13 It can result in   14 litter

Pulling it all together
Review
Exercise 1
Suggested answers
1 The graph highlights information about how many students of French and Spanish studied in UK universities, over a six-year period between 2010 and 2016.
2 The graph illustrates information about the amount of electricity which was used in the UK and the USA, over a 15-year period between 2000 and 2015.

Exercise 2
1 what stands out   2 there; upward trend
3 saw; period   4 Another; point   5 had more; than   6 more popular than

Exercise 3
1 There was a sharp increase in the prices of mobile phone contracts
2 Exports of cheese from the UK to France increased substantially.

Exercise 4
1 After increasing considerably to 600,000 in 2016, sales of sports watches went up slightly to 650,000 in 2018.
2 Having soared to 1.4m a year in 2015, the number of people participating in park runs levelled off until 2016.

Exercise 5
1 The number of visitors to the Science Museum went up sharply to 4.1m in 2015, after which the figure rose steadily to 4.1m in 2017.
2 The number of visitors to the Tate Modern gallery fell slightly to 1.8m in 2014, at

which point there was a levelling off for the next three years.

Exercise 6
See the key for Exercises 1 and 2 on page 83.

Exercise 7
See the information box on page 85 for an outline of the technique.

Final practice essay
Exercise 2
Sample answer
The graph shows information about how many people travelled to Thailand and the Philippines, over an eight-year period between 2010 and 2018.
Overall, what stands out from the graph is that there was an upward trend in the number of travellers to the Philippines, but the number of people travelling to Thailand saw a considerable decrease over the period. Another interesting point is that Thailand had more travellers than the Philippines in 2010, but in 2018 the Philippines was much more popular than Thailand.
In detail, the number of travellers to Thailand started at around 3.2m in 2010, and then remained stable until 2012. Having fallen sharply to approximately 1.6m in 2015, the figure then levelled off until 2016. Finally, there was a gradual fall to just over 1m in 2018.
However, if we look at travellers to the Philippines, the figure began at about 2.1m in 2010, after which there was a steady rise to 2.8m in 2012. After dropping slightly to about 2.7m in 2013, the number then rose dramatically to just under 4m in 2015, after which it levelled off until 2017. Finally, the figure went up significantly, finishing at 4.4m in 2018.
(196 words)

Unit 7
Writing Task 1: Comparative graphs
Model essay
Exercise 1
1 Engineering (men) and education (women)
2 Education
3 Men: four (business, marketing, sales and engineering)
  Women: three (education, medicine and advertising)
4 It was the same.

Exercise 2
1 There are four paragraphs: 1 Introduction, 2 Overview, 3 Describes the jobs with more men, 4 Describes the jobs with more women, plus law at the end.
2 Paragraph 3: three sectors
  Paragraph 4: four sectors
3 It is a topic sentence telling the reader what the paragraph is about.
4 X and Y were equally popular.
5 *were employed in, had jobs in*

Grammar: Comparative structures
Exercise 1
1 slightly   2 considerably, significantly
3 much

Exercise 2
2 Marketing was far/much more common for men than women.
3 Medicine was slightly more common for women than men.
4 Business was considerably/significantly more common for men than women.

Exercise 3
1 A far higher percentage of men than women worked in engineering.
2 A slightly higher percentage of men than women had jobs in sales.
3 A considerably/significantly higher percentage of women than men were employed in advertising.

Exercise 4
1 Three times as many women as men worked in advertising.
2 Three times as many women as men worked in education.
3 Seven times as many men as women worked in marketing.

Exercise 5
D percentage, higher than that
E more, than, had
F equally popular

Exercise 6
2 Much more men than women had jobs in engineering.
3 The percentage of women who were employed in education was far higher than that of men.
4 Considerably/Significantly more men than women had jobs in business.

Exercise 7
Suggested answers
1 Twice as many men as women studied Spanish.
2 French was far more popular for women than men.
3 Slightly more women than men chose Russian.
4 Mandarin was equally popular for men and women.
5 A slightly higher percentage of women than men studied Cantonese.
6 The percentage of women who studied Korean was considerably higher than that of men.

Language for writing about numbers
Exercise 1
the figures being 14% and 2% respectively
at 12% compared to 6%
The figures were 19% and 17%.
at 12% as opposed to 4%
The former figure was 30%, while the latter was 10%.
at 8% each

Exercise 2
2 A slightly higher percentage of women than men worked in medicine, at 19% as opposed to 17%.
3 Far more men worked in marketing than women. The former figure was 14%, while the latter was 2%.
4 Engineering was much more common among men than women, the figures being 21% and 4%.
5 The percentage of men who worked in sales was slightly higher than that of women, at 7% compared to 6% respectively.
6 Far more women had jobs in the education sector than men. The figures were 30% and 10%.

Exercise 3
Suggested answers
1 Twice as many men as women studied Spanish, with figures of 28% and 14%.
2 French was far more popular for women than men, the figures being 23% and 11%.
3 Slightly more women than men chose Russian, at 6% compared to 5% respectively.
4 Mandarin was equally popular for men and women, at 20% each.
5 A slightly higher percentage of women than men studied Cantonese, at 5% as opposed to 4%.
6 The percentage of women who studied Korean was considerably higher than that of men. The former figure was 9%, while the latter was 2%.

Exercise 4
1 d   2 a   3 b   4 c   5 e   6 e

Other comparative language
Exercise 1
Suggested answers
1 A one-bedroom flat in country A is twice as expensive as in country C.
2 A man's haircut costs slightly more in country B than in country A.
3 A woman's haircut costs the same in country A as in country B.
4 A burger and fries is much cheaper in country C than in country A.
5 A double espresso is half the price in country C as in country D.

Exercise 2
1 twice, as   2 quite   3 as, as   4 nearly
5 half, as

Exercise 3
1 d   2 a   3 c   4 b   5 e

Exercise 4
1 A burger and fries is not quite as expensive in country C as in country D, at £2.50 and £3.
2 A one-bedroom flat is half as expensive in country C as in country A, at £300 and £600.
3 A man's haircut in country C is not nearly as expensive as in country B, at £6 and £21.

4 A burger and fries is twice as expensive in country A as in country D, at £6 and £3.

5 A woman's haircut is as expensive in country C as in country D, at **£15**.

Exercise 5
Suggested answers

1 A woman's haircut is much/far more expensive in country B than in country C, at £45 and £15.

2 A double espresso is considerably/ significantly more expensive in country B than in country C, at £3.10 and £2.

3 A double espresso is slightly more expensive in country B than in country A, at £3.10 and £3.

4 A burger and fries is much/far more expensive in country A than in country C, at £6 and £2.50.

Exercise 7
Sample answer

The table highlights information about how much money people paid for a selection of items in four different countries in 2017. Overall, what stands out from the table is that country A and country B were generally the most expensive, while the cheapest country was country C. Another interesting point is that rent was by far the biggest cost among the five items.

In details, if we look at rent, it was twice as expensive in country A as in country C, at £600 and £300 per month respectively. Regarding a woman's haircut, it was as expensive in country A as in country B, the figure being £45. The lowest price was in countries C and D, at £15 each.

In terms of a men's haircut, it was slightly more expensive in country B than country A, at £21 compared to £20 respectively. A men's haircut in country C cost half as much as in country D, at £6 as opposed to £12. As regards a burger and fries, it was not quite as expensive in country B as in country A. The former figure was £5.50, while the latter was £6. Finally, espresso prices did not vary as much as the other items, with the highest price being £4 in country D and the lowest £2 in country C.
(220 words)

Vocabulary for pie charts and ratios
Exercise 1

1 most   2 highest   3 least   4 second
5 lowest   6 top   7 ranked   8 equally
9 bottom   10 place, followed

Exercise 2

2 The least popular sector for internships for women was engineering, at 2%.

3 PR and law were in third place with 12% each, followed by banking at 10%.

4 The sector with the highest percentage for women was journalism, at 20%.

5 Publishing ranked second, with 14%.

6 Engineering came bottom of the chart, with 2%.

7 PR and law were equally popular, at 12%.

Exercise 3

1 a fifth, one in five   2 a quarter, one in four
3 a third, one in three   4 (a) half, one in two
5 two-thirds   6 three-quarters

Exercise 4

1 A quarter of / One in four   2 a tenth of / one in ten   3 One in   4 a fifth of / one in five   5 a tenth / one in ten   6 one in

Exercise 5

1 most   2 quarter   3 followed   4 place
5 ranked   6 equally   7 tenth   8 ten
9 seventh   10 lowest

Exercise 6
Suggested answer

If we look at the chart for women, the sector with the highest percentage for women was journalism, with one-fifth, while publishing ranked second at 14%. Law and PR were in joint third place, with 12% each. One in ten women did internships in banking, closely followed by marketing at 9%. The least common field for work experience for women was engineering, with just 2% of the chart.

Exercise 7
Sample answer

The table highlights information about the percentage of women and men who started jobs in nine fields of work in the UK in 2018. Overall, what stands out from the table is that human resources was the most common industry for women, while IT was more popular than the other fields for men. Another interesting point is that the industry with the biggest difference between the genders was IT.

As regards men's employment, the most popular sector was IT, with just under a quarter, followed by marketing and sales in second place with 14%. Engineering ranked third, with 11%, and then science and law were equally popular, with just under a tenth each. Just over one in 20 men were employed in teaching, while graphic design came seventh, with 4%. The sectors with the lowest percentage were banking and insurance, and medicine, at 3% and 2% respectively.

If we look at the chart for women, the sector with the highest percentage for women was human resources, with one fifth, while medicine ranked second at 14%. Marketing and sales and teaching came close behind, with 13% and 12%. Just over one in ten women worked in banking and insurance, followed by science at 8%. The least common field for work for women was engineering, with just 2% of the chart.
(219 words)

Introductions and overviews for comparative essays
Exercise 1
Suggested answers

1 The graph shows information about how many people studied part-time at university in the UK in 2018.

2 The graph highlights data about the number of concert tickets which were sold at the O² stadium in 2018.

3 The chart gives figures about how much solar energy was produced in Chile and Argentina in 2017.

4 The graph illustrates information about the amount of water which was used in Spain and Italy in 2018.

Exercise 2

1 The highest numbers for men and for women, and the profession with the biggest difference

2 Overall, what stands out from the graph is that … , Another interesting point is that …

Exercise 3
Sample answer

The table illustrates data about the percentage of English mother-tongue men and women who studied nine selected foreign languages at the London School of Foreign Language Studies in 2018. Overall, what stands out from the table is that Spanish was the most popular language for men, while French was more popular than the other languages for women. Another interesting point is that the biggest difference between the genders related to Spanish.

Listening Part 3: Sentence completion
Skills focus
Exercise 2

1 full-time salary   2 travel expenses
3 marketing manager   4 local newspaper
5 permanent job   6 30

Exercise 4

1 wealthy families   2 journalism
3 compulsory   4 stop

Reading: Summary completion with a wordlist
Skills focus
Exercise 2

1 1 a noun   2 a plural noun   3 a noun
   4 an uncountable noun

2 *Key words:* 1 issue   2 all   3 sufficient
   4 how much

3 *Possible synonyms:* 1 problem   2 everyone
   3 enough   4 the amount of

4 *Possible answers:* 1 poverty/unemployment
   2 men/women/citizens   3 food/money/
   benefits   4 money/time

Exercise 3

1 poverty   2 citizens   3 food   4 money

Exercise 6

1 tax   2 benefits   3 government
4 temporary   5 huge   6 tried

Speaking Parts 1, 2 and 3
Grammar: Cleft sentences
Exercise 1
Suggested answers

1 … would like to work as a doctor is to help people / is so that I can help people.

2 … is most important in a job is the possibility of promotion.

3 … is the least important is flexible working hours.

4 … need (to do) to become a lawyer is (to) get a good Master's degree.

5 … really enjoyed was dealing with people.

6 … found was that it was really boring and repetitive.

Grammar: Using comparatives
Exercise 3
1 not nearly as good
2 as
3 not as well-paid as
4 far better with money than I am
5 a much better understanding
6 not quite as sure about it as

Pulling it all together
Review
Exercise 1
with figures of, as opposed to, compared to, The figures were, The former figure was … while the latter was …

Exercise 2
Suggested answers
2 A packet of cigarettes is not nearly as expensive in country A as in country B, at £3 and £9. / A packet of cigarettes costs three times as much in country B as in country A, at £3 and £9 respectively.
3 A litre of petrol is half as expensive in country A as in country B, at £1 and £2.
4 A cheese sandwich is as expensive in country A as in country B, at £2.
5 A loaf of bread is twice as expensive in country A as in country B, at £2 and £1.

Exercise 3
1 first place   2 bottom   3 second most
4 highest/largest/biggest/greatest

Exercise 4
1 a tenth / one in ten
2 25% / a quarter
3 50% / one in two
4 three quarters / three in four
5 (approximately) a/one third / one in three

Exercise 5
1 What I like best/most about being a nurse is the feeling of helping others.
2 What motivates me to be a primary school teacher is knowing I'm making a difference to a child's life.

Final practice essay
Exercise 2
Sample answer
The bar graph shows information about the percentage of men and women who studied nine selected subjects in the UK in 2018. Overall, what stands out from the graph is that IT was by far the most popular subject for men, while business was more popular than the other subjects among women. Another interesting point is that the biggest difference was represented by IT.

As regards the details, there were four subjects which were studied by more women than men. Music was far more popular for women than men, at 14% compared to 3%. Similarly, considerably more women than men studied business, with figures of 18% and 10%. Twice as many women as men chose English. The figures are 12% and 6% respectively. Finally, a significantly higher percentage of women than men studied Spanish, with 11% and 3%.

By contrast, men outnumbered women in four of the other subjects. Four times as many men as women studied IT, the figures being 24% and 6%. Engineering was also far more popular for men than women, at 14% and 2%. Regarding law, slightly more men than women studied it. The former figure was 14% and the latter was 13%. There was a similar pattern for science. Science was slightly more popular for men than women, at 9% compared to 8%. Finally, economics was equally popular for men and women, at 9% each.

(230 words)

Unit 8
Writing Task 1: Maps
Model essay
Exercise 2
2 They have been cut down and new houses have been built.
3 It has been turned into flats.
4 A bike-rental scheme has been introduced.
5 There is a lot more accommodation now than in 2000.
6 New cafés and bars have been opened.

Exercise 5
1 There are four paragraphs: an introduction, an overview and two paragraphs describing the main changes.
2 modern, developed
3 More accommodation and entertainment facilities; fewer trees and green areas
4 There are three changes in paragraph 3 and four in paragraph 4.
5 a have been cut down (x2), have been constructed, has been built (x2), have been opened
   b one change has been … , the last few years have seen … , a significant change is … , A further important development is …
   c making it easier for people to get around the city centre by bike, meaning that the beach area is now a nicer and more interesting place to go out
   d In 2000, there did not use to be a hall of residence, but … ; There used to be trees … , but …

Language for describing changes in maps
Exercise 1

Make bigger	Add something new	Take away something	Change one thing into something different
enlarge, expand, extend	build, construct, erect, introduce, open	cut down, demolish, knock down, pull down, remove	convert, make into, pedestrianise, redevelop, replace, turn into

Exercise 2
1 You can cut down trees, but not buildings.
2 *Enlarge* and *expand* mean 'make bigger' and *extend* means 'make longer'. For example, you can extend a train line by building new stations on the end of it.
3 A road
4 You introduce a scheme, like the bike-rental scheme in the maps. You can't introduce buildings.

Exercise 3
2 have been opened   3 has been introduced
4 has been converted into new flats   5 near the seafront has been pedestrianised   6 have been cut down, has been built

Exercise 4
Suggested answers
1 The old train station in the north-west has been knocked down, and a new train station has been constructed.
2 The trees in the north-east have been cut down, and new houses have been built.

Exercise 5
1 Sentence A is used to describe things which are in the first map, but which have been removed in the second, whereas sentence B talks about things which are not in the first map, but which appear in the second
2 Sentence B
3 Sentence A

Exercise 6
Suggested answers
1 There did not use to be a bike-rental scheme, but a new one has been introduced in the city centre.
2 There used to be a bank in the south-west of the city, but it has been pulled down and replaced by flats.
3 There used to be trees in the north-east of the city, but they have been cut down, and new houses have been built.
4 There did not use to be any bars or cafés in the city, but new ones have been opened in the area near the beach.

Exercise 7

Verb	Noun
construct	construction
convert	conversion
cut down	cutting down
demolish	demolition

enlarge	enlargement
erect	erection
expand	expansion
extend	extension
introduce	introduction
knock down	knocking down
modernise	modernisation
open	opening
pedestrianise	pedestrianisation
pull down	pulling down
redevelop	redevelopment
remove	removal
replace	replacement

Exercise 8
2 the erection of a new tower near the beach
3 the introduction of a bike-rental scheme in the city centre
4 the opening of new bars and cafés along the seafront
5 cutting down of the trees, building of new houses
6 the conversion of the bank in the south-west into flats / the conversion into flats of the bank in the south-west
7 the pedestrianisation of the road near the seafront
8 removal of the trees to the east of the city centre, opening of a new library

Exercise 9
1 change, been   2 Another   3 interesting development   4 further   5 significant
6 striking   7 noticeable improvement
8 few, seen

Introductions and overviews for map essays
Exercise 1
Suggested answers
describe: *show, highlight, illustrate*
the main: *the major, the most important, the key*
changes: *developments*
happened: *occurred, taken place*
between … and …: *from … to … , over a period between … and …*

Exercise 2
Suggested answer
The maps highlight the key developments which have taken place in Westville between 2000 and today.

Exercise 3
1 what stands   2 become   3 modern*
4 developed*   5 more   6 fewer
* Grammatically, these two answers could be swapped, but this is the order from the model essay.

Exercise 5
1 making it easier   2 meaning that, nicer, more interesting

Exercise 6
Suggested answers
1 … making it safer for people to walk near the beach.

2 … meaning that it is cheaper for students to live in the area.
3 … making it easier for young families to find a place to live.
4 … meaning that there are now more trains going to London every day.

Two maps in the past
Exercise 1
1 No, because the time period is finished in the past.
2 You need to use the past simple passive most of the time, and you can also use the past perfect passive in some cases.

Exercise 2
Suggested answers
1 was built/constructed/opened   2 were cut down, was constructed

Exercise 3
Suggested answers
1 The trees in the east of the city were cut down, and new tennis courts were constructed.
2 The old car park was demolished, and an indoor market was opened in its place.

Exercise 4
1 they had been cut down, had been built
2 a new one had been built
3 by 2018, it had been knocked down
4 by 2018, new ones had been constructed

Exercise 5
Sample answer
The maps highlight information about the key developments which happened in Jolyton, over a ten-year period between 2008 and 2018.
Overall, what stands out from the maps is that Jolyton became much more urban and developed, with more transport and sport facilities, and fewer trees and open spaces. In detail, one significant change is that a new shopping centre was built in the north-west of the city. In addition, the old car park in the east was demolished, and an indoor market was built, meaning that there were far more places to go shopping in 2018. There used to be houses in the north-east, but they were demolished and replaced by new flats. A further striking development is the knocking down of the disused factory in the west of the city and its replacement by a community centre.
If we look at the south of the city, an interesting development is the building of a new airport in the south-east. There did not use to be a station in the south of Jolyton, but the railway was extended and a new station was built, making it easier to commute to the city centre. Finally, in 2008, there were trees in the south-west of the city, but by 2018 they had been cut down and a new football stadium had been erected.
(221 words)

Listening Part 4: Predicting answers
Skills focus
Exercise 1
costs (and the impact of rising costs on city dwellers), transport, leisure opportunities, multi-culturalism

Exercise 2
1 The answer will be a verb, as it follows *to*, and will be something that can be done to rent and bills.
2 London is likely to be more expensive than a generation ago, as prices usually rise over time.
3 The answer will be an adjective, as it follows *very*, and will describe the population.
4 Possible synonyms: *really, extremely*
6 The answer will be a noun, as it follows *a process of.*
7 Possible synonyms: *poorer, less affluent, less wealthy*
9 The answer will be an adjective, as it comes between *a* and the noun *amount.*
10 Possible synonyms: *set, agree*

Exercise 3
1 cover   2 mixed   3 gentrification
4 maximum

Skills application
Exercise 1
5 variations   6 dirty   7 twice   8 remove
9 copied   10 playgrounds   11 200 / two hundred   12 overseas   13 common language

Reading: Table completion
Skills focus
Exercise 2
Advantage: benefit, bonus, plus point, pros
Disadvantage: cons, downside, drawback, negative point
Verdict: conclusion, opinion, view

Exercise 3
Gap 2 will be a noun or pronoun because it precedes a verb.
Gap 3 will be a noun or the *-ing* form of a verb because it follows *for*.
Gap 4 will be a noun because it follows *outstanding*.
Gap 5 will be an adjective because it describes something that Dubai is in summer.
Gap 6 will be a noun that can follow *in*.

Exercise 4
Suggested answers
2 may = might / can; poor = bad / not good
3 Very good = great / excellent
4 Outstanding = excellent / brilliant
5 Often = generally / usually
6 Suitable = good for / appropriate

Exercise 6
1 monuments   2 Weather   3 historical places   4 shopping (malls)   5 unbearable
6 winter and spring

Skills application
Exercise 1
1 success   2 films and advertisements
3 24 hours   4 volume of passengers
5 reliable   6 Driverless trains   7 reluctant
8 beauty

Speaking Part 2
A city you enjoyed visiting
Exercise 2
Why he went there: had friend working there who had invited him
When he went and for how long: one week in June last year
What he did there: strolled around the city, ate good food, saw tourist attractions, took bus tour to see sights, took lots of photos, bought souvenirs, relaxed on the beach, swam in the sea, hung out with his friend
Why he enjoyed visiting it: spending time with his friend

Exercise 3
1 going, tell   2 reason   3 thing   4 Another
5 highlights   6 well, also   7 had, would

Exercise 4
1 took   2 went   3 arrived   4 hadn't
travelled   5 met   6 was working   7 hated
8 decided   9 had   10 went   11 had just
finished   12 didn't have   13 (had) told
14 bought

Speaking Part 3
Talking about improvements
Exercise 1
1 would, invested   2 wish, would
3 were/was, would

Exercise 2
2 so that   3 in order to

Pulling it all together
Review
Exercise 1
1 A new football stadium has been built on the outskirts of the city.
2 The old factory in the south of the city has been knocked down, and a science park has been constructed.

Exercise 2
Suggested answers
1 There did not use to be a Lebanese restaurant in the city centre, but a new one has been opened.
2 There used to be a pub near the beach, but it has been turned into an art gallery.

Exercise 3
Suggested answers
1 One change is the opening of a new library in the middle of the town.
2 A striking development has been the cutting down of the trees in the north-east of the city, and the building of a new shopping centre.
3 A further change is the introduction of a new recycling scheme in the city.
4 One significant change is the conversion of the village hall into a café.

Exercise 4
The two structures are:
- *making it* + comparative + *for … to …*
- *meaning that* + clause.

Exercise 5
Suggested answers
1 … there is more choice of places to eat out.
2 … to get to the city centre quickly.

Exercise 6
1 a new one had been built   2 had been knocked down, had been erected

Exercise 7
1 It **would** be good if the government **invested** more money in healthcare.
2 I **wish** the government **would** invest more money in education.
3 If it **was/were** up me, I would increase tax on petrol.

Final practice essay
Exercise 2
Sample answer
The two maps highlight the main developments which have happened in Ironbridge over the period between 2010 and today.
Overall, what stands out from the maps is that Ironbridge has become much more developed and urban, with more entertainment facilities and places to shop, and fewer trees and green areas.
In detail, if we look at the north of the city, one change is that the church in the north-west has been knocked down, and a library has been built in its place. In 2010, there did not use to be an Arabic restaurant in the town, but one has been opened north of the city centre. A further important development is the cutting down of the trees in the north-east, and the building of a new football stadium.
As regards the south of the city, a significant development is that the old sports centre in the south-east has been converted into a pub. There used to be trees in the south-west, but they have been cut down, and replaced by a new shopping centre, making it easier for people in the town to do their shopping in one place. Regarding the city centre, the last few years have seen the introduction of a bike-rental scheme. A final change is the construction of some new houses just east of the city centre.
(222 words)

Writing Task 1: Future plans and predictions
Model essay 1
Exercise 2
1 English in 2030, Arabic in 2040
2 The number of students will increase sharply.
3 The figure is going to decline steadily.
4 It will fluctuate.
5 It is going to remain stable.
6 *will* future, *be going to*

Exercise 3
1 *the number of students who will study three languages*
2 The first point is the future trends of the three languages, and the second highlights the fact that Arabic is going to overtake English at the end of the period.
3 *Overall, what stands out from the graph is that …*; *Another interesting point is that …*
4 The future perfect (*will have become*)
5 Paragraph 3 is about English and Arabic, and paragraph 4 is about Spanish.
6 *Regarding … , As regards … , If we look at …*
7 *approximately, around*
8 *after which*
9 *at the end of the decade*
10 Future tenses: *will, be going to*, future continuous (*will be learning*)
Future expressions: *is set to, looks set to, is estimated to, according to predictions, is likely to, predictions show that*

Language for future trends graphs
Exercise 1
2 The number of students of Arabic is going to drop considerably.
3 There will be a dramatic increase in the number of students of English.
4 The figure for Spanish will decrease gradually.
5 There is going to be a steady increase in the number of students of Arabic.

Exercise 2
Suggested answers
1 The number of students of English will rise considerably, from 500m in 2030 to 700m in 2034.
2 There is going to be a slight fall in the number of students of Arabic, from 420m in 2030 to around 360m in 2032.
3 The number of students of Spanish is going to go up sharply, from around 150m in 2034 to 400m in 2036.
4 There will be a dramatic increase in the number of students of Arabic, from 400m in 2038 to approximately 750m in 2040.

Exercise 3
Suggested answers
1 There will be a gradual drop in the number of students of English, from 700m in 2034 to around 650m in 2036.
2 The number of students of Arabic is going to decline steadily, from 500m in 2034 to 400m in 2038.

3 The number of students of Spanish is going to fall dramatically, from 400m in 2036 to 200m in 2040.

Exercise 4
1 According   2 looks   3 likely
4 Predictions   5 estimated/expected   6 set

Exercise 5
2 Predictions show that there will be a slight fall in the number of students of Arabic to 360m in 2032.
3 The figure for Spanish looks set to rise sharply to 400m in 2036.
4 The number of people learning English is estimated to drop gradually to 650m in 2036. / It is estimated that the number of people learning English will drop gradually to 650m in 2036.
5 According to predictions, there is going to be a steady decline in the number of students of Spanish to around 150m in 2034.
6 The figure for Arabic is/looks set to go up sharply to 750m in 2040.

Exercise 6
Suggested answers
1 500m people will be studying it   2 650m will be learning it   3 just over 400m people will be studying it   4 only 200m will be learning it

Exercise 7
Sample answer
The table shows information about how many people are predicted to speak three languages, Welsh, Breton and Gaelic, over a ten-year period between 2030 and 2040. Overall, what stands out from the table is that there will be upward trends in the number of speakers of Breton and Gaelic, while Welsh is likely to see a slight drop over the period. Another interesting point is that in 2030, Welsh is predicted to be the most commonly spoken language, but by 2040, Breton will have become more popular than the others.
In detail, regarding Welsh, 1.2m people will be speaking it in 2030, and then it is likely that the figure will fall significantly to 0.5m in 2036. At this point, the figure will level off until 2038, after which it will recover to 0.9m in 2040.
If we look at Breton, the number is set to begin at 0.6m in 2030, and then according to predictions it will rise to 1m in 2034, at which point it is going to level off. The last four years of the period are likely to see a significant rise, with the figure finishing at 1.8m in 2040. Regarding Gaelic, in 2030 only 0.2m people will be speaking it, but predictions show that the figure will increase considerably to 0.6m in 2034. Despite a slight dip to 0.5m in 2036, it is then estimated that there will be a dramatic increase to 1.2m at the end of the period.
(245 words)

Model essay 2
Exercise 1
1 Seven
2 It will become much more developed, with more facilities for sport and study.
3 The library is going to be extended. The lecture hall will be converted into an IT suite.
4 The trees are set to be cut down, and a gym/sports hall will be built in their place.
5 New things: hall of residence, lecture theatre, cycle path, IT suite, restaurant, gym/sports centre
6 There will be a cycle path running from north to south, making it easier to get around the campus by bike.

Exercise 2
1 Six
2 *the houses […] are going to be knocked down*; *a new hall of residence will be built*; *a new lecture theatre will be constructed*
3 The future perfect passive (*will have been converted*)
4 *Another striking change is the creation of a cycle path.*
5 *meaning that there will be more space for students to study*; *making it easier to cycle around the university*
6 *the campus is going to become much more developed*; *one change will be that …*; *the library is set to be expanded*; *It is also planned that a new lecture theatre will be constructed*; *the trees in the south-west are due to be cut down*
7 *one change will be that …*; *Another important development is that …*; *It is also planned that …*; *Another striking change is …*; *Finally, …*
8 By using the phrase *If we look at the south part of the campus* at the beginning of the paragraph.

Language for future maps
Exercise 1
1 An IT suite is going to be built in the south of the campus.
2 The trees in the south-west will be cut down, and a gym will be built.
3 A cycle path running across the university is going to be created.
4 The lecture hall will be turned into an IT suite.
5 A new restaurant is going to be opened in the south-east of the campus.
6 The library in the north-east of the campus will be expanded.

Exercise 2
Suggested answers
1 By 2035, a new restaurant will have been opened in the south-east of the campus.
2 By 2035, the student houses in the north-west will have been pulled down and replaced by a hall of residence.
3 By 2035, a new lecture theatre will be been constructed in the east of the campus.
4 By 2035, a new cycle path will have been built in the middle of the campus.

Exercise 3
1 A new supermarket is due to be opened in the north of the campus.
2 A new student nightclub is set to be built on the edge of the campus.
3 It is planned that more computer facilities will be built.
4 A new car park is scheduled to be constructed.
5 New tennis courts are due to be built next to the university gardens.
6 A brand new doctor's surgery is set to be opened.

Model essay 3
Exercise 1
1 *how many people studied …*
2 The most popular subject in 2010 and 2018; the largest change between the two years
3 Comparative
4 It compares the changes between 2010 and 2018, so trend language.
5 *If we look at 2010, …*; *As regards the changes in 2018, …*
6 The past perfect is used in the second part of the sentence, because of the time linker *by 2018*, which requires the past perfect.

Exercise 2
Suggested answers
2 … by 2018, the figure had fallen slightly to 16%.
3 … by 2018, the number had risen dramatically to 11%.
4 … by 2018, the figure had decreased considerably, to 5%.

Exercise 3
Sample answer
The table highlights information about how many 18-year-old pupils in an English-speaking country sat an Advanced Level exam in ten foreign languages in two time periods: 2012 and 2017.
Overall, what stands out from the tables is that the most popular language in 2012 was French, but in 2017 more students took Spanish than the other languages. Another interesting point is that the biggest change related to Spanish, which increased dramatically over the period.
If we look at 2012, French was considerably more popular than Spanish, with figures of 50,000 and 32,000 respectively. Slightly more students took German than Mandarin, the figures being 11,000 and 10,000. Latin and Portuguese had an equal number of students, at 8,000 each, while twice as many pupils took Polish and Cantonese as Japanese, at 2,000 compared to 1,000.
As regards the changes in 2017, French fell significantly, from 50,000 to 34,000. By contrast, the figure for Spanish went up dramatically, rising from 32,000 to 68,000 in 2017. In 2012, 10,000 students took Mandarin, but by 2017 this figure had jumped to 22,000. Finally, there was a considerable increase in the figure for Arabic, which increased from 4,000 to 10,000.
(195 words)

Listening Part 3: Matching information
Skills application
Exercise 1

1 D   2 F   3 G   4 A   5 C

Exercise 2

1 3/three   2 taxes   3 email/e-mail
4 50,000   5 jobs

Exercise 4

1 costly   2 state-of-the-art   3 slash the
ticket prices   4 outskirts   5 a shortage of
housing   6 refurbished   7 host   8 deadline
9 objections   10 influx

Reading: Matching headings and multiple-choice questions
Skills application
Exercise 1

A iii   B vii   C ii   D vi   E iv

Exercise 2

1 C (The text says *very few people had
mobile phones*. A is incorrect because it
was very few and not zero, and B is
incorrect because the text says *they
certainly did not have access to emails and
images on them*.)

2 B (The text says *This is predicted to have
positive and negative impacts*. A is
incorrect because *the so-called 'gig
economy' […] is predicted to expand*. C is
incorrect because the paragraph describes
both positive and negative impacts, not
just positive ones.)

3 C (The text says *Home schooling, for
instance, is already rising in popularity, and
this is set to grow dramatically*. A is
incorrect, because home schooling is
already rising in popularity, so it is more
popular now that it was, not less. B is
incorrect *because the vast majority of
children will attend normal schools*.)

4 A (The text says *These days, travellers have
a much bigger variety of flights, hotels and
holiday types to choose from*. B is
incorrect, because although low-cost air
travel is mentioned, there is nothing about
it being over or not. C is incorrect because
although the text says that travel websites
are a trusted way of choosing a holiday, it
does not say that people will use them
more in the future. If anything, the text
suggest that people *will try to book directly
with each other … without going through
accommodation websites*.)

Speaking Part 3
Future predictions
Exercise 3

1 highly likely   2 good chance   3 definitely
4 see, working   5 doubt   6 predict   7 not
much   8 unlikely

Exercise 4

will: 1, 2, 3, 4, 5, 6, 8
won't: 7, 9

Exercise 5

1 know   2 50-50   3 wait   4 impossible

Speaking Part 1
Your future plans
Exercise 3

1 'll get   2 short-term   3 lined up   4 plan
5 is to   6 'll have started   7 to be running
8 have met   9 one day

Exercise 4

1 c   2 b   3 d   4 a

Pulling it all together
Review
Exercise 1

1 The number of students of Turkish looks
set to rise significantly to 120 million.

2 According to predictions, there will be a
sharp rise in the number of students of
Japanese to 60 million.

Exercise 2

1 A new shopping centre is due to be built in
the city centre.

2 One change is that by 2040, a new
swimming pool will have been constructed
on campus.

3 A new IT suite is set to be built on campus.

4 One development is that by 2040, the
trees in the south of the city will have been
cut down and new flats will have been
built.

Exercise 3

1 highly   2 chance   3 see   4 much

Final practice essays
Exercise 2

Sample answers

1 The table highlights information about
how many students are predicted to study
three languages, Korean, Italian and
Turkish, over a 16-year period between
2034 and 2050.
Overall, what stands out from the table is
that there will be upward trends in the
number of students of all three languages,
and that Korean will see the biggest
increase over the period. Another
interesting point is that Turkish is estimated
to be the most popular language in 2034,
but by 2050 Korean will have become the
number-one language.
In details, regarding Korean, the number is
set to begin at 50m in 2034, and then the
number is going to rise steadily to 70m in
2038. At this point, there is likely to be a
sharp increase to 140m in 2040, after
which the figure will level off. Despite a
slight dip to 130m in 2046, according to
predictions, the figure will then soar to
270m at the end of the period.
If we look at Italian, the number looks set
to fall significantly from 100m to 65m in
2038, at which point it is going to level off
until 2042. Subsequently, predictions show
that the figure will go up steadily, finishing
at 160m in 2050.
Finally, the figure for Turkey will start at
110m, and then there will be a steady
increase to 170m in 2040. The number of
students is then estimated to drop

significantly to 130m in 2046, before rising
sharply and finishing at 200m in 2050.
(247 words)

2 These maps illustrate the expected changes
that will take place in the centre of a city
between now and 2040.
Overall, what stands out from the maps is
that the city centre will become far more
developed and modern, with more
transport and cultural facilities, and fewer
trees and open spaces.
If we look at the north of the city, one
change is that the trees in the north-west
are going to be cut down, and a new
sports centre will be built in their place.
Another development is that the museum
to the north of the park looks set to be
expanded. It is also interesting to note that
by 2040, a cycle path will have been built,
making it easier to cycle across the city
centre to the park.
In terms of the south part of the city, one
expected development is the knocking
down of the old factory south of the park,
and the construction of new flats. A new
bus station is expected to be built in the
south-west, meaning that it will be easier
to travel to and from the city centre. Finally,
an art gallery is due to be opened in the
south-east part of the city centre.
(204 words)

Unit 10

Writing Task 1: Describing a process
Model essay
Exercise 2

5 Grind   6 Put, label   7 Pack   8 Deliver
9 Buy, take   10 Fill, add   11 Heat
12 Pour, drink

Exercise 3

1 Three paragraphs; in the model answers in
Units 7–9, there are four paragraphs.

2 Because there are two separate parts to
the process.

3 In the first stage; Once; after that; Having
been … , then; Subsequently; Finally; to
begin with; after which; After; When; The
final stage is

4 Present simple passive

5 *If we look at*; used to introduce the second
part of the process

6 It rounds off your answer.

Grammar: Present simple passive
Exercise 1

In each case, sentence b is better because the
object of the sentence (*Boxes of coffee* and
The coffee beans) is the most important part
of the sentence, and the subject is not
important. Therefore a passive sentence is
better.

Exercise 2

2 The coffee beans are picked from the trees.
3 The coffee beans are dried in the sun.
4 The beans are roasted.
5 The coffee packets are labelled.
6 The coffee beans are cleaned.

7 The coffee is packed into boxes.
8 The bottom part of the coffee pot is filled with water.
9 The coffee pot is heated.

Exercise 3

Verb	Past participle
sell	sold
put	put
throw away	thrown away
sow	sown
hold	held
buy	bought
grow	grown
cut	cut
take	taken
choose	chosen
leave	left

Exercise 4
1 Coffee is grown in Brazil.
2 The coffee beans are ground (by a machine).
3 The coffee is put into packets.
4 The bad coffee beans are thrown away.
5 The coffee is bought (by customers).
6 The coffee is taken home (by customers).

Grammar: Present perfect passive and participle structures
Exercise 1
2 When the bad beans have been thrown away, the good beans are cleaned.
3 After the beans have been roasted, then they are ground.
4 Once the coffee pot has been filled with water, it is heated.
5 When the boxes of coffee have been delivered to supermarkets, then they are put onto the supermarket shelves.
6 After the packets of coffee have been packed into boxes, then they are delivered to supermarkets.

Exercise 2
1 Having been picked, the coffee beans are placed in a basket
2 After being roasted, the beans are then ground.
3 Having been filled with water, the coffee pot is then heated.
4 After being packed into boxes, the packets of coffee are then delivered to supermarkets.
5 Having been delivered to supermarkets, the boxes of coffee are then put onto the shelves so that customers can buy them.
6 After being dried in the sun, the coffee beans are then roasted.

Linking phrases
Exercise 1
Linking phrases to describe the start of the process
In the first stage, …
Initially, …
The first stage is that …
To begin with …
Linking phrases to describe the next stage of the process

After that, …
… , after which …
… and then …
At this point, …
Following this, …
In the next stage, …
Next, …
Subsequently, …
The following step is that …
The next step is that … Then …
Linking phrases to describe the end of the process
Finally, …
In the final stage, …
The final stage is that …

Exercise 2
Suggested answer
The first step is that the kettle is filled with water, and then it is boiled. After that, a tea bag is put into a cup, and then hot water is poured into the cup. In the next stage, the tea bag is removed, after which milk and sugar are added to the tea. Subsequently, the tea, milk and sugar are stirred with a spoon, and then the final stage is that the tea is drunk.

Introductions and overviews for process essasys
Exercise 1
1 the process of growing coffee
2 the steps involved in making a cup of coffee
3 the first stage and the last stage
4 gerunds (*-ing forms of the verbs*)

Exercise 2
1 to   2 made   3 growing   4 which
5 involved in   6 making

Exercise 3
1 The diagram shows information about the process of growing coffee.
2 The diagram highlights information about the steps involved in growing coffee.
3 The pictures illustrate information about the stages of growing coffee.
4 The pictures show information about the process by which coffee is grown.

Exercise 4
Diagram can be rephrased as *pictures* or *illustration*.
Shows can be rephrased as *highlights, illustrates, gives* or *demonstrates*.

Exercise 5
Suggested answers
1 The pictures illustrate information about the process by which tea is made.
2 The diagram highlights information about the process of producing tomato ketchup.
3 The diagram shows information about the steps involved in making a tennis racket.
4 The illustration highlights information about the how mobile phones are produced.

Exercise 6
1 stages   2 starting   3 picking   4 finishing
5 drinking

Exercise 7
Suggested answers
1 The diagram illustrates information about the steps involved in producing chocolate bars. There are ten stages in the process, starting with planting cocoa seeds and finishing with eating chocolate.
2 The illustration gives information about the process by which potato crisps are made. There are 12 stages in the process, starting with harvesting potatoes and finishing with eating crisps.

Reading: Completing a flowchart
Skills focus
Exercise 1
Suggested answers
1 *Become* would be followed by an adjective such as *famous, well-known*, etc. or a noun such as *the boss / the manager*. A possible synonym for *deciding* could be *choosing*, and for *getting rich, becoming wealthy / earning lots of money*.
2 Possible synonyms for *First of all: At the start, Initially, At first, The first thing you need to do*
3 A noun follows a pronoun.
4 A noun starting with a vowel follows *an*. A synonym of *good-quality but inexpensive* could be *cheap and cheerful*. You would expect the answer to be different because it's something that you need to decide between.
5 Possible synonyms for *find: discover, locate, identify, see*

Exercise 2
1 the boss   2 decision   3 concept
4 upmarket   5 gap

Skills application
Exercise 1
1 experience   2 professional designer
3 warm   4 welcoming   5 quality staff
6 excellent references   7 Marketing
8 interview   9 samples

Speaking Part 2
Grammar: Linking phrases
Exercise 1
1 terms of   2 regarding   3 think about
4 Talking   5 What I really   6 Another thing

Grammar: Modal verbs to talk about the past
Exercise 1
1 must/might have been   2 would have been   3 must have been   4 would have been

Exercise 2
1 These two phrases are used to say more or less when something happened in the past.

2 No, the speakers are not 100% sure when these things happened, which is why they use these two phrases.

Exercise 3
1 it   2 I

Listening Part 2: Sentence completion
Skills focus
Exercise 1
Suggested answers
1   new management/bosses
2   new food / a new selection of dishes
3   a new building/restaurant

Exercise 2
1 D (The Tokyo House)   2 A (A Taste of Italy)
3 C (The Parisien Bistro)

Exercise 5
1 50% / fifty percent   2 craft beers
3 omelette   4 ingredients   5 apples
6 jazz band

Skills application
Exercise 2
1 D (The Thai Temple)   2 A (The Pancake Palace)   3 C (The Argentine Steakhouse)
4 C (The Argentine Steakhouse)   5 B (Tang's Chinese)   6 D (The Thai Temple)

Exercise 5
1 backpacking   2 authentic   3 nutritious
4 tourists   5 chilli-eating / chilli eating
6 (vegetarian) red curry

Pulling it all together
Review
Exercise 1
1 The tea seeds are planted.
2 The tea leaves are picked and put into a basket.
3 The tea leaves are packed into boxes (by the farmer), and the boxes are put onto a lorry.
4 The tea boxes are delivered to supermarkets (by lorries), where they are bought (by customers).

Exercise 2
1 Once the coffee beans have been washed, they are then dried in the sun.
2 When the packets of coffee have been filled, they are labelled.
3 After the coffee beans have been roasted, they are ground.

Exercise 3
1 Having been unloaded from the lorry, the coffee is put onto the shelves for customers to buy.
2 After being loaded onto a lorry, the packets of coffee are then delivered to supermarkets.

Exercise 4
Regarding … , If I think about … , Talking about …

Exercise 5
1 I must/would have been about 11 or 12 years old.

2 It must/would have been about 2001 or 2002.

Exercise 6
1 See page 138 for a summary of techniques for dealing with flowchart questions.

Final practice essay
Exercise 2
Sample answer
The pictures illustrate the stages by which potato crisps are made. There are 15 stages in the process, starting with harvesting potatoes in a field and finishing with customers buying crisps in supermarkets.
In the first stage, potatoes are harvested in fields, and then they are packed into trays. The trays of potatoes are then transported to a factory by lorry. Once the potatoes have been sorted, and any bad potatoes have been thrown away, the good potatoes are cleaned. Subsequently, they are sliced, and then oil is heated in a deep fat fryer. Having been fried for ten minutes, the slices of potato are removed and left to cool.
The next stage is that salt and flavourings are added to the potatoes, and then they are put into packets. After being packed into boxes, the packets of crisps are then loaded onto a lorry, which delivers them to supermarkets. Finally, the crisps are stacked onto supermarket shelves, where they are then bought buy customers. This completes the process of making crisps.
(172 words)